Baby
Steps™
to
Happiness

John Q. Baucom, Ph.D.

Baby
Steps™
to
Happiness

John Q. Baucom, Ph.D.

STARBURST PUBLISHERS™

P. O. Box 4123, Lancaster, Pennsylvania 17604

Acknowledgments

The author thanks: LA, Shannon McKnight, and Bud Ragan for the formation of the early stages and the proposal of this book; LA, Shannon McKnight, Roy Glenn, Carol Rogers, Harrison, Clairalyn, and Jeremy for typing, editing, and proofreading; Roy Glenn, Bud Ragan, Carol Rogers, and Keppy for finding and editing quotes; Butch Simpson, Barry Wagner, Roy Glenn, Michael Alfono, Lois Smith, Edwinna Bierman, Benjamin, Chip, Valerie, and Sheri for inspiration.

Dedication

This book is dedicated to Shannon McKnight, without whom this work would not have been possible.

To schedule Author appearances write:
Author Appearances, Starburst Promotions, P.O. Box 4123
Lancaster, Pennsylvania 17604 or call (717) 293-0939.

Credits:
Cover by David Marty Design
Unless otherwise noted, or paraphrased by the author, all Scripture quotations are from the King James Version of The Holy Bible.

First Printing, December 1996

ISBN: 0-914984-86-1
Library of Congress Catalog Number 96-68842
Printed in the United States of America

Table of Contents

Foreword

This book is entitled **Baby Steps to Happiness.** The title is used because there are occasions when one "big step" is simply too much. However, there's a more important reason to call them baby steps. When a baby is learning to walk she toddles, teeters, and often *falls down and goes boom*. Yet nobody frowns and complains, "You'll never make it. Why don't you give up?" Instead, we applaud and say, "Way to go—good girl (or good boy)." Each new step is applauded along the way.

The same is true with *Baby Steps to Happiness.* You will toddle before you walk. You will occasionally fall down and *go boom*. There may be times when you want to give up stepping at all and simply crawl. But as you'll discover later, it's important to surround yourself with the kind of people who will applaud, encourage, and help you get back to baby stepping once again. These steps take practice. When you first learned to walk you didn't take one step and then start running. You practiced. This book is purposefully designed to follow the same model. Sometimes you'll need to read the same thing over again two or three times. Occasionally, you will find similar ideas stated in different form. The book is purposely written that way, to follow the baby step model.

Each baby step is designed to mean one thing at a superficial level, and something entirely different if you look more deeply. Some of the baby steps are simple, concrete, and to the point. Others contain a staggering degree of depth that could be entire philosophies on their own. It is suggested you read the book completely through twice. The first time is a preview. Highlight the material you find particularly applicable to you, and spend more time with it later. The second time you read it to master the step. This book is about happiness, *one baby step at a time.*

A little and little, collected together, become a great deal; the heap in the barn consists of single grains, and drop and drop make the inundation.

—Sa'di

Foreword

In preparing to write this book I came up with a design that is simple and pragmatic. Each baby step is covered in three paragraphs per page, four pages per chapter. Each page is self-contained and can be read independent of the others. Each four-page baby step is self-contained as well. You can read one page, one baby step, or several baby steps at one time. Or you can stop at any point along the way, place the book down, pick it up later, and continue to read without a disruption in your flow of thought.

The chapters have been organized sequentially. They are divided into what makes sense. Yet you don't have to read them the way they are structured. You can read them out of sequence if you wish. The material will still be immediately applicable and easily understood. It's designed so that a reader who has never studied "happiness" at all can understand each concept along the way. If you have spent substantial time already on this concept you may choose to jump ahead, or skip around. That's fine, the material will still be useful.

Every baby step is written using a metaphor or slogan. The slogan was chosen because it contains truth about the particular baby step and is easy to remember. I suggest when you find one that you really need to focus on, to write it down on a small card and carry it around with you. Look at it often. Flash cards—post card size—are available from the author. They contain graphic illustrations of each particular baby step and will reinforce your learning. Tapes are also available for each baby step. The tapes complement the material in the book. They do not duplicate it. The tapes will also be helpful as you focus on the baby steps. A workbook has also been prepared to compliment each baby step. It includes journal activities, self-help questionnaires and other activities—two pages per step—to clarify each concept presented. See end of foreword for ordering information.

Do not despise the bottom rungs in the ascent to greatness.

—Publilius Syrus

Foreword

Little is actually known about the topic of "happiness." The research done on this subject is dwarfed by that done on illness. The actual studies done on happiness will fill only several file folders. In contrast, however, the research on depression would fill a warehouse. I think the reason is because there are so few happy people available to be researched. Yet the number of depressed people is phenomenal.

One of the basic flaws in behavioral sciences over the years has been to define happiness as "the absence of illness." Since so much time has been spent studying depression and other forms of mental illness, researchers have virtually no understanding of happiness. They have therefore defined "normal" as the *absence* of depression or other emotional disturbance. It's not defined as the *presence* of anything. Therefore what we call "normal" is actually mediocre. Normal is the absence of depression, not the presence of happiness. Most studies trying to measure mental health use this as a base line for their research. Therefore, to people who are searching for happiness, the entire system is flawed. By definition, happiness is considered abnormal and in some cases is actually defined as pathological.

Happiness is also misunderstood because of the way it has been commonly defined. Happiness and success are actually two totally different concepts. Happiness and wealth are different as well. Although you can measure someone's assets and gauge an individual's success, happiness is not something which can be measured in the laboratory, or produced by a pill. In fact, it's difficult to observe at all. It's something you experience internally on a subjective and individual level. As a result, it does not lend itself easily to research. It's also not something you can achieve and then hang onto. You can't really own it. You can only experience it. This book will help you do that. And we believe it can only be done *one baby step at a time.*

The kingdom of heaven is like a mustard seed, which a man took and planted in his field. Though it is the smallest of all seeds, yet when it grows it is the largest of garden plants and becomes a tree, so that the birds of the air come and perch in its branches.

—Matthew 13:31-32 NIV

Foreword

How long would it take you to learn a foreign language? It probably would depend on how well you needed to learn it. If you needed to learn it to live in a foreign country, it would take a bit longer. To have a conversational knowledge of a foreign language could take as little as a few weeks or months.

You speak the language you do, simply because you grew up around it. You listened, you practiced, and ultimately you mastered the language as your own. You also learned a particular dialect, accent, or inflection. Short of some impediment such as cleft palate or lisp, the way you speak has everything to do with where and how you grew up. If you grew up in Japan, even as a child of American parents, you might think, drink, and speak excellent Japanese. Though you appear occidental in your physical features, you are purely Asian in your thinking. In the same way, if you grew up in an unhappy environment, you may have learned unhappiness extremely well. You may think, dream, and speak excellent unhappiness. But the good news is, you can learn to speak a foreign language.

How long will it take? It depends on how long you work. How do you learn it? The same way you learn to speak a foreign language. You listen to tapes, you read books, you look at flash cards, you watch videos, you go to seminars, and then you visit the foreign country—the place where happy people are. *Baby Steps* is designed to help you accomplish that. We have audio cassettes, video cassettes, and flash cards available. Obtain these by writing Dr. John Q. Baucom at the address listed below or call the phone number. Learning a foreign language is not necessarily easy. Learning happiness will not be easy as well. It takes practice. One of the the best ways to succeed is one Baby Step at a time.

Human Resource Center
7433 Preston Circle
Chattanooga, TN 37421
(423) 855-5191

Introduction

Have you ever wondered why you're not happy? Or have you ever wondered why you're happy some of the time, but can't seem to sustain it? Perhaps, like me, you have noticed there are very few people who describe themselves as actually being happy. I've investigated these questions most of my adult life. When I was a teenager there was a popular song about happiness. One chorus went something like this. *". . .if you want to be happy for the rest of your life, don't make a pretty woman your wife. From my personal point of view, get an ugly girl to marry you. . ."*

The sad part is the advice presented in that song is probably as valid as most other advice given in the past about the subject of happiness. Although our Declaration of Independence grants each of us *". . .life, liberty, and the pursuit of happiness. . ."* most people have no idea how to actually go about the work of pursuing it. *Baby Steps to Happiness* suggests that not only can you pursue happiness, you can literally *make* yourself happy. This book begins where Thomas Jefferson's promise ended.

Many years ago at a seminar, a man lamented to me that he was a life-long pessimist. "I'm a pessimist. I've always been one. My parents, my grandparents, everyone in my family are pessimists." To him, pessimism—unhappiness—was terminal. It was genetic, permanent, and not optional. The idea that he could learn to *make* himself happy was foreign. When I began to convince him he could be happy, he thought I was joking. Before our discussion was concluded however, he was a believer. And after living in what he thought was "terminal pessimism" for over sixty years, he has become a very happy seventy year old. He simply had never imagined that happiness was an option. It was for him. And it is for you. *You can make yourself happy*. That's the purpose of this book.

Happiness is neither virtue, nor pleasure, nor this thing nor that, but simply growth. We are happy when we are growing.

—**William Butler Yeats**

Introduction

Before you actually begin to read *Baby Steps*, I want you to know the premise upon which this book is based. I do have biases, both personally, and as a writer. There are three assumptions I made when writing this book that are essential to understanding *Baby Steps to Happiness*. Grasping these elements ahead of time will help you make your own happiness far more quickly.

The first assumption is that life is composed of a continuous series of struggles. The way you respond to these will have a big impact on the early stages of your happiness. The second bias I have is that we all make mistakes. Welcome to the club! The way you respond to these mistakes will deeply affect how quickly you learn about happiness. The final bias I have is, most people give up too quickly. For some, learning to be happy is like learning a foreign language. It may take some study and practice. But the good news is, it's a language you *can* learn.

Begin today. It takes about a minute to read a page, and less than five to read a chapter. Give yourself that much of a chance. You're worth far more than a minute a day. But begin by investing that minimum. The return on your investment will convince you to commit more. You can make yourself happy—one baby step at a time. Have fun!

Life is difficult. This is a great truth, one of the greatest truths. It is a great truth because once we truly see this truth, we transcend it. . .Because once it is accepted, the fact that life is difficult no longer matters.

—M. Scott Peck, M.D., *The Road Less Traveled*

1

Beginning the Journey
to
Happiness

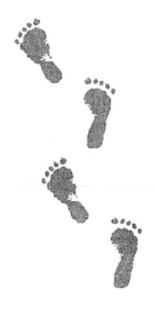

The Journey of a Thousand Miles Begins Now

HAVE you had a life-changing experience? Like skiing down a mountain when suddenly there is an avalanche. Or were you thrust into a situation where you had to save another's life, or they yours? There are many experiences that can create change in your life. For example, there was a man who was struck by lightening while riding a horse on a road. While he lived to tell the story, the trauma of that experience, combined with divine intervention, resulted in a tremendous personality change. A few others have experienced such dramatic change—but only a few.

Most permanent change is like weight loss. Experts say the only healthy way to lose weight and keep it off *is to do so slowly*. One pound per week seems to be the mutually-agreed limit. Sure, there are crash diets, water loss and starvation routines, but *true* weight loss must occur one pound at a time. Lasting personality change occurs the same way. Stopping a habit is often quite simple. Anyone who served in the military can recall making numerous habit-pattern changes. You learned to salute, say, "Yes, Sir," and "No, Sir," and march in formation. And you learned each of these things very quickly. Neither psychotherapy nor support groups were required. You simply did it. After several months you returned home on leave but *didn't* march into your mother's kitchen, or salute your father. A therapist wasn't required to adapt. Those are simple behavior changes. And they're remarkably easy.

Other change, however, is more difficult. You can change what you do or don't do quite easily. Changing *who you are*, however, is like losing weight. It takes a while. One "pound" per week is about all you can handle. It took years to gain the weight. It'll take time to lose it. In the same way, it took years to become who you are. It'll take a while to change. You create permanent change in your life *one baby step at a time*. Any change is possible when you look at it from that perspective.

Wash you, make you clean; put away the evil of your doings from before mine eyes; cease to do evil . . . .
—Isaiah 1:16

The Journey of a Thousand Miles Begins Now

TO make the journey, start with the first step. In the summer of 1959, I was a youngster living in Greensboro, North Carolina. Dwight Eisenhower was president. We owned a Studebaker. And Ray Charles was singing *What Did I Say?* on the jukebox. I was swimming with my father at a local swimming hole called Ritter's Lake. There was a multi-level diving tower in the middle, with four platforms beginning at water level. The top platform was probably twenty feet high and had been taunting me for weeks! On this occasion my father had particularly encouraged me to dive from the top level.

I swam to the tower and began by diving off the lowest platform. Then I proceeded to the second with no problem. When I got to the third level, I jumped off, then returned and dove on the second attempt. I finally climbed the ladder to the fourth level and paused. My dad smiled and waved. I glanced back at the water, jumped in feet first and swam to where he watched. We spoke for a few minutes and he encouraged me to go ahead and make the dive. I returned to the tower, counting each step as I climbed. I continued counting as I walked to the edge of the fourth platform and leaned into a dive without even pausing for contemplation.

I was so ecstatic I laughed out loud on the way down. My father was even more excited than I. Later he told me I could do anything I wanted in life by following the same pattern. "You started off at the bottom level, and then went up to the second, and the third, then the fourth. Then you jumped instead of dove. One small step at a time and you can accomplish anything . . . ." I nodded my head agreeably but was perplexed by his reaction. For some reason, that accomplishment gave him more excitement than anything else I'd ever done. I didn't understand it at the time. Unfortunately, within a year he died. Thirty-five years later, I understood. The truth is you can accomplish any goal by taking baby steps, "one small step at a time . . . ."

Begin where you are; work where you are; the hour which you are now wasting, dreaming of some far off success, may be crowded with grand possibilities.

—Orison Swett Marden

The Journey of a Thousand Miles Begins Now

YOU have probably heard the old saying, "A journey of a thousand miles begins with one step . . . ." If you want to create change, the first step is probably the most important. Momentum from the first step makes the second and third much easier. This quote can be traced to Lao Tze, a 6th century B.C. Chinese philosopher. The most accurate translation states, "The journey of a thousand miles must begin with one step . . . ." Actually I like that version better. It places the emphasis where it belongs. For change to occur in your life, you must take the first step. Waiting doesn't help. Worrying only magnifies it. Blaming makes it more complicated.

Changing all at once can seem intimidating. Let's face it, you can really get discouraged if you think of an entire thousand-mile journey. The sheer volume of necessary change can be downright frightening. The greater the change—the greater the stress. So you may look at the thousand-mile journey and decide it's too far. As a result you may never take the necessary first step, and fail to do what you must to succeed. As a result, you'll never reach the goal.

Don't make this mistake. Take the first baby step in your thousand-mile journey. You'll hear the haunting whine at some level exclaiming, *"It's too far, too much, too big, etc."* Ignore it. The momentum for change begins with your first baby step in the direction of your goal. Don't look at the thousand-mile journey. Look three feet in front of you—one baby step ahead on the trail. It's not intimidating. It's not a thousand miles. It's one baby step. And you can take it.

God always gives a greater blessing to humble beginnings than to those that start with the chiming of bells.
                                        —St. Vincent de Paul, *Life and Works*

The Journey of a Thousand Miles Begins Now

OCCASIONALLY, change can seem impossible. A lady came to see me for counseling and described her plight in-between sobs. At the young age of twenty-six she found herself fifty pounds overweight and incredibly lonely. She had little formal education, few employable skills, and was thirty-five thousand dollars in debt to charge card companies. Her depression had become so overwhelming she had decided to commit suicide. Instead of attempting to convince her the problems were minor, I encouraged her to accept the problems she described as massive. It was easy for me to agree that facing these problems head-on, all at once, was a tremendous task.

"Look at yourself," I suggested. "I agree you're in an awful situation. It feels impossible to you, doesn't it?" She nodded her head in agreement. She trusted me because I didn't lie to her and attempt to encourage her naively, as others had. By gaining her trust she was willing to listen as I described how I completed a book on deadline. I explained, when thinking of finishing the entire book as one task, I was overwhelmed. But by breaking it down to merely four pages per day, it became apparent I could finish the book within three months—well before deadline. *Completing the book* was a task I didn't know if I could achieve or not. Four pages per day anybody could do. She began taking baby steps immediately. She lost weight before resolving the debt. But eventually she did both.

Don't worry about mammoth change. Just go for one baby step at a time. Choose one task you would like to accomplish in the next four weeks. It could be something you've been putting off, such as cleaning out the garage. It could be something like learning to watercolor. For the first week simply gather the materials or do the research for the task. Buy boxes and organizers for the garage. Arrange for watercolor painting instruction or purchase supplies. On week two spend a small amount of time beginning the task. Follow up for week three and four. Try *one* baby step. The other 999 miles will take care of themselves.

Don't deny the existence of a mountain in your life; deny its authority to stay, and refuse to allow it to stop the plan of God in your life.
—Jesse Duplantis

Happy Is Not What You Are—
It's a Series of Things You Do

HAPPY is not what you are. It's a series of things you do. You can't be happy without doing the necessary things. Confusion arises because people define happiness—like their favorite food—in different ways. As an example, if you asked ten people their idea of a perfect meal, you'll get ten different answers. Who's right? They all are. The perfect meal has to do with your individual taste.

Happiness is the same way. One person's definition of a perfect meal, is another person's idea of garbage. Similarly one person's idea of happiness, may be your vision of boredom. Who's right? Both of you! Can circumstances make you happy or unhappy? No. Circumstances can influence happiness. It's unlikely you'll be blissfully happy in the face of adversity. As an example, to be happy when someone dies is inappropriate. In those circumstances, you do what's necessary to be happy later. You grieve. Someone who grieves is obviously unhappy. But once you do the necessary grieving, you regain your happiness. Grieving, in this case, is one of the things you *must do* to maintain happiness.

In any circumstance there are actions you can take to increase your happiness. Happiness is not in circumstances. It's in doing. And it's your doing. It's not up to your spouse, your hormones, or your parents. Only *you* can make *you* happy. And the way you make yourself happy is in the series of things you do.

Though our character is formed by circumstances, our own desires can do much to shape those circumstances; and what is really inspiring and ennobling in the doctrine of free will is the conviction that we have real power over the formation of our own character . . . .
—John Stuart Mill

Happy Is Not What You Are—It's a Series of Things You Do

I got my first exposure to "doing" on a combat patrol during the Vietnam War. We trudged through the terrarium-like jungle near the North Vietnamese border. The triple-canopy jungle cast a sultry emerald-colored fog amid the 100-degree midday sun. It was 1969, and I was acting as liaison with a Korean special operations group.

As we lumbered through the milky haze, my heart raced to keep pace. We had waltzed right into an ambush. Two of the Koreans were wounded. As I carried Choi I wondered at times if I was dreaming. But my drumming pulse reminded me it was all too real. Lieutenant Park stopped in front of me, dropping to one knee. He peered ahead intensely. Catching up with him I adjusted Choi's body on my shoulder as I passed my AK-47 rifle from one hand to the other. Then I carefully laid Choi down to check his wounds. "He OK?" Park asked. I nodded and answered that he would live. Park responded, "You do right thing, you be alive. You do wrong thing, you dead. Choi do wrong thing." He accented his last comments by drawing a forefinger across his throat like a knife. Similar to most Koreans I'd gotten to know, he made his point clearly.

I learned a great deal from the Koreans I worked with during the war. Lieutenant Park's comments were priceless. *You do right thing, you be alive. You do wrong thing, you dead.* The same is true with any goal. Happiness is not what you are. It's a series of things you *do*. It's the *doing* that makes the difference. In combat, do the right thing and you're alive. In life, *do* the right thing and you're happy. Happiness is not an assumption. It's baby steps taken on the journey to happiness.

If I then, your Lord and Master, have washed your feet; ye also ought to wash one another's feet. For I have given you an example, that ye should do as I have done to you . . . If ye know these things, happy are ye if ye do them.

—John 13:14–15, 17

Happy Is Not What You Are—It's a Series of Things You Do

HAPPINESS is in what you do. It is not something you own. It's more like reaching your ideal weight. If you return to bad habits, you'll easily gain the weight back. And this can occur all within a matter of weeks. Happiness is the same way. You actually have to work on it rigorously. As a society, we accept the idea you must exercise to remain fit. However, we reject the idea of exercising emotionally to remain happy.

Instead, most people just assume happiness happens. If you want to be happy, you must do what's necessary. It's not unusual for a person to change his lifestyle after a heart attack in an attempt to avoid additional problems. Similarly, you may need to adjust your lifestyle to avoid an emotional coronary. Some time ago I was talking to a man who said he wanted to be an author. I began asking questions about his writing habits. Before I even finished the first question, he held up his hand and interrupted. "—No, no," he shook his head. "I didn't say I want to write. I hate writing. I just want to be an author." Well, so do I. And maybe I missed his point. But I do think writing is necessary to become an author.

Yet as a society we've become like this man. We want money, but don't want to earn it. We want success, but aren't willing to make the sacrifices for it. And we want happiness, yet fail to do what's necessary to gain it. We fail to take the baby steps. Happiness is a series of things you *must* do. There's nothing to prevent you from experiencing it but yourself, regardless of money, genetics, or ethnicity. Don't look for happiness. You'll never find it that way. *Do the things* and happiness will follow.

I made a resolve then that I was going to amount to something if I could and no hours, nor amount of labor, nor amount of money would deter me from giving the best that there was in me. And I have done that ever since, and I win by it. I know.

—Colonel Harland Sanders

Happy Is Not What You Are—It's a Series Of Things You Do

HAPPY is not what you are. It's a series of things you do. The popular psychology of blame, attempts to convince you it's your parents' fault. Don't buy into it. If you grew up in a crazy home, suffered abuse, or grew up in poverty, it traumatized you. But it doesn't have to destroy your life. As a therapist, I've worked in various hospitals, drug treatment centers, and counseling clinics. I have seen people overcome horrifying childhoods and become extremely happy adults. I've also seen the opposite extreme. Childhood trauma does not predestine you to adult misery.

Too many people—many of them well-intentioned counselors—excuse today's emotional laziness by blaming yesterday's mistakes. It simply doesn't have to be that way. The psychology of blame has become common, and there's certainly enough to go around. It's become a quiz-show atmosphere, but instead of *Wheel of Fortune*, it's Wheel of Blame. From ACOA to CODA, to TMJ, OCP, PMS, and of course my favorite "alphabet soup"—ADD. The list seems to be endless. I want to let you in on a secret. After over twenty years as a consultant, educator, and writer, I've discovered the truth! *There are no **functional** families! I've never seen one.* **All families are dysfunctional.** *Welcome to the club . . . .*

Happiness is not coming from a functional family. It's not something you inherit from your past. It's a series of steps. It's things *you* do. Quit blaming the past. Accept responsibility for your happiness by changing what you do today. Take this baby step by making a list of things *you* need to do to be happy on a daily basis. As an example, if you need to get up in the morning and jog, pay your bills on time, or you need some quiet time or prayer each day to be happy, then include these. Follow up by scheduling time for each activity you've listed on your daily calendar. Then try it out for a week. Happy is not what you are, it's a series of things *you* do.

First say to yourself what you would be; and then do what you have to do.

—Epictetus

Know What's Really Important

KNOW *what's* **really** *important.* Over the years I've talked with literally thousands of people in therapy, on radio talk shows, and during seminars. Few actually knew what was genuinely important to them on a deep personal level. There are ways to analyze it. And there are ways you can discover what's really important to you. But very few people spend the time to understand it.

You need to know this at a level of depth. Most people can give superficial answers. They don't usually reflect the truth. What are examples of something that's really important? The answer is actually inside of you. What's really important to one person can be extremely insignificant to another. One conclusion the author of Ecclesiastes came to was most material pursuits are folly. A similar conclusion was presented in the movie *Don Juan DeMarco. There are only four questions of value in life—what is sacred, of what is the spirit made, what is worth living for, and what is worth dying for? The answer to each is the same—only love.* A friend of mine who had seen many friends die in Vietnam and his own six-year-old son die in a tragic auto accident had another criterion. "If there's no blood shed, and nobody's dead, it's no big deal . . ." *Know what's really important.*

The problem is there is no universal criterion for measuring importance. It's a decision you have to make individually. Certainly, there are those who would be glad to tell you what to think, feel, or do. And, in their opinion, what's important to them *should* be important to you as well. But if you honestly want to understand what's really important, you're going to have to do something dangerous. You're going to have to think deeply on your own. Don't wait for blood shed or until someone dies. Do it now. It's also a baby step in the right direction.

How desperately difficult it is to be honest with oneself.
—Edward Benson

Know What's Really Important

I first began thinking about "what's really important" when I attended a seminar many years ago. The speaker used an illustration to make his point. He said it was not original, but it still accomplishes more clarity than other analogies I've heard. The speaker placed a plank of wood the dimensions of a diving board on the floor. He asked one of the participants if he would walk the length of the plank for a fifty-dollar bill.

The participant readily responded that he would. The speaker then went through a methodical series of escalations. Each successive time he increased the plank height and the ante! From the floor, to between two tables, he continuously increased the risk and the reward. Each time the participant would hedge, the speaker increased the payoff by adding another zero. Over time the height raised to the 40th floor of a nearby building. The reward for walking the plank was raised from $50 to $500, then $5000, and eventually to $50,000. At the 40th floor the participant refused to walk the plank even for $5 million.

Finally the speaker said "Okay, you won't walk the plank for five million dollars. Now let's change the rules. Let's say this time I've got your five-year-old daughter and I'm hanging her out the window on the 40th floor. You're on one side of the plank and I'm on the other. If you don't walk it, I'm going to drop her." The participant not only said that he would run across, but promised he would also beat up the seminar leader when he got to the other side! This is a way of knowing what's really important. His daughter was of far more importance to him than five million dollars. What would you walk the plank for? What would you come close to walking the plank for? Think about it. It's an important baby step on the road to happiness.

For where your treasure is, there will your heart be also.
                                              —Matthew 6:21

Know What's Really Important

HOW do you learn what's *really* important? Sometimes we learn best during times of trauma. This is probably more true for men than women. For some reason it often takes trauma for a man to learn what's important to him. Somehow when you get hit "upside the head" it opens your mind. I'm not sure how that works, but it seems to be the case.

I learned what was really important during the birth of my first child. He almost died during delivery. I remember literally running into my mother on the way to neo-natal Intensive Care. I explained to her what had happened. I told her I would do anything for the child to live, including giving my blood, heart, or even my brain. I knew I was willing to die to save his life. To me that's what was really important. What are you willing to die for? If you're honest you might say, not much! There are probably few causes, slogans, or battle cries you would willingly give up your life to perpetuate. But there are some. And the closer you would go to the point of death for that cause, the more important it really is.

Few would say they were willing to die for money, realizing that after dying they wouldn't be around to enjoy it. I've never heard a woman say she wanted her epitaph to be, "Sally sure did maintain her ideal weight" or "Doesn't she look great? She's buried in her high school prom dress." I've never heard anyone say they were willing to die to pay their bills, or a funeral speaker intone solemnly, "He carries a good credit rating with him to his grave." However many people react as if these were life-and-death issues. What's really important? What would you walk the plank for? What would you die for? What would you want on your tombstone? These are the things you need to focus on to decide what's really important. *Know what's really important.* It will help you chart your baby steps on the road to happiness.

Ninety percent of the world's woe comes from people not knowing themselves, their abilities, their frailties, and even their real virtues.
—Sydney J. Harris

Know What's Really Important

I believe in foxhole conversions. Unfortunately, many people
need pain to learn what's really important. I've seen many people
who've suffered heart attacks, or been close to death, and as a result,
changed permanently. A lady who I met initially through a radio
talk show described living with an abusive husband for twenty-eight
years. He had tortured her in every imaginable way but she refused
to end the relationship.

Finally, she had enough pain. It happened after she had attempted suicide and was laying near death in a hospital emergency
room. When her husband came to visit, he didn't offer condolences
or ask what he could do to help. Instead, he began complaining,
"Why did you do this to me? Who's going to cook for me while
you're in the hospital? Who's going to wash my clothes?" The pain
of this insult was enough for her to finally create change. Others
can learn to create change by taking another approach. "What does
this (job/experience/relationship) add to the quality of my life?"
When I asked one young man, he responded, "Absolutely zero!"
He ended up getting out of a dead-end career. A person who had
been through a house fire shared this criterion. After evacuating
his family and pets, he had at the most, sixty seconds before the
entire house collapsed. The things he decided to rescue in that final
minute were *really* important to him.

What would you salvage if the roof was about to cave in and you
had already evacuated your family? What would you grab in the final
minute? Know what's really important. "What would I walk the plank
for? What am I willing to die for? What would I like my epitaph to say?
What does this add to the quality of my life? If I had sixty seconds,
what would I take?" Take this baby step today by listing the answers
to the questions in this chapter. You will become a lot happier knowing
where to spend your time and efforts. *Know what's really important.* It's
a vital step on the road to happiness.

---

*If a man knows not what harbor he seeks, any wind is the right
wind.*

—Seneca

Learn to Drive Your Own Bus

A friend of mine working the baby step program had a fascinating dream. Probably inspired by the movie *Speed*, she dreamed she was on a bus careening out of control. But in her case the driver was the problem, not a bomb. However, a faceless rescuer did end up throwing her off the bus before it crashed and burned. As we discussed the dream I asked if she recognized the bus driver. "It looked a lot like my ex-husband," she explained. "But a bit more maniacal. This guy was really nuts! My 'ex' was only half crazy!"

Learning to drive your own bus is a major concept in the baby step program. It involves learning to take control of your own happiness. With many people this is a brand new experience and involves new habits. Learning to take control of your own bus—happiness—is a difficult process. When you let others drive, you go wherever they take you. But that's only part of the problem. There is also a part of you that's determined to drive your *own* bus over the cliff. It can be a major part, or just a small portion. But there's a self-destructive element that can occasionally take over the wheel and steer you toward the nearest cliff. Learning to drive your own bus means slowing your vehicle, and getting it under your conscious control.

As a consultant who has worked with people since 1974, I believe each of us, probably in any given twenty-four hour day has moments of crystal-clear thinking. We also have moments—maybe only a few—of complete irrational craziness. When you have your brief losses of sanity, you need to take yourself out of the driver's seat and say, "No, I don't need to be driving now." On these occasions, choose someone you can trust—a designated driver—to help you through your tough moments. Yet make sure your designated driver is rational. If you make the mistake of allowing a "maniacal ex" to hijack your bus and your mental health, you'll pay severe consequences. When you're in control and in good shape, you drive it. When not, have a few designated drivers who can take over and steer you out of harm's way.

Be wise in the way you act toward outsiders; make the most of every opportunity.

—Colossians 4:5 NIV

Learn to Drive Your Own Bus

PART of driving your own bus is learning to control it. Part of achieving your own happiness is learning to control it as well. To accomplish this, it's important to define happiness as occurring within you. Happiness can't come from outside of you. Your boyfriend or girlfriend can't provide it. A pill or drink won't create it. There are several things you can do, however that will.

Happy people make their own standards and live by them. If their life standards are that of a church or some other organization, the happy person has internalized them as his or her own. They have consumed the standards, and aren't chasing them. They're living them. The individual is driving the bus, not chasing it. Several other factors are of equal importance. One of them is developing confidence and security in your ability as a "driver." You need to let go of any cynicism you may have—especially directed toward yourself. This results in a feeling of self-control and belief that your life has meaning. Former author and journalist Norman Cousins wrote, "You feel most insecure when obsessed with your fears . . ." Learning to drive your own bus means overcoming fears you'll careen out of control and developing a sense of security in your own skills.

Another key to driving your own happiness bus is accepting and enjoying what you are—especially your faults and mistakes. This drive is going to be filled with blunders. Accepting and learning to expect it is a major baby step. In doing so your security level in getting behind the steering wheel will be vastly improved. Philosopher and president of Harvard University at the turn of the century Dr. William James once wrote, *How pleasant is the day when we give up striving to be younger—or slender! Thank God when we say these illusions are gone . . . .* Give up your illusions. Set reasonable standards while keeping your dreams, and enjoy each step of your journey along the way. By doing so you'll take control of your bus and ultimately take control of your life.

The first essential, of course, is to know what you want.
—Robert Collier

Learn to Drive Your Own Bus

THERE was a time in my life, when I would have never dared speak in public, talk on the radio, or risk writing a book. I did my job quietly. I taught at a small college, and worked in hospitals developing alcohol and drug treatment centers. Then I was given a wake up call. Similar to my friend at the beginning of this baby step, it came in the form of a dream.

In my dream I had died and was waiting at "the pearly gates." It looked like a surreal scene from Woody Allen's movie—*Love and Death*. Clouds floated up to my knees as I waited in line for my moment with St. Peter. I wasn't scared or nervous. In fact, for once in my life I was patient waiting in line! Finally it was my turn. I told St. Peter my name. He pulled out a stack of computer printouts about six inches thick, and began reading them aloud. After a few moments he quit reading, and looked up. "But those aren't really important . . . ." Then he reached down and picked up another stack of printouts, this one over four feet tall. He rested his hand on top of the stack and looked at me curiously. *This however, is a list of things you could have done with the gifts God gave you! This is what's really important. Your sins can be forgiven. These can't . . . .*

My pounding heart jolted me awake. I was soaked with sweat and thought I was having a heart attack. After a few panicky minutes I called a friend on the phone and calmed down. Later that week I discussed my dream with several other friends and began changing my life. One of the results is this book. It's important to pay attention when your bus is going the wrong direction. Whether your wake up call is a dream, feedback from one of your designated drivers, or from hitting bottom, pay attention. A wake up call is either your subconscious mind's, or God's way of getting your attention. It's an alarm letting you know there's a problem ahead. If you ignore it you may end up self-destructing. It's much easier to slow the bus down, pull to the side of the road and change directions. Learn to drive your own bus. You'll be happier as a result.

It you don't run your life, somebody else will.
—John Atkinson

Learn to Drive Your Own Bus

LEARNING to drive your own bus can be difficult and laborious. Though liberating in its outcome, the process itself can be exhausting. If you're like most people, you've spent a lifetime letting others drive. Caretaking, trying to please, and denying responsibility has become an accepted way of life in modern society. Deciding to take control can have adverse consequences. The biggest problem will likely be that people who drove your bus in the past are going to object.

There are several things you can do to help make progress. Begin by visualizing yourself crawling behind the wheel, successfully slowing the bus down, and steering it in the direction you want to go. I suggest seeing it multi-dimensionally—actually seeing, hearing, smelling and touching. The more comprehensive your visualization, usually the more successful it will be. Prayer and meditation can also be very helpful. Ask your higher power for assistance as you take control of your life and happiness.

Make a list of people who create negative influences in your life. Do what a friend of mine did. Divide them up into two lists—assassins and idiots. Assassins are those who purposely want to hurt you. They're malicious, insensitive, and will go out of their way to cause you pain. The idiots on the other hand, are sometimes well-meaning but bumbling. Steer completely away from the assassins. Try to educate and reform the idiots. If you can't convert them, say good-bye to them as well. Make a third list which are your designated drivers. Enlist them as your allies in this process. You'll need all the help you can get. Get the most reliable of your designated drivers to help hold you accountable. If they hear you blaming and projecting responsibility, ask them to let you know. If they observe you becoming mentally lazy, invite them to give you a wake-up call. If they think you're developing any dependencies, ask that they point them out immediately. Taking control of your happiness is like any other habit. It's something you can learn. Feedback and accountability will help you learn more quickly.

The only true measure of success is the ratio between what we might have done and what we might have been on the one hand, and the thing we have made and the thing we have made of ourselves on the other.
—H.G. Wells

Happen to Life Instead of
Letting Life Happen to You

IT'S not the *things that happen to you* that are important. It's how *you happen to things* that really matters. Your *reaction* defines your mood, attitude, and behavior. In fact, your reaction to events is of vastly more importance than reality. At times, reality seems almost irrelevant. How you react or happen, is within your control. What occurs around you is not.

Most people are familiar with examples of "eyewitness" accounts. Though two eyewitnesses observe the same accident, they report incredibly contrasting versions of events. Yet, they're supposedly describing the same accident. Who's right? Is anybody right? Within their subjective emotional reality, people respond differently. Their individual reaction is based on how they perceived an event. As far as eyewitness accounts are concerned, each person would pass a lie detector test, even though they may record conflicting accounts of the same event. That's how believable subjective perception is.

How you react to a series of events on an emotional level is everything. It's not the event that matters. If you approach life with a healthy attitude, even in the face of adversity, you can still be happy. This is true, even if the events are overwhelmingly stressful. It's not what happens to you that matters, it's how you react to it. We say, go *do to* a situation, rather than allowing the situation to do something to you. Don't sit around and let things happen. Go out and happen to things. In this way you begin to define your reality before it defines you. We think it's a healthy approach, and an important baby step on the road to happiness.

Consistent winners refuse to wait for breaks to happen. The unexpected is part of their game plan and they thrive on the element of surprise. They'll "go for broke" any time, anywhere. Their performance implies that there is no tomorrow.

—Jack Whitaker

Happen to Life Instead of Letting Life Happen to You

YEARS ago we learned about life in a different way. I spent most of my life as a child and teenager on a rural North Carolina farm. As youngsters we learned to *happen* to life. Television stations that existed in those days couldn't reach our isolated mountain village. There was time for play, but we had to *happen* for play to occur. Passive entertainment was limited to reading and listening to clear-channel radio at night from such faraway mystical locations as WLS Chicago, KDKA Pittsburgh, and KMOX St. Louis. These powerful signals rocked us to sleep each night. It was our way of maintaining contact with the universe.

We also learned if we were going to survive the harsh Appalachian winters, we had to *happen* to life. In the spring we planted potatoes, tomatoes, and onions. I crawled on my hands and knees through tall rows of corn weeding them on hot July afternoons. We pruned the apple trees each spring, picked and canned apples in the fall, and ate them all winter. We grew celery in the summer and packed it in barrels of sand. Somehow it was edible till the next spring. Potatoes that we dug in late summer were covered with lime and lasted till the next year. We cut the sprouts off them and started the entire process over again.

And we *happened* to the livestock as well. Two cows provided milk, cream, butter, and cheese. Hens gave us eggs, and sheep gave us their wool that we sold to buy school clothes. But none of them did anything passively. If I purposely didn't *happen* to "Bessie's" udder we had no milk to drink. Wool isn't shed by the sheep naturally. Somebody had to *happen* to shear it. If the chickens starved or froze to death, we could starve. And if I didn't *happen* to some trees we all could have frozen to death and starved as well, since we cooked over a wood stove. In those days we *happened* to life naturally. We learned in the most honest ways. It was a dramatic and effective way to internalize this Baby Step. Passivity is a dangerous habit. Happen to things. It's a tremendous stride toward happiness.

An idle soul shall suffer hunger.

—**Proverbs 19:15**

Happen to Life Instead of Letting Life Happen to You

BEHAVIORAL scientists refer to a concept called "locus of control." Locus is a combination of the words location and focus. In science the term is used to describe "place." That's consistent with its meaning in original Latin. Your place—or locus—of control is an important concept, because in many ways it determines how you react when adversity occurs.

Your locus of control is going to be predominately internal or external. Most people will be seventy percent in one direction and thirty in the other. If your locus is internal, you're more likely to be centered on what's happening inside of you. If your locus is external, you'll be more focused on things around you. The person who has an external locus will be perpetually reacting to events going on around them. Consequently, these people feel out of control. Externally-locused people obsess on what others proscribe as their limits. Their obstacles become paramount, and as a result, possibilities are limited.

People with an internal locus of control are more focused on what's going on inside. By shifting your locus to be more internally-based, you begin to empower yourself. This perspective gives you a sense of personal control of your life. And that's not an illusion. You experience personal control, because frankly, you have it. You have control of yourself. You can begin this very moment to become internally locused. Begin by making a decision that you're going to switch the power over to your internal circuit, more than to the circuit of things around you. It's an important baby step in your journey to happiness.

There are two big forces at work, external and internal. We have very little control over external forces such as tornadoes, earthquakes, floods, disasters, illness and pain. What really matters is the internal force. How do I respond to those disasters? Over that I have complete control.

—Leo Buscaglia

Happen to Life Instead of Letting Life Happen to You

WHEN you shift to an internal locus of control, your individual reaction automatically grows more important than things that happen to you. This will lead to a higher degree of trust in your own experience. You'll have fewer questions as to whether or not what you're experiencing is valid. You'll be less waffling in your decision making. You'll grow less affected by other's emotions as a result. When people question your reality, you may entertain their doubt intellectually, but will not be affected on a disabling emotional level. You simply know whether or not your experience is questionable.

This will ultimately lead to the ability to "reframe" things that happen to you. Reframing takes an event which could be potentially destructive, and "reframes" it as a learning experience. Reframing is the art of taking something interpreted by most people as devastating, and putting a new frame around it. Instead of junk, it then can become not only usable, but art! With an internal locus of control, undue criticism from others grows irrelevant. You reframe criticism, mistakes, and temporary failures as learning experiences. Happy people (HAPs) do have bad moments. They simply define them as ways to build happiness muscles. Yes, HAPs do have doubts. Yet they're based more on intellect, and less on emotion. Yes, HAPs do *like* the approval of others. They just don't *need* it.

By developing an internal locus, you react less. You don't wait for things to happen. You are perpetually happening to things. You can begin to practice this baby step by reframing a negative experience. Describe one occasion in the last seven days where you were externally controlled. Determine how you would replay that situation and be more internally driven. Rehearse your response so the next time it occurs, you can change your locus. This is not an easy baby step. It will not make you popular. People won't like you more if you master this step. It empowers you, not them. It gives you the sense of control, not others. They won't like it. But you'll be far better off on the road to happiness.

Man is not a creature of circumstances. Circumstances are the creatures of men.

—Benjamin Disraeli

2

Choosing the Direction
to
Happiness

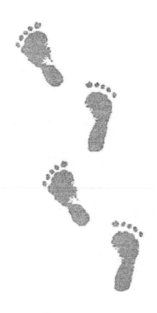

Your Accomplishments Will Seldom Exceed Your Expectations

YOUR accomplishments will seldom exceed your expectations. Expectations are important in various ways. If your expectations are unrealistic at either end of the spectrum, you're probably headed for disappointment. As an example, if you have an expectation life will be easy or you'll be taken care of, you're treading on very dangerous territory. On the other hand, if you expect life to be unfair and you can never succeed, you probably won't. Or if you're convinced everyone is out to get you, somebody probably will.

Your best chance for happiness occurs when your expectations are high for yourself, low for others, and optimistic about life in general! If you expect too little from yourself, high achievement is unlikely. If you expect too much from yourself, disappointment is awaiting. Appropriate expectations are an important ingredient for happiness. In actuality, people's expectations are usually too low for themselves and too high for others! Either way, it's a mistake. Contrary to what some philosophers suggest, I really don't believe expectations *determine* outcome. I do think they establish parameters of the outcome. Merely having high expectations will not make you successful. Yet if they're too low, they may prevent you from succeeding as much as you would have liked.

Make the expectations for your own performance high. You can control how you perform. Have little or no expectations for others. You can't control what they do, so don't try. Make your expectations boundaries you attempt to exceed. If you become frustrated or guilty, investigate whether your expectations are realistic. Adjust them as necessary. Consider realigning them, but realize your accomplishments will rarely exceed your expectations. When you truly understand this you're on the way to happiness.

Dream lofty dreams, and as you dream, so shall you become. Your vision is the promise of what you shall one day be; your ideal is the prophecy of what you shall at last unveil.

—James Allen

Your Accomplishments Will Seldom Exceed Your Expectations

APPROPRIATE expectations can lead to peace of mind. If you're deeply disappointed in life, it's probably due to some unrealistic belief developed in your past. Usually it results from a feeling of entitlement. These originate from a belief that you are entitled to privilege without earning it. This is often due to being spoiled or overly indulged in early childhood. If you feel entitled, you are probably headed for a major disappointment. Such unrealistic expectations can be adjusted. And if you are going to have any degree of happiness, it's necessary to do so.

Other unrealistic expectations often revolve around intense emotion. I had a long series of discussions with a close friend who was in love with a severe alcoholic. She was constantly wanting to know how she could "fix" the relationship. She would call me on the phone and talk as long as I would listen. Finally, one day in frustration, I blurted out the truth. "If you expect a healthy relationship you'll have to find a healthy person to have it with. You have defined what you have with this man as 'normal.' The insanity you're experiencing is 'normal' for him. If healthy is what you're looking for, you're going to have to find someone else."

She didn't like the answer, but at least it helped her see the light. If you expect healthy fruit to grow from grossly unhealthy seeds, you're expectations are wrong. You will definitely be disappointed as a result. In my friend's case, expecting a roller-coaster relationship would have led to happiness. A roller coaster ride was exactly what she got. Expectations are important. Appropriate expectations are even more important. Make your expectations high, but also keep them realistic.

We lift ourselves by our thought, we climb upon our vision of ourselves. If you want to enlarge your life, you must first enlarge your thought of it and of yourself. Hold the ideal of yourself as you long to be, always, everywhere—your ideal of what you long to attain—the ideal of health, efficiency, success.

—Orison Swett Marden

Your Accomplishments Will Seldom Exceed Your Expectations

THERE'S a Greek myth about a sculptor named *Pygmalion*. He chiseled a statue of the perfect lady, and then fell in love with it. Obviously, he could expect nothing in return from his marble statue, so his love had to be altruistic. The goddess of love was very impressed with this young sculptor's altruistic belief about love. In response, she brought his statue to life and they "lived happily ever after."

Years later George Bernard Shaw adapted this myth to a play he entitled, *Pygmalion*. The play was turned into a musical entitled, *My Fair Lady* and the rest, as they say—is history. Incidentally, a screen writer did a modern-day variation on the *My Fair Lady* theme and called it *Pretty Woman*. In each of these adaptations of the original myth, one person's deep beliefs changed both of their lives. In the original Pygmalion myth the statue became a person. In *My Fair Lady* the street urchin Eliza Doolittle passed herself off as a duchess at a royal reception. The prostitute—pretty woman—developed a healthy relationship and married a millionaire. These transformations were possible due to the powerful beliefs of another person.

Several years later I conducted a teacher-training workshop. I spoke to the teachers about the power of deep belief. One of the ladies came up with an ingenious way of implementing it. At the beginning of the school year she would kneel and whisper in her first graders' ears, *You've got to be special to be in my class. I only get the really smart students.* Each child reacted with pleasant surprise upon discovering they were "special." She ended up having far less difficulty in her classrooms than any other teachers. She also started receiving phone calls from parents telling her they were glad someone finally recognized their children were so smart! It turned out to be a win/win situation. Beliefs can do that in children. They can do it for you too. Develop positive beliefs about yourself, and you can change your own life.

Where there is no vision, the people perish.
—**Proverbs 29:18**

Your Accomplishments Will Seldom Exceed Your Expectations

NEGATIVE beliefs and expectations can also have powerful results. They will create cynicism and stress at the least. At the worst, they can be a set up for absolute failure. One of the most powerful things you can do in a relationship is to remove expectations. At times this can have an almost comical effect. The other person will often be puzzled. She may search for clarification in an attempt to get you to place expectations on her. In the long run however, removing expectations frees her to be independent. It allows her to determine how she will behave in the relationship. And it can be a liberating, if puzzling, gift.

As far as expectations about yourself are concerned, I suggest keeping them *high*. But at the same time, *make certain they're within the realm of your control*. Let's face it, if you expect to jump off a thirty-story building and fly away you'll be disappointed. That's not only an unrealistic expectation, but a dangerous one. There's a difference between having high expectations, and having delusional ones! Having expectations that are high, based on performance is one thing. Having high expectations about *getting high*, jumping out of a thirty-story window and flying, are another. I suggest having high expectations, instead of getting high.

But make your expectations reality based. With apologies to some, regardless of how "clear" you get, you will never walk through walls. Don't expect to. You can walk on coals, sleep on a bed of nails, bungee jump, and meditate. You still can't walk through walls. Your accomplishments will seldom exceed your expectations. Keep your expectations high, but make them realistic. For this baby step, list five areas in your life where you're disappointed with the results. Examine your expectations to determine if they're too high for others, too low for yourself, or unrealistic generally. Raise those expectations you have control over and lower expectations where you have little control. It's a baby step on the journey to happiness.

The cities and mansions that people dream of are those in which they finally live . . . .

—Lewis Mumford

Live the Life You Have Imagined

LIVE the life you have imagined. Actually most people are living lives others imagined for them. I once spoke to a physician in therapy who led what most people described as a magnificent life. He had a beautiful wife, a huge mansion, and the finest of cars. He had talented children who were quite successful and happy. But he was miserable. His only passion was playing the piano. He was a physician because his parents had wanted him to be. He continues to be one to please his wife and creditors.

Who imagined the life you are living? Who currently owns your life? For some people it's their spouse or parents. Others are living the life their *kids* imagined for them. Still others allow their job to determine how life should be led. For some it's creditors who make these decisions. With others, it's the illusion of security—the job, retirement down the road, insurance benefits. For some people it's none of the above. Perhaps it's the way you were raised or unfinished business from the past. In reality, too few experience the life they actually imagined. Some try. Most become discouraged by the obstacles encountered and quit. Others have good intentions but get sidetracked.

Set aside some time to take inventory of your life. Ask the question, "Who owns my life? What controls my life? If I'm not living the life I imagined, who imagined it for me?" Then begin to list the changes needed to refocus. The changes may be small, but the consequences will be enormous. Live the life you've imagined. Thoreau tells us if you do you will experience success never before imagined.

If one advances confidently in the direction of his dreams, and endeavors to live the life which he has imagined, he will meet with a success unexpected in common hours.

—Henry David Thoreau

Live the Life You Have Imagined

IT'S easy to *think* about living the life you have imagined. But too often the tyranny of the familiar prevents you from actually doing it. You can grow familiar with virtually any kind of dysfunction. Since what you practice, you become, unhappiness can be self-perpetuating. Whatever it is you are currently doing, you probably practiced for years. As a result, you define it as normal. You can grow cozy in it, regardless of the pain. We are incredibly adaptive creatures as returning prisoners of war and concentration camp victims have proven. Misery, pain, and abuse can become defined not only as normal, but desirable. This can be the case simply because of the familiarity.

In all honesty some people just want control. Even if it's painful, as long as they're in control it's acceptable. Some will occasionally exchange control for what is perceived as "a good deal." But they soon orchestrate events to get control, and their pain, back. These people have gown so familiar with pain, they'd rather have it, as long as it is accompanied by the illusion of control. At times this becomes an addiction to affliction. They'd rather have their familiar pain than risk the unfamiliar. "The devil you know is far better than the devil you don't know. . . ." This is true even if the unfamiliar looks quite promising and rewarding. With these people, it's the lack of predictability that's the problem. I've actually heard dozens of people echo this sentiment. *If it weren't for my pain, then I'd have nothing.* They become so familiar with affliction they grow addicted to it. Unhappiness reproduces itself as a result.

The tyranny of the familiar is that it grows to be a friend. Just as a deadly drug seduces an addict, so can pain. Addiction to affliction is a common malady. Don't be common. And don't get stuck in the familiar. Be one of the few who walks away from it and risks the possibility of unfamiliar success and happiness. Don't choose the familiar life. *Live the life you have imagined.*

If I had to choose between pain and nothing, I'd always choose pain.

—William Faulkner

Live the Life You Have Imagined

IF you're not living the life you have imagined, perhaps you need to check your thermostat. You may have set it too low! It's similar to the relationship between a thermostat and a central heating and cooling system. If it becomes too warm or too cool, the thermostat will trigger the correct system and return the temperature within the comfort zone. You can adapt to unhappiness the same way. If you experience more pleasure than you think you have a right to, the thermostat can kick in and you end up self-sabotaging! Comfort zone is a powerful concept.

I had a friend who was a military policeman on a U. S. base in Ethiopia. He described the adaptability of the human spirit in a memorable way. He explained they adapted to a different kind of comfort zone in Ethiopia. Since the equatorial climate is extremely hot they grew accustomed to heat. One night it got down to sixty-eight degrees. He described his friends putting on sweaters and thinking they saw ice forming on mud puddles. They had adapted so successfully to sweltering 100°F heat, that 68° seemed to be freezing. While they knew logically it was impossible for ice to form, it was a good illustration of how people can adapt to a very unusual comfort zone.

This is the same way people end up repeating unhealthy behavior patterns over and over again. They find themselves in the same circumstances, simply with different people. Some actually live the same year forty times, instead of actually living forty years. This is how one man ended up quitting five jobs in a row saying his bosses were unfair. His comfort zone had adapted in an unhealthy way. Instead of having five different jobs, he lived the same job five different times. But this is unnecessary. The good news, is your comfort zone can change in either direction. You can adapt to the familiarity of affliction and define it as normal and functional. Or you can change your thermostat setting. If you're tired of misery, make a dramatic change. Change your internal thermostat setting and live the life you have imagined. Grow comfortable with pleasure for a change. It'll be a baby step in the right direction.

No servant can serve two masters, either he will hate the one and love the other, or he will be devoted to the one and despise the other . . . .
—Luke 16:13 NIV

Live the Life You Have Imagined

IT could be that instead of leading the life you had imagined, you are living the life your family imagined for you. Perhaps you're leading the life your mother and father imagined—or even your grandparents. Or it could be you're trying to reconcile your parents' unfinished business in your own life. This is a fairly common path but not one I would recommend. The late Doctor Murray Bowen came up with what he called "the multi-generation transmission process." Bowen believed behavior and emotions are learned through generations. He suggested most people robotically repeat the patterns of their family past.

To Bowen, the cure was what he called differentiation. This process is becoming *different* from your family of origin and living the life you have imagined. Bowen considered this to be a life-time work. After all, you spend upwards of twenty-plus years becoming like your family. To expect to give up the multi-generation transmission process easily is naive. Bowen's concept of differentiation is actually deep and complex. Differentiating yourself is far more difficult than it sounds. It's similar to the concepts of, "separation and individuation." It's becoming an individual—as difficult as that may seem.

Live the life you have imagined. Forget about the one imagined for you by others. Think about what you would like to do with your life. If you could spend your time doing anything you wanted, how would you spend it? Make a list of at least twenty things you would do if there were no limits placed on you. The list might include big things like taking a vacation to Europe or quitting your present job and working for yourself. Smaller dreams might include painting your kitchen a different color or landscaping your yard. Choose one dream from the list and make a small gesture toward nurturing it. Using the examples above, you might subscribe to a travel magazine, take a class in small business management, pick out the paint color, etc. Live the life you have imagined. Only you can determine what that is. Only you can imagine it. And only you can take control of your life.

The imagination equips us to perceive reality when it is not fully materialized.

—Mary Caroline Richards

You Can't Have a $50,000 Car and a $50,000 Marriage

You can't have a $50,000 car and a $50,000 marriage . . . The energy it takes to achieve one major goal, is often so great it can exclude having the energy required to achieve another major goal. A $50,000 car requires $50,000. That's a lot of money, time, energy, and concentration. A "$50,000 marriage" requires equal commitment. In most settings those two goals would be mutually exclusive.

I know few people who can successfully pursue both. And the ones that do, paid the price when they were younger. They usually went through two or three other marriages while amassing their fortune. I like to say you can have *anything* you want, but you can't have *everything* you want. If you want money, you can earn it. If you want a quality marriage, you can work for it. If you want to balance your marriage and your earnings, you can do that too. But to say you want to excel at everything is to succeed at nothing. When going on a journey, you can't go north and south at the same time.

Goal setting is very important. And I do believe you can have anything you want. But you can't have everything you want. If you want a $50,000 marriage, good for you. If you want a $50,000 car, good for you as well. You probably will not have both, at least early in life. Choose your goals wisely, then pursue them energetically. At the same time, realize prioritizing one goal higher, may automatically exclude a lower-priority goal. If you're willing to pay the price, you can achieve your primary goals. But spreading yourself too thinly will result in frustration and a feeling of failure. *You can't have a $50,000 car and a $50,000 marriage.* Prioritize your goals, and you're well on the journey—baby stepping your way to happiness.

We live in a vastly complex society which has been able to provide us with a multitude of material things, and this is good, but people are beginning to suspect that we have paid a high spiritual price for our plenty.

—Euell Gibbons

You can't have a $50,000 car and a $50,000 marriage

YOU can have one of them, but you must plan first. Most people spend more time planning a vacation than planning their lives. One lady I know plans her vacations six months in advance. She plans every minute, including who she's going to be with, what she's going to do, and what she's going to take. She literally leaves nothing to chance. When she arrives at her vacation site, she's unable to relax. She's busy following the schedule.

I believe in goals. And I believe in planning. I think it's important to have strategic plans, quarterly objectives, and monthly projects. I also believe in having a daily plan with prioritized activities. But I don't believe you should become enslaved by your goals or plans. A goal should provide direction. It needs to be broad-based and general. Goals provide you with a broadly-defined area you pursue in life. Narrowly-focused goals can result in limiting your boundaries. If you're narrowly obsessed with a pinpoint goal, you may miss opportunities which could result in the same long-term accomplishment. By becoming too obsessed, you miss the big picture, and end up thinking dichotomously.

As an example, the goal of taking a trip to Atlanta is reasonable. A goal of flying to Atlanta arriving exactly at twelve noon, going directly to the Omni to attend a 12:30 p.m. meeting, is an unreasonable goal. If your flight's delayed, you might resort to dichotomous thinking and not go at all. If your goal is simply to get to Atlanta, on the other hand, your options are still open. You can drive, take an alternate flight, catch a train, hitchhike, or ride a bicycle. Somehow you'll still get to Atlanta. You may not arrive precisely at 12:01 p.m., but you'll be there. This is the beauty of goals. They provide general direction. But don't make the mistake of being so locked into a particular sequence of steps that you miss the big picture. And the big picture is arriving at your destination. The way you get there may surprise you.

When one door closes, another opens. But we often look so long and so regretfully upon the closed door that we do not see the one which was opened for us.

—Alexander Graham Bell

You can't have a $50,000 car and a $50,000 marriage

THE emphasis here is placed on prioritizing. Frankly, I'd like both. I'd really like to have a $50,000 car and a $50,000 marriage, and a $50,000 family, and $50,000 kids, and $50,000 extra. Sure. I'd like to have it all! I found out the hard way that's impossible. You have to decide what's really important in your life. And what's really important must reflect your primary beliefs.

Primary beliefs act as the internal guidance computer on an airplane. The jet may be off course as frequently as 92% of the time. But the internal guidance system makes momentary corrections that redirects the aircraft back on course. You ultimately arrive at the proper destination. Your beliefs respond the same way. But there are times when a minor correction won't suffice. I've heard airline pilots say when faced with a massive storm they can't go around or above, they'll go back to where they started. They won't even attempt to go through a storm. The risks are too high. They fly back to the point of origin, and make the trip another day. They don't give up on their goal. They simply delay it. And they have good reason. Too many of their friends have self-destructed by being so locked into the plan they missed the big picture.

Goals need to provide you a general direction. Don't be imprisoned by them. Don't make foolish decisions based on a planning session you did in a sterile environment. The storms of reality will often present themselves to you. Make the intelligent choice. *You can't have a $50,000 car and a $50,000 marriage*. Those are different goals. Choose all your goals wisely, and then pursue them energetically. Be ready to take an alternate route if necessary. If you can't, turn around and go back to your origination point. It's not only a baby step on the journey to happiness. It's a safe course to follow.

What good is it for a man to gain the whole world, and yet lose or forfeit his very self?

—Luke 9:25 NIV

<u>You can't have a $50,000 car and a $50,000 marriage</u>

IF you pursue a goal inconsistent with your beliefs, you will always fail. As an example, if a man's goal is to purchase a $50,000 car, but he doesn't want to sacrifice family time to earn the money, he'll not likely afford a $50,000 car. Yet in this example, he isn't a failure. His goal of buying the expensive car was inconsistent with his belief system. He believed his family was important. Marriage was important. Parenting was important. Children were important. Making money was *also* important.

In this case, the "*also*" is the qualifier. His primary beliefs included family, marriage, and parenting. His secondary beliefs were "*also*" about money. Your goals need to be consistent with your beliefs. Primary goals will only be achieved if they're absolutely reflected by your *primary beliefs*. If they're inconsistent, you may end up sabotaging your goals. The easy tip-off here is the "also" beliefs. They are often the after thoughts. In the movie *Under Siege* Steven Seagal played the role of a Navy Seal who was spending his twilight tour as a cook on a Navy battleship that gets hijacked. After watching him in action, a playboy bunny, stranded with him on the vessel says, "I thought you were a cook." Seagal deadpans back to her, "I *also* cook." *Cooking* was his secondary *also* specialty. His primary specialty was being a Navy Seal!

How do you know what your primary beliefs are? You can begin to understand these by stating the preamble to your life. The preamble to the US Constitution describes what we'll fight for. The preamble to your life can be the same thing. Take a sheet of paper and write down the following sentence twenty-five times. I believe _____ is important. Leave a space to fill in the blank later. Then set aside thirty to forty-five minutes and fill in the blank twenty-five times. After doing so go back and prioritize your responses. Let your "number one" reflect your most fervent belief. "Number two" is your second most significant belief. And so on, down to number twenty-five. The first ten will be your primary beliefs, the last fifteen are your "also" beliefs.

I'd rather have roses on my table than diamonds on my neck.
—Emma Goldman

Have a Reason to Get Out of Bed Each Morning

HAVE a reason to get out of bed each morning. Like other baby steps discussed thus far, this one is a continual process. Certainly it refers to having a reason to get out of bed on a daily basis. But it also refers to a larger reason to get out of bed. In many ways it answers the question, "Why get out of bed and live at all?" On the other end of the spectrum, it's a baby step you can use with more frequency. Having a reason to get out of bed is never-ending.

What is your reason for getting out of bed? For some it's other people. She gets out of bed to parent her children. He gets out of bed to please his spouse. Or she looks to her job as the reason to get out of bed. None of these really work. In fact, if any of those is your reason to get out of bed, you may have big problems facing you down the road. Your children will grow up. You will quit, get fired or retire from your job. Your spouse will leave, or one of you will die. If you die first, you'll ultimately die alone anyway. Your reason for getting out of bed needs to come from within. And it needs to be something over which you have some control. Having a reason to get out of bed drives you. It propels you forward.

Having a reason to get out of bed—a HARTGOB—is different than a goal. A goal is something external. A HARTGOB is internal. It's why you got up this morning. And on a larger scale it's why you're alive. HARTGOB is perpetual. It's why you're doing what you're doing each moment of the day. It helps you understand why you react the way you do. It can become the source of energy that propels you through life. *Have a reason to get out of bed each morning.* Think about it, focus on it, and keep it in front of you. It's a major baby step on your road to happiness.

Many persons have a wrong idea of what constitutes true happiness. It is not attained through self-gratification but through fidelity to a worthy purpose.

—Helen Keller

Have A Reason to Get Out of Bed Each Morning

THE term MAJOR HARTGOB describes your sense of life mission or purpose. The parameters of MAJOR HARTGOBs are intentionally wide. The term *minor* hartgob refers to smaller segments of time and intermediate-length projects. MAJOR HART-GOBs are about your life. Minor hartgobs are measured in weeks or months. Your MAJOR HARTGOB helps you answer the question why am I here—at all? It attempts to help you focus on the purpose of your life's work. It takes a long time to figure out, and some people eventually give up. But it's a worthwhile endeavor.

Virtually every major corporation will have a MAJOR HARTGOB. Often they call it a mission statement. It keeps them focused. In the same way you need to have one for your life. Minor hartgobs are short term. But they do need to reflect and be consistent with MAJOR HARTGOBs. Some people literally take this to an extreme. They ask the question, "What does this period of my life have to do with the reason I got out of bed?" If it doesn't reflect the larger statement, many will then change what they're doing and adjust their behavior. Minor hartgobs can change depending on circumstances. As an example, the minor reason to jog may have to do with your physical health. The minor reason you go to work can have to do with your financial stability. Yet both can reflect your MAJOR HARTGOB. You can't achieve your MAJOR HARTGOB if you're not healthy and free from worry about finances.

It's important to realize minor hartgobs change, and occasionally, your MAJORS may as well. As you develop and learn more about yourself it would not be unusual to discover you want to shift your MAJOR HARTGOB in some way. I recommend you review your MAJOR HARTGOBs at least annually and your minor ones on a daily or weekly basis. *Have a reason to get out of bed each morning.* It's a major baby step on the road to happiness.

The soul that has no established aim loses itself.
—Michel de Montaigne

Have A Reason to Get Out of Bed Each Morning

1994 was a tragic and strange year for football fans. There were deaths, arrests, and a great deal of disappointment. Then to top everything else, CBS lost the NFL broadcast rights. Football fanatics began having strange cases of a new non-viral epidemic called *PMSS*—Post Madden Shock Syndrome. The question was not, "What's going to happen to the NFL?" It was, "What's going to happen to John Madden?"

Some suggested he run for president. To his credit Madden didn't want to take a step backward, and declined the nomination. Instead he signed a contract with Fox Network for thirty million dollars. A friend of mine asked the "question of the year" after reading about Madden's fortunes in "USA Today." *How can a man get paid so much for doing something he loves?* Without trying to sound like a smart aleck I suggested the answer was in the question. In Madden's case, it's *because* he does what he loves that he gets paid so much. Madden discovered his HARTGOB years ago. After signing the Fox contract, I heard him interviewed on a network talk show. Madden told the host he does the very same thing he has been doing since first grade. He's watching, talking, and living, the game of football. He's having fun. And he gets paid a lot of money to let us watch him have fun.

I doubt John Madden's MAJOR HARTGOB has changed much since first grade. His minor hartgobs have probably changed—little league, junior high, high school, college, professional, coaching, commentator of—*football*. As he got older, the minor hartgobs changed until his team eventually won the Super Bowl. Yet his major HARTGOB remained consistent. I suggest you follow the Madden formula. Generate a MAJOR HARTGOB for your life. Make certain you love what you do and do what you love. You may not love all the minor hartgobs along the way. But if you love the MAJOR you will succeed. And if you love it as much as John Madden you'll probably also be wealthy.

Once a person says, "This is who I really am, what I am all about, what I was really meant to do," it is easier to decide how to spend one's time.

—David Viscott

Have A Reason to Get Out of Bed Each Morning

YOU have likely heard the story of Victor Frankl. Dr. Frankl was an Austrian psychiatrist who spent several years in Nazi concentration camps. He survived and later became a best-selling author and leading philosopher of our time. His classic book, *Man's Search For Meaning* has been quoted and cited. Among other things, Dr. Frankl suggested it was his ability to find meaning in the persecution he suffered, that gave him the will to survive.

I heard Dr. Frankl speak many years ago. I didn't meet him personally, though I did participate in an impromptu question-and-answer session after his presentation. One person asked Dr. Frankl how he could possibly find meaning in a concentration camp. Dr. Frankl quickly answered that the reason he got out of bed each morning was to live. By living he could prevent the Holocaust from ever happening again. Later he looked at several of us and suggested the meaning was in the very conversation we were having. Dr. Frankl's MAJOR and minor HARTGOB was very clear, even in the most tragic of circumstances.

This ability to find meaning in suffering is one of the keys to happiness. HARTGOB can help you do that. It can become an extremely important process. I recently spoke to a man during a radio talk show who expressed a similar sentiment. He said he looked on his time in jail as the most positive thing he had experienced. It was a small price to pay, he explained, for the freedom he later experienced by learning about life. He developed a minor hartgob for his jail time and turned it into a positive learning experience. Find meaning in your life. Think about your reason to get out of bed, both for your life and the next three months. Actually write down your major and minor HARTGOBs. Edit and refine them. Try them out for a few weeks and then write them again. This is an important baby step on the road to happiness.

The man who plants and the man who waters have one purpose, and each will be rewarded according to his own labor.
                                              —1 Corinthians 3:8 NIV

3

Practicing Happiness Skills

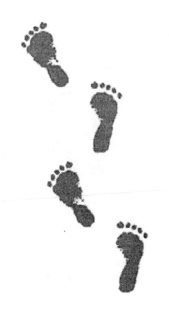

Schedule Your Pain and Pleasure

SCHEDULE *your pain and pleasure*. Most people, including "shrinks" squench up their noses at this baby step. One thing they do agree to however, is that happiness is most often achieved when you schedule a frequent number of minor "fun" experiences with more widely-spaced more intense peak ones. Your happiness can improve by increasing the frequency of events most people designate as small pleasant experiences.

Researchers suggest, as an example, rather than waiting for the "big ship to come in," go swimming in your local pool on a day-to-day basis. Frequency seems to be the most important factor. These small experiences can be anything you define as pleasant. A good time with friends may be included. A date with your spouse, daily exercise, or hobbies you enjoy, could all be considered small pleasant occasions. To others, daily prayer, honest conversations with caring friends or a weekly visit for a therapeutic massage might qualify. It's important to participate in some such event on a frequent basis. Schedule something just for the purpose of fun regularly. Don't wait until you can afford to do something huge. Do several small things instead.

The incredibly intense experiences are important as well. Yet they require a bigger budget and more planning. These intense experiences could include an occasional romantic weekend get away, a vacation, or some other major event you've been planning. Yet the key is to focus on the *frequency of small experiences*, not the intensity level of the more occasional ones. Learn to take tremendous pleasure in your smaller accomplishments. If you do, you will have far more happiness. Schedule your pleasure. It will help you take control of your happiness.

When schemes are laid in advance, it is surprising how often the circumstances will fit in with them.

—William Osler

Schedule Your Pain and Pleasure

OKAY. I know. This is a book about happiness. So why would I suggest scheduling pain? Won't that take care of itself? Unfortunately, if you don't take care of your pain, it may take care of you! Scheduling pain is a very important key to enjoying life. As an example, probably everyone has attended a funeral. That's a painful experience, but one that was scheduled. You schedule an appointment to go to a dentist. That can be exceedingly painful! Yet it's something you not only schedule, but pay for as well! What kind of a deal is that?

The answer is simple. If you schedule a little suffering now—going to the dentist as an example—you avoid immense pain later. That's the key. If you schedule your pain and suffer a small amount now, you avoid even greater pain later. Scheduling a painful experience is like insurance. So, feel a little pain. Some people would say I take this to a bizarre extreme. I schedule a time every twenty-four hours to worry. I literally sit down and worry for two minutes every day. That way if problems intrude when I'm trying to focus on something important, my mind is free to realize it's not important to worry about them now! I'll be worrying about them at six o'clock in the morning, as an example. If you do this, it will help you let go of negative thoughts during your productive time.

I have a friend who is a highly successful salesman. He gave me an example of how this principle works for him. When somebody tells him a phone number he will remember it to a fault. The phone number will intrude upon his thoughts while he is trying to think of something else. He'll wake up at three o'clock in the morning thinking of nothing but the phone number. This continues until he writes it down. Then he lets go of it. His mind has placed it in a category and he can go on. In this case the category is his Rolodex. That's why we suggest scheduling your pain. Schedule your worry time as well. It will free you to be happier along the way.

Remember that pain has this most excellent quality: if prolonged, it cannot be severe, and if severe it cannot be prolonged.
                                                                —Seance

Schedule Your Pain and Pleasure

DR. B. F. Skinner spent most of his life as a researcher and teacher at Harvard University. His influence was over far more than merely his students. He published many scholarly articles. He authored several books. There have been biographies written about him as well as educational films about his accomplishments. He was an extremely productive and brilliant man. Dr. Skinner is responsible for what is now called behavior modification. His study in this area has influenced psychotherapy, teaching, and probably every aspect of modern American life.

His concept of positive reinforcement is probably the most powerful tool uncovered in the study of human behavior. He suggested positive reinforcement as the way to increase learning. By utilizing positive reinforcement, pigeons have learned to play Ping-Pong, chimpanzees and gorillas have learned sign language, and dolphins have been trained to locate scuba divers and submarines on the ocean floor. These accomplishments probably sound phenomenal, but positive reinforcement is a relatively simple process. It involves rewarding desired behavior with whatever the person—or gorilla—defines as rewarding. The question arises, how does this influence happiness?

When you begin to schedule your pain and pleasure, be sure to include positive reinforcement on a daily basis. Reward yourself for minor achievements. Remember to use frequent positive consequences for accomplishment along the way. Make a list of things you consider to be rewarding or reinforcing. Make sure you, or someone, rewards you for achieving small goals each baby step along the way. Regardless of your age or stage in life, if you do this you will be much happier. Schedule you pleasure. You'll have more fun. Schedule your pain as well. You'll have more happiness.

Six days you shall labor, but on the seventh day you shall rest; even during the plowing season and harvest you must rest.
—Exodus 34:21 NIV

Schedule Your Pain and Pleasure

IT'S important to do a daily scheduling period of pain and pleasure. If you do this, you'll accomplish a great deal more. As a result you'll have more pleasure from each baby step along the way. Most people do their daily planning in the morning. I think it's better to do it the last thing before bed. A brief planning session at night will ignite your subconscious in a positive way. If you plan your next day before going to bed it's likely you will end up having creative ideas about how to accomplish those goals the following morning.

I actually spend ten to fifteen minutes each night planning the next day, and probably five minutes again the following morning prioritizing. This is one of the ways I accomplish much of my creative work. If you schedule this way you leave far less to impulse, guesswork, and old habitual patterns. At first, you may have to go to the extreme of planning each *hour* of the day. If you do so it will not be a loss. Let's face it, most of us have more painful habits than pleasant ones. It's too easy to slump back into the old ways that kept us unhappy to begin with. So if it requires scheduling your time hour by hour it's really not such a bad idea.

During your planning period be sure to include positive reinforcers. Use charts, graphs, or any form of record keeping to mark your positive steps. Give yourself daily and weekly rewards for achieving your happiness goals. The key is in finding what's specifically rewarding to you. This kind of planning really works. If chimpanzees and gorillas can learn to speak in sign language, you can learn to be happy. Schedule your pain and pleasure. Don't ignore the pain. Go ahead and suffer. Go ahead and worry. Schedule a definite time each day to take care of the negative things and then let go of them. Schedule time to have fun as well. Take this baby step today by scheduling something painful you've been avoiding. Then follow through and do it. Afterwards reward yourself with a positive experience. Consider purchasing a day planner product of some type and learn to use it to *schedule your pain and pleasure.*

Our greatest danger in life is in permitting the urgent things to crowd out the important.
—Charles E. Hummell

What You Practice You Become

WHAT you practice you become. Most of us begin "practicing" by observing our parents. I've always respected the influence of parental modeling. I didn't actually realize its importance until I wrote my first book. While researching teenage suicide I discovered the power of modeling. The factor which best predicted the child who would have problems with suicide attempts turned out to be quite surprising. It wasn't drug use, or emotional problems in the child. In fact, the most valid factor had nothing to do with the child at all. It was depression in the mother.

Apparently, a child can grow up watching the primary caretaker in a depressed state, and model her behavior. The factor which most accurately predicted drug addiction in children was tranquilizer use by the mother. Similarly, the most valid predictive factor for self esteem in children, was happiness in the mother. In families where traditional roles were reversed, the father's behavior was more important. Perhaps the real power of modeling is that it's unintentional. Children don't consciously copy parental behavior. Since it's primarily unconscious, normal defense mechanisms are lowered. We know, as an example, that abused children often become child abusers of the next generation. Children who grow up with parents who beat each other frequently become spouse beaters as adults. This is the seductive strength and power of modeling.

As a child, you grow up observing. At first it's innocent and passive. Eventually you begin to watch more closely. Then you consciously begin to copy. All the while you're subconsciously modeling. As you model even more, you begin to practice the behavior. As you practice, you refine it. Eventually you become good at it. Ultimately, over time, you *become* the behavior. You're no longer observing, or copying violence. You become violent. It's true. *What you practice you become.* It's wise to begin practicing happiness.

You can preach a better sermon with your life than with your lips.
—Oliver Goldsmith

What You Practice You Become

WHAT you practice you become. If you practice any habit repeatedly you become it. If you spend a great deal of time with fear, you will become fearful. On the other hand, if you spend a great deal of time practicing happiness, you will become happy. Technology now tells us, when you think about something repeatedly, you are perfecting it. Your brain can't tell the difference. This means you can mentally practice being happy, and eventually achieve it. Even when you don't *feel* happy, it's more likely to occur if you visualize it.

Recently researchers in the behavioral sciences have discovered there is absolutely no difference between mental and physical practice. The mind doesn't know the difference between mental imagery—or exaggerated thoughts—and real practice using the body. Various scientific studies have proven this to be true. What you practice you become. William James says you become what you think about the most. Thinking is practice. It works with astronauts, actors, and athletes. It can also work for you.

This is the power of visualization. Throughout these chapters, suggestions are made to use visualization as a means of creating change. Sometimes real practice is unavailable. When this is the case, visualization will serve just as well. If you cannot practice happiness at this point in your life, visualize it instead. Imagine it. Experience it multi-dimensionally. Imagine yourself hearing, tasting, smelling, seeing, and touching happiness. It will work for you and ease the way on your journey toward happiness.

For imagination sets the goal "picture" which our automatic mechanism works on. We act, or fail to act, not because of "will," as is so commonly believed, but because of imagination.
—Maxwell Maltz

What You Practice You Become

MANY years ago an extremely intelligent lady came to see me for psychotherapy. She was a college teacher who had completed all but her dissertation toward a doctorate in theology. She was brilliant, witty, and entertaining, but in trouble. She was experiencing "writer's block." She had a severe case of it. At times she felt stupid, incompetent, and unworthy. Though she was a successful teacher, her self image was not successful at all. If the block continued, it would result in the loss of her teaching position.

She didn't have the luxury of long-term therapy. The dissertation deadline was rapidly approaching. Her goal was completion, not contemplation. She needed to finish the requirements or lose her degree. I began by developing a strategy to help her overcome writer's block. At the same time I suggested when her dissertation was complete, she enter a longer phase of psychotherapy. Then her goal would be to prevent such problems from occurring in the future. She agreed.

The regimen was fairly simple. She followed it like a trooper, and that was the key to her success. I suggested she get up at five a.m. and within a matter of minutes be out the door exercising, either jogging or fast-walking. I instructed her to repeat the following phrases each time her left foot hit the ground. The phrases included: *I can write; I'm creative; I deserve it; I'm intelligent* . . . . This was followed by an additional thirty minutes of guided imagery I had done for her on a tape. She visualized not only writing, but getting her dissertation approved as well. She visualized her nameplate on the door with Ph.D. after her name. She imagined her students calling her "Dr." instead of "Ms." Within a matter of days she was able to begin writing again. In less than a year she received her doctorate. By changing what she practiced, she changed what she became. It wasn't that difficult, but it did require a great deal of discipline. The same thing can work for you. *What you practice you become.* So be careful what you practice.

Visualize this thing that you want. See it, feel it, believe in it. Make your mental blueprint, and begin to build.
                                        —Robert Collier

What You Practice You Become

CHARLES Horton Cooley was a sociologist in the early years of this century. His most significant contribution was what he called the looking-glass self. Cooley suggested that self-image is formed by responses from others. In his theory, other people hold up a mirror or "looking glass" to you by their responses. If their reaction is positive you think more highly of yourself. If the responses are unfavorable, you begin to think negatively. While in reality, self-image is probably far more complex than that, it's a good place to start.

Happiness is learned. Therefore, if you learn to be unhappy, you can change that at any point or age in your life and learn to be happy. The other good news is, as an adult you can carefully choose whose mirror you look into. Who are the people you will empower in your life? When someone holds up that negative mirror and the looking-glass self you see is miserable, what are you going to do? If you are serious about change, the only option you have is to look elsewhere. Frankly, other people often will not change. Regardless of what you do, some people are invested in holding up a negative mirror and keeping you unhappy.

What you practice you become. Decide what you want reflected in the looking glass and then begin to surround yourself with those who provide that reflection. This can be accomplished in a number of ways. Choose your friends very carefully by encouraging interaction with those that hold up a positive mirror. Limit your contact with those who respond critically to you. Listen to esteem-building cassettes on a regular basis. Go to seminars, read positive literature and get counseling as needed. You can't control the reflection someone is holding up to you. But you can choose *where* you look. What you are experiencing today may not be totally your fault. However, what you become from this point forward is pretty much up to you. *What you practice you become.* Be careful what you practice.

What goes into a man's mouth does not make him "unclean," but what comes out of a man's mouth, that is what makes him "unclean."
—Matthew 15:11 NIV

Do What You Need to Do, Not What You Want to Do

MANY years ago I needed a friend to talk to. I called someone and talked to her for quite a while. She listened, empathized, and nudged me like a good friend would do. Then she asked the important question. *So, what are you going to do?. . .* After thinking for a few moments I told her what I wanted to do was to go home, eat some Cherry Garcia®, then go to bed and feel sorry for myself. However what I *needed* to do was something different. I told her I needed to go home and ride my exercise bike 'til I was totally exhausted. Then I probably needed to beat the punching bag until I passed out on the floor. *That sounds like a good idea,* she responded. *Why don't you do that?*

And that's exactly what I ended up doing. It was one occasion when I was able to appreciate this particular baby step. Doing what you *need* to do is not often the same as what you *want* to do. In the beginning practices of this baby step you may have to ask yourself repeatedly, "Am I really doing what I need to do? Or am I falling back into the 'want to' trap?" After awhile, those two can become the same thing. But at first they'll be different.

Doing what you *want*, is giving in to the pleasure principle. We as humans seek pleasure. We like to please ourselves. And on rare occasions the pleasure principle and need will coincide. It's a sign of growth to put off short-term wants and respond more to your needs. It won't be easy at first. Like any other skill it's something you're going to have to practice. By doing what you *need* to do now, you avoid difficulty later. By doing what you want to do, you create momentary pleasure, but more complications later. Eating several bowls of ice cream would have given me great pleasure. Within hours however I would not only have had stomach cramps, but probably been hung-over as well. Additionally, it would have added more unwanted weight to slow me down on the road to happiness.

The price of greatness is responsibility.

—Winston Churchill

Do What You Need to Do, Not What You Want to Do

SOUTHERN lore is filled with wisdom. One bit of that wisdom focuses on doing what you need to do, not what you want to do. *When you're up to your rump in alligators, it's easy to forget your original objective was to drain the swamp.* On one level the lesson focuses on urgencies. When you're beating off alligators, it's easy to forget the big picture. Alligators come in many forms but the common denominator for all is, they're urgent. When the alligator's snapping at you, he demands your attention. Responding to urgency is like that. You have to focus on them, but they have the possibility of taking your attention away from where it needs to be.

On the other hand there's a deeper meaning. To me it's far more profound. There's an interpretation of this saying I've never heard discussed. There are two very important questions. What were you doing in the swamp? And why were you trying to drain it anyway? It's not possible to drain a swamp. It's not like your bathtub. There's no plug to pull. What were you doing there? Maybe the journey into the swamp was a mistake to begin with. Just maybe—I could be wrong—you didn't need to be there at all.

When you get into a southern swamp, you will end up fighting alligators. The best plan is to learn from your mistake. Hopefully it won't take too many bites before you decide to stay away. In the midst of an alligator-induced emergency, you don't have the luxury of philosophy. But when you wade out of the mire ask yourself, "What the heck was I doing in there to begin with? And why was I trying to drain the impossible?" It's easy to get caught up in the trivial instead of pursuing the profound. Urgencies have a way of reaching out and biting you. You can confuse the ringing phone, the interruption, and unnecessary self-imposed deadlines as important. At times they seem to be what you need to do. And it's true, when alligators are snapping at you, you want to get away. But don't confuse urgencies with the bigger issues. Stay out of the swamps to begin with. And when you end up in one, don't try to drain it. You'll get bitten!

I feel the responsibility of the occasion. Responsibility is proportionate to opportunity.
—Woodrow Wilson

Do What You Need to Do, Not What You Want to Do

COMEDIAN Richard Pryor told a poignant story that occurred when he was rehabilitating from his severe burn injury. Former professional football player Jimmy Brown had come to talk to him. Pryor described Jim as confronting him about his self-destructive streak. Pryor reminisced in interviews about Brown questioning him repeatedly. *What you gonna do?* Trust me. When Jim Brown asks questions, people pay attention.

So. *What you gonna do?* . . . I suggest doing what needs to be done, not necessarily what you want to do. Face your problems. Don't run from them. Regardless of how far you go on the baby step journey there will always be problems. Don't obsess about them. But don't run from them either. Schedule time to deal with the things that are unpleasant. And then do them. One of the processes I found helpful is to pray about whatever problems are confronting me. Then I get silent and listen. The more silent I can become during those few minutes, the better. I try to avoid talking to myself. Instead, I try to listen. When you're tensely overwhelmed by the immediate problem, it's difficult to think creatively. It's in these quiet moments when I usually have found solutions.

It's too easy to seek escape from problems the easy way. Alcohol and drugs are not the solution though they're often advertised as such. One lady who was visiting me for psychotherapy was confronted by her angry father. "Why don't you go to a real doctor and get some drugs and deal with your problem the right way?" he screamed at her. That seems to be the consensus of many people. In many cases however, medication is no different than any other means of escape. Do what you need to do. Face your problems. If a temporary crutch is absolutely required, then use it. But don't become dependent. Your leg will never get healthy that way. Give your body time to rehabilitate. Give your mind the same gift. Seek silence. It's salve for your mind and will help you focus on what you need to do.

The word meditation is rather an abused word . . . It would be much better to use the words "quiet time," in which a person shuts out the noise of the world, enters into himself and judges himself not by his press clippings, but how he stands with God.
—Bishop Fulton J. Sheen

Do What You Need to Do, Not What You Want to Do

DO what you need to do, not what you want to do. Respond to the important, and don't be overwhelmed by the urgent. There is much out there to be overwhelmed with. One of the biggest mistakes that can occur is not knowing how to selectively focus. This is where prioritizing and planning play such an important t role. Plan each day where you intend to expend your emotional energy. You have a limited supply. Like a scuba-diving tank, when your tank's empty, the air is gone.

Scuba diving is relatively harmless. There are obvious dangers but the accidental injury rate is actually very low. You learn that if you stay too deep, for too long, you can get into trouble. When you surface you have to do so very slowly and make periodic stops along the way. These are called decompression stops. The longer you stay down, the slower you have to surface. This gives your body time to acclimate to the change in pressure. If you come up too quickly you can, at one extreme, experience a great deal of pain. At the other extreme, you can experience a great deal of pain, and then die. Decompression stops are a very important part of scuba diving safety.

I think decompression stops are an important part of life as well. If you go too deeply, and stay too long, you can get into real trouble. Come up slowly, and take some decompression stops along the way. Occasionally this may mean just sitting around and "chilling out." It can help you to acclimate to a different kind of pressure. Transitions such as from home to the work place, and the work place to home, are often places you may need periods of decompression. Think about your daily rituals and design decompression stops where they're lacking. Allow spouse, co-workers and children the same privilege. Take this baby step today by scheduling decompression stops for one week. Remember there are life transitions that also require decompression. When changing careers, moving, or going from one stage in life to the next, some period of decompression will probably be necessary. Do what you need to do. Be easy on yourself and schedule time to adjust. To avoid burnout take time for decompression. It's an important stop on the journey to happiness.

For they have sown the wind, and they shall reap the whirlwind.
—Hosea 8:7

Enjoy the Journey As Well As the Destination

HAPPINESS is a journey. It's really not a destination. It's a never-ending path. Therefore it's very important to enjoy the scenery along the way. Don't get me wrong, there are distractions and obstacles on the path ahead. There will be stops, rests, and quite a number of unexpected challenges. The important part of this however, is the journey. And it is to be enjoyed each step of the way. Happiness is also a continuous process. You don't simply arrive at happiness and then sit back and take a rest.

It's the same as breathing. You just don't breathe once and then relax and decide you don't have to breathe anymore. Happiness is ongoing and perpetual. There are many things like that. You eat, sleep, and drink fluids perpetually. Happiness should be in the same category. Besides being ongoing and continuous, there's another problem. In the absence of a conscious positive thought, it is likely negative energy will take over. Negative, miserable, and unhappy stimuli predominate society. If you don't continuously make happy or peaceful choices, it's too easy for negativity to take control and determine the outcome for you. If you arrive at a destination and then quit traveling, you'll be subject to whatever happens to you in that place. The same is true with happiness. It's important to make ongoing, continuous, and happy choices.

The journey to happiness is perpetual. It's not easy, but can be tremendously pleasurable. Work at making it fun. The two concepts are not a paradox. Many years ago Vernon Howard said, "The easy road now, leads to the hard way later. The hard road now, leads to the easy way later." The journey to happiness sometimes requires difficult choices. But the choices can be difficult *and* happy at the same time.

The fact remains that the overwhelming majority of people who have become wealthy have become so thanks to work they found profoundly absorbing . . . The long-term study of people who eventually became wealthy clearly reveals that their "luck" arose from the accidental dedication they had to an area they enjoyed.

—Srully Blotnick

Enjoy the Journey As Well As the Destination

ANY journey requires preparation. If you're traveling by car you have to get it ready. If you're flying you have to purchase your ticket and make other preparations. If you're hiking, you have to get the right equipment, and make sure you're in shape for the trip. The same is true with this journey. There are preparations to make before you travel. The first quality you need to pack for your journey is *attentiveness*. You have to pay attention and make sure you remain on the proper route.

The second quality is *commitment*. The reality is, any journey will present its obstacles. If your commitment is weak, it's too easy to quit. Your happiness will have to be one of the most important things in your life. There's a story of the conquest of the Aztec Indians by Cortez in 1519. After his troops landed, Cortez burned all eleven ships. He told his men, "We either die here together or we win the battle and go home together. There is no turning back." That illustrates commitment. Incidentally—they won the battle.

Flexibility is also a requirement. Athletes understand the value of flexibility. They spend a great deal of time stretching their muscles to make them flexible. This makes them less likely to get injured. Flexibility on the journey to happiness provides a similar quality. The more flexible, the less likely you are to get unnecessarily injured. *Openness* is an important quality as well. The kind of openness required is that of not criticizing the path just because it may be new, or something you're unaccustomed to. *Courage* is important. As you continue the journey, you'll stand out. You will be different. There will be those people who simply won't like you, unless you go back to the way you were before. Therefore, along with courage, *perseverance* to stay on the path will be necessary. Stay on the courageous journey to happiness. Pay attention. Be committed. Remain flexible and open. And make it an important part of your life. If you do this, you will have a successful journey.

I have learned, in whatsoever state I am, therewith to be content.
—Philippians 4:11

Enjoy the Journey As Well As the Destination

FOR most of my early childhood I lived with my grandparents. They were wonderful loving people. They owned a small farm and would be described today as "country folk." To exist, was to work. We all worked in the garden, and we all worked with livestock. And we all—including men—cooked.

Supper preparation began at three in the afternoon. If we were going to have chicken, there was no visit made to Colonel Sanders. Instead, we had to convince the chicken to give her life for our supper. That took awhile and was often quite dramatic. If we wanted potatoes we didn't go to the grocery store. We either went up to the garden and dug them up, or climbed under the house, sifted through the lime and found potatoes which looked edible. If we wanted bread, someone had to make it—the old-fashioned way. Working the dough, cutting out biscuits and baking them, was a major ordeal. But the food was delicious and there was always plenty of it. I learned implicitly from my grandparents that if anything was going to be good, it was going to take awhile.

Life has changed since then. I remember several years ago my youngest son asked if we could go get a Happy Meal. But only if there "wasn't too long a line in the drive through." His idea of excellence was not only a Happy Meal, but one you didn't have to wait for. Our society has developed a microwave mentality where quick and quality are synonymous. If we have to wait for it, we don't want it. If we have to work for it, it's not worth the effort. Many Americans have come to believe that if it doesn't *come to you*, it just wasn't meant to be. On the journey to happiness, there is no such thing as quick. There is no room for a Happy Meal mentality. And there certainly is no microwave formula. It is a lifetime journey. It is perpetual, ongoing, and fun every step along the way. Enjoy the journey as well as the destination. You'll be far better off on this baby step to happiness.

Happiness is not a state to arrive at, but a manner of traveling.
—Margaret Lee Runbeck

Enjoy the Journey As Well As the Destination

HAPPINESS will never *belong* to you. You can't catch it. You can't own it. You don't deserve it. And no one else is going to give it to you. It's a journey, and all you can do is take one baby step at a time. Different people take different paths. Jockey Bill Shumaker took one path and later sued the state of California claiming the roads were not safe for him to drive on while intoxicated. The Menendez brothers chose a different way. They claimed it wasn't their fault they killed their parents. Their actions were due to the abuse they suffered during childhood. Lorena Bobbitt, Tanya Harding and many others chose their paths.

Each of these people claimed, "It's not my fault." And all of their stories are tragic. It's terrible Bill Shumaker is paralyzed due to his traffic accident. But he made the choice to drink and drive. The Menendez brothers may end up wasting their lives in jail. But they made the decision to kill their parents. The Bobbitt fiasco speaks for itself. But the reality is none of these people have taken responsibility for the path they chose. The journey to happiness is your responsibility. No blame is allowed. It's easy. Get ready. Put on some comfortable shoes, and start baby stepping down the path. Only you can make this journey for yourself. No one else can do it for you. You can't blame your parents, the traffic engineers, or your ex-spouse. Get on the road to happiness and enjoy each step.

This journey is most successfully made one baby step at a time—a small step. It's nothing grandiose, dramatic, or histrionic. It's simply putting one foot in front of the other and deciding to enjoy life. You can practice this baby step by deciding to find happiness each day. Start a daily "happiness list." Simply be aware of the joy and wonder of daily living and write your observations down on paper. By doing this you will eventually realize each step along the way is fun. *Enjoy the journey as well as the destination.* It will make life more pleasant, one baby step at a time.

Get happiness out of your work or you may never know what happiness is.

—Elbert Hubbard

4

Doing the Work
of
Happiness

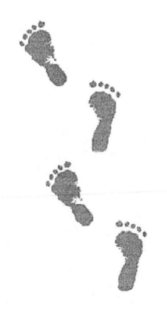

If You Want Different Results, Do Things Differently

IT'S common among twelve-step groups to hear people discussing this baby step. They use different formats than we do. The comments are a bit more negative. I often hear " . . . One definition of insanity is doing something over and over again and expecting different results..." In the Baby Step program we believe the power of being "for" something is exponentially greater than being "against" something. We try to give you something to achieve, rather than something to avoid. So we say, if you want different results, do things differently. Another way of saying this is, if it's not working, change it.

If your life is unsatisfying it's absolutely necessary to change what you're doing. If you don't you'll get identical results—regardless of how many times you redo it. Apparently that's difficult for most people to figure out. So they go through life repeating the same mistake one miserable time after another. And they whine about things not working out. *Things* never work out. *Things* are inanimate. They can't change. Either you change and work things out, or you don't. And if you don't *things* will eternally remain the same.

It doesn't take too many times sticking your hand in a waffle iron before you decide to do things differently. You look at the smoldering waffle marks on both sides of your hand and try something else. Regardless of how many times you stick your hand in there you're always going to get burned. To change the results you must do things differently. I suggest going through life making whatever necessary mistakes you must along the way. But learn from them, and change. Don't do the same thing, the same way, next time. If you want to avoid a great deal of pain, learn from your own mistakes and from the mistakes of others. Then you'll be a true champion. If you want different results do things differently. If you want even better results learn from the mistakes of others. Just insure you model after the ones who have already learned how to do things differently.

The dogmas of the quiet past are inadequate to the stormy present. The occasion is piled high with difficulty, and we must rise to the occasion. As our case is new, so we must think anew and act anew. We must disenthrall ourselves.

—Abraham Lincoln

If You Want Different Results, Do Things Differently

IF you want different results, do things differently. If something you're doing is not working for you, change it. Don't do the same thing over and over and expect different results. Some people have been doing the same thing for so long they don't know how it's possible to change. It is, but will take persistence and practice. The results, to some small degree, will change instantly. But doing things differently, even with different results, is difficult to stick with.

There is a story that Pablo Picasso was approached by a lady in a Paris restaurant. She was flattering and complimentary. After gushing over him for a few minutes she handed him her napkin and asked him to draw something. "Anything," she pleaded. "Just draw something. I'll pay whatever you ask." Reluctantly he took the lady's napkin, scribbled something on it for a few minutes and passed it back to her. "That'll be fifty thousand dollars," he told her. "But maestro," she whined. "It only took you a few minutes." After pausing Pablo Picasso shook his head. "No," he responded. "You don't understand. It has taken my entire life."

Picasso's life story is a commentary on this baby step. For years he got frustrating results. Then he tried doing things differently. But it took his entire life to achieve the results he wanted. The good news is he kept doing things differently and the entire world benefited. Picasso obviously made it look easy. Most masters do. But it only looked easy, because he kept changing until he got different results. We need to follow the same model. Do things differently. If the results aren't right, do things differently again. And even again if necessary. The results will change when you do.

Whatsoever thy hand findeth to do, do it with thy might; for there is no work, nor device, nor knowledge, nor wisdom, in the grave, wither thou goest.

—Ecclesiasties 9:10

If You Want Different Results, Do Things Differently

IF you want different results, do things differently. It makes sense to most people. But for some reason, it's difficult to practice. I discussed this baby step during several different counseling sessions with one lady. Over the years she'd been married to three alcoholic wife-beaters in a row. That was an interesting indicator that she was having difficulty with this baby step. But it was only the surface-level problem. The truth was even more fascinating.

Not only had she been married to three of these cretins, the sequence of events was enthralling. Each of the men claimed to be teetotalers during their courtship. There was no evidence of drinking or violent behavior until well after each of the three marriages had occurred. She was faithful to each husband up to the point that he entered treatment for alcoholism. Incidentally, she paid for two of them to be hospitalized, and only divorced each of them after they had sobered up. Before the ink was dry on the divorce she began a relationship with a successor and repeated the pattern.

She entered counseling after the third marriage ended. Her explanation was she wanted to try something different. We both agreed it was about time. But her attempt at getting different results was a farce to me. After her fourth visit this very resourceful woman informed me she had "gotten it." She was complimentary of my skills as a therapist and claimed I had worked miracles. In fact, she had decided to change her career and become an alcoholism treatment counselor. Regardless of my objections she rationalized it was a good choice. I could have gagged. Literally within months she was working at a treatment center in Atlanta. As of this writing she works as a recovery specialist. Now she is abused by alcoholic men full time, and gets paid for it. She doesn't have to send them to treatment. She doesn't have to marry them. They come to her. Those are not different results. They are worse results. I still want to gag.

One must never lose time in vainly regretting the past nor in complaining about the changes which causes us discomfort, for change is the very essence of life.

—Anatole France

If You Want Different Results, Do Things Differently

IF you want different results, do things differently. If what you're doing doesn't work, change it. Try doing what works for you. Some people legitimately have no idea what works. They had role models that didn't teach them how to experience success, happiness, healthy relationships, or anything else of value. If that is your case, there are alternate ways of learning that are quite effective. Books, tapes, seminars and counseling are all available. There are biographies of people that are great learning tools. The writings of philosophers and theologians are also filled with good information. In today's marketplace all of these items are available at reasonable prices. It does take time to learn, but there is a shortcut that some people find saves them a great deal of pain. Find a happy person and do what they do.

Act *"as if"* you are happy. You can immediately begin to create different results by acting "as if." You can stand erect and hold your shoulders back. When you walk, act as if you have a purpose. You're going somewhere and you have something to do once you arrive. You can hold your head erect and look straight ahead. When you see people looking at you, return the glance. Look them in the eye, smile, and slightly nod your head. If eye contact bothers you at this point, look at their forehead. When you shake hands, do so firmly. Lead an active life and participate in opportunities to network with friends and associates. You can exercise daily, moving large muscle groups of the body. You can laugh often, even if you have to search for something funny. Go to a comedy club or find stand-up comedy on television. Even forcing yourself to smile can increase your happiness temporarily.

This is not faking. It's actually acting "as if." And if you do so, this can result in legitimate neurological and biochemical changes that will increase your measurable happiness. In fact, if you act "as if" long enough, you will ultimately find it's natural to feel happy without acting at all. You may be skeptical of this idea at first. But actually, try it for three weeks. You can create permanent change. Do something different, if you want different results.

Change not the mass but change the fabric of your own soul and your own visions, and you change all.

—Vachel Lindsay

If They Knew How Much Work It Took, They Wouldn't Call It Genius

"IF people knew how hard I have to work to gain my mastery, it wouldn't seem wonderful at all." That statement came from Michaelangelo, often described as the most profound genius in the history of mankind. He was an artist, sculptor, musician, athlete, and had many other talents. But most of all, he was a worker. Work is the missing element from most people's descriptions of genius. Thomas Edison said genius is 1% inspiration and 99% perspiration. It's the perspiration that most people leave out.

Those people who do work are usually dismissed as being talented, gifted, or "natural." To me that's an insult. On a personal level, I've seen this happen with my own children. They happen to be great athletes and students as well. People call them lucky, naturals, or gifted. I despise those descriptions. What these people don't see is the work my children put into their endeavors. They're good athletes because they spend two hours per day, twelve months per year, lifting weights, working out, and running hills. They make good grades because they study five nights per week—even during the summer. They are "gifted" because, instead of watching TV on weeknights, they spend time reading—even when there's no homework. My children work. That's the reason they succeed.

You'll find this philosophy compatible to all high achievers. Einstein worked himself to the point of exhaustion. His productivity was not because he was brilliant, but because he worked. The same is true of successful coaches. Dan Gable, who has one of the highest winning percentages in all of inter-collegiate athletic history, is a committed worker. His wrestling teams are winners because they do the work no one else is willing to do. Whether in sports, business, or art, the same principle is true. If you want to be successful, do the work. Do you want to be happy? Work at it. It's the work most people are not willing to do that'll make the difference in your life.

Remember this: Whoever sows sparingly will also reap sparingly, and whoever sows generously will also reap generously.
—2 Corinthians 9:6 NIV

If They Knew How Much Work It Took, They Wouldn't Call It Genius

IF they knew how much work it took they wouldn't call it genius. I'm told it was Picasso who echoed Michaelangelo's comment. It's not just "working" that makes a difference. It's focused work. Every successful corporation makes New Year's Resolutions. They call their resolutions a strategic plan. The point where they differ, is in following through. They make other commitments to help accomplish their strategic plan. Workers are guided by quarterly, monthly, and weekly objectives. Yet it's not the planning that makes the difference. It's the work that follows the planning.

This has been found to be true with all HAPs I have studied. HAPs aren't scared to work. The testimonials to this are phenomenal. Picasso's and Michaelangelo's comments are reflected by those of actor Paul Newman, *It's always been 10% talent and 90% hard work . . . .* All great winners agree, the common element to success is working at it. Unfortunately, work ethic is uncommon in modern-day society. If you work toward a goal you can usually achieve it. Certainly there has to be a small degree of inherent talent to make it possible. Yet "natural talent" is likely the most unimportant factor. And what appears to be natural, usually isn't that at all. It's the result of years of work. Too often, lack of talent is given as an excuse for lack of time spent toward achieving the goal.

Through a combination of hard work and smart eating, one friend of mine lost a little over 90 pounds in a year. People began talking about how lucky he was to have a "high metabolism." He laughed and told me his high metabolism hit at five thirty in the morning and eleven o'clock at night when he was on the track doing laps. "High metabolism never seemed to visit me at Taco Bell!" he laughed. It was the work that made the difference. But others dismissed it as high metabolism. You don't develop a high metabolism by pushing a remote control. It's all in the work. It's an important baby step on the journey to happiness.

You can't ever work too much because there's no such thing as being in too good condition. You can't ever get too strong. You can't ever wrestle too much because you can always do better.

—Dan Gable

If They Knew How Much Work It Took, They Wouldn't Call It Genius

I suggest falling in love with your work. When you do this you have a tremendous advantage. Your work becomes play. It becomes something you would do for free. It's easy to find happiness at work if you're blissful while doing it.

Many years ago I met a man in my mother's hometown named Buddy Holt. Buddy was quite impressed with me, but it had nothing to do with me, personally. It had to do with my mother. They had attended high school together and, according to him, if it hadn't been for my mom he would have never graduated. He claimed to have copied her papers all the way through high school and suggested she even completed his term papers for him. "She's the hardest-working woman I know," Buddy declared. Apparently, he'd learned a great deal about work himself since that time. He owned several businesses in his home town and had been elected to several public offices, including mayor. Probably because of my mother he began waxing philosophical about how to be successful. I listened intently, and hopefully learned something from our discussion. I think his formula works.

According to Buddy Holt, if you want to be successful, find something you love doing. And then do it passionately. *Forty hours a week will help you be average. If you work a forty-hour week you'll be able to keep up with everybody else and get by. If you want to get ahead you've got to work longer than that. For every hour you work over forty hours, the odds are the more success you'll experience. The secret is loving what you do. If you love what you do, it won't seem like work at all. It will seem like play . . . .* That's what he did. Buddy found something he loved, then poured his heart into it. I think it's good advice. Love your work and happiness will be a by-product of it.

The dictionary is the only place success comes before work. Hard work is the price we must all pay for success. I think we can accomplish almost anything if we are willing to pay the price. The price of success is hard work, dedication to the job at hand, and the determination that whether we win or lose, we have applied the best of ourselves to the task at hand.

—Vince Lombardi

If They Knew How Much Work It Took, They Wouldn't Call It Genius

SIGMUND Freud was asked to describe the necessary ingredients for happiness. His brief response was "love and work." By love, he was referring to relationships. By work, he was talking about your life's work. The concept of life's work is an important one. View your life as an opportunity to accomplish great things. Your life's work may not have anything to do with your job at all. Contemplate the meaning of your life. After your lifetime is spent, what will you leave behind as a legacy? What have you given back to the world?

You can achieve anything you want. You have to get absorbed in it. It may be necessary to get so involved in what you're doing that you lose track of time, and even forget where you are. When you enter this "zone" you are on target. At this point you are truly beginning to love your work and you will ultimately be successful. The fascinating by-product of this approach is that happiness will follow you. People who make happiness their only goal can become narrowly self-absorbed. They lose sight of what's going on around them. Ultimately, they perish without achieving anything of significance. By falling in love with your work, it is more likely that you will not only experience success at work, but happiness as well. Happiness is actually a by-product of living a full life which includes love and work.

If you choose what you want carefully, then do the necessary work, there is no doubt about achieving the goal. You must get absorbed in it however, and love what you are doing. Follow the same plan as do all major corporations. Determine what is your mission, or life's work. Then don't let a single day go by that you do not accomplish a small activity toward achieving your goal. Even if it's making a phone call, or writing a thank-you note, do something on a daily basis that moves toward your life work. The more, the better. It can become a series of baby steps on your road to happiness.

The average person puts only 25 percent of his energy and ability into his work. The world takes off its hat to those who put in more than 50 percent of their capacity and stands on its head for those few-and-far between souls who devote 100 percent.
—Andrew Carnegie

Love to Win More Than You Hate to Lose

LOVE to win more than you hate to lose. This is something I first heard from a good friend who unfortunately made the opposite choice. As a result, although he was an Olympic-caliber competitor, he shortened his amateur wrestling career. He hated losing so badly he quit wrestling. As a former Marine Corps officer and college football player, I am one of those who used to despise losing so badly, I'd get physically sick when we did lose. Losing is not fun. I encourage my children to win. However, I'm very careful today how I define winning. I'm glad I grew beyond that "disease."

To me, there's nothing more enjoyable than totally preparing for and burying myself in an event. I do my best to prepare for it, then see it to fruition. To me, *this* is winning. At this point in my life, winning is making a speech, conducting a seminar, or meeting the deadline on a writing project. I don't define winning as whether or not the crowd laughs at my jokes, or how many of my books actually sell. Those are things out of my control. Winning is meeting your responsibilities and doing your best at living life. Winning is about far more than sports.

Love to win more than you hate to lose. Unfortunately many people do just the opposite. They hate to lose more than they love to win. As a result, they often give up not only on the event they're preparing for, but life as well. If you hate to lose more than you love to win, you will give up on relationships once your heart is broken. You will never work again, once you lose your first job. You'll never drive your car again after getting a flat tire. It's a miserable place to be. I suggest loving to win more than you hate to lose. Winning is the process of simply keeping on trying. It's getting up after the fall, brushing yourself off, and climbing on that horse one more time. *Love to win more than you hate to lose.* If you do, there is no quitting.

To fail is a natural consequence of trying. To succeed takes time and prolonged effort in the face of unfriendly odds. To think it will be any other way, no matter what you do, is to invite yourself to be hurt and limit your enthusiasm for trying again.

—David Viscott

Love to Win More Than You Hate to Lose

I celebrate my children's losses, as much as I do their victories. Don't get me wrong. It's tough on kids when they lose. But I see it as an opportunity to learn a lesson. They prepare to win. They love to win. But they actually learn more from losing. In reality, we all need to learn how to lose. It's something we reluctantly face as adults.

Our society is filled with people who claim they fear commitment. What they really fear is loss. They haven't learned how to lose without being devastated. They haven't learned to cope with loss. It's one of the most important things you can learn. Author Kenny Roberts tells an incredible story on one of his cassettes. He claims a *Wall Street Journal* article stated that most people who lose money on investments, do so by trying to avoid loss. Apparently, he explains, these people make a classical blunder. Their decisions are based on the fear of losing money, instead of the desire to earn it. There is a big difference in those two approaches. They're trying to avoid losing, instead of winning.

When I first heard Kenny say this I was taking my children to school. As I listened I rewound the tape and played it back again three times in a row. I asked my children to explain what Kenny had just said. One said that was why University of Tennessee lost to Alabama in football. *They're trying to avoid losing, instead of winning,* he suggested. *They get conservative and lose the game.* His brother claimed it was the same in wrestling. Some people try to avoid losing the match, instead of going all out for the win. They end up losing anyway. I agreed with both of them. It took awhile for me to make an attempt to explain that the same principle applies in marriage, careers, and virtually all of life. Initially, I wasn't very successful. Yet the principle transcends investments or sports. Being "for" something—*for a good relationship*—is positive energy. Being "against" something—*against divorce*—is negative energy. Positive attracts; negative repels. If you want to accomplish something, *love to win more than you hate to lose.*

The greatest mistake a man can make is to be afraid of making one.
—Elbert Hubbard

Love to Win More Than You Hate to Lose

AS I indicated earlier, I'm very proud to be a combat veteran of the Vietnam War. I have no shame or embarrassment about what I did during that time in my life. Like other Americans, we were doing a job we felt was honorable. The people I knew were soldiers, not politicians. And all of us believed in what we were doing.

In many ways I think we missed the point of the war. Today, as I look back on it, I'm not sure we were sent there to win. But at the time, all the Americans I knew believed in the cause we represented. The problem is, however, we misunderstood not only the goals, but the philosophy. The North Vietnamese and Viet Cong thought they were fighting *for* their country. We, on the other hand, were fighting *against* communism. Guess what? The positive cause outlasted the negative opposition. Something happens when you love to win more than you hate to lose. When you love to win you're harnessing a positive force. Hating to lose harnesses negative energy. But negative energy expends itself quickly. Positive energy not only persists, but perpetuates itself.

All of my heroes throughout history have said the same thing. Winston Churchill, Albert Einstein, Thomas Edison, William James, all of them say it eloquently. Churchill, however, summed it all with poetic simplicity, "Never, never, never! Never, give up." That's the message of loving to win. It propels you in a positive way to never give up on achieving your goal. *Love to win more than you hate to lose.* Then on the occasion you do lose, you'll continue the journey. If for no other reason you'll continue because you want to win again.

Compared to what we ought to be, we are only half awake. We are making use of only a small part of our physical and mental resources. Stating the thing broadly, the human individual thus lives far within his limits. He possesses power of various sorts which he habitually fails to use.

—William James

Love to Win More Than You Hate to Lose

ON January 21, 1991 ABC News reporter Bill Redeker was interviewing an unidentified Marine general in the Persian Gulf. In response to Redeker's question as to how to handle the shock of battle the general asked his marines to remember one word, a word marines don't use very often. The word was love. *And love was what you use to overcome the feelings of fear which are natural. Sometimes I've got to really prompt guys. What would cause a woman, a mother, to run out, ninety-eight pounds, and pick up an automobile off her child? Love. What would cause a marine to jump on a hand grenade, killing himself in order to save his fellow marine? Love. They don't fight because they hate the enemy. They fight for their buddies. They fight for love . . . .*

I've never talked to a true combat veteran who said he fought because he hated the enemy. I've never spoken to an athlete who said he won by hating his competitor. I've never spoken to anyone who said he or she stayed happily married simply by hating divorce. You must love to win more than you hate to lose.

Love to win more than you hate to lose. If you want to move toward a goal—any goal—you have to desire it. You have to love it. Don't attempt to motivate yourself by avoiding loss. That will only set you up for failure. Love to win. Want to achieve your goal. Have a compelling desire to excel. It's a positive force and will attract success to you. If the driving force in your life is fear of failure, you will focus on and experience fear. Ultimately, you will fail as a result of the negative energy created by obsessing. Identify an area in your life where you've experienced undesirable results because you've been afraid to lose. Change this around by being "for winning." Do something positive in this area each day for a week and observe the results. *Love to win more than you hate to lose.* It's an important baby step on the road to happiness.

If someone strikes you on the right cheek, turn to him the other also. And if someone wants to sue you and take your tunic, let him have your cloak as well. If someone forces you to go one mile, go with him two miles.

—Matthew 5:38–42 NIV

That Which Does Not Destroy You
Really Does Make You Stronger

HOW long does it take you to get in shape? How long would it take you to prepare for a marathon? Part of the answer depends on the kind of condition you were in when training began. In some cases it would be a matter of weeks. In other cases it might take years to get in competitive condition. In either extreme, a great deal of pain would be involved. Without some stress, your muscles atrophy. For muscular development to occur you either . . . *use it or you lose it* . . . . The same thing is true of happiness. Emotional pain, struggle, and suffering, stress the happiness muscles. If followed by a period of recovery, you will be happier.

If you are like most people you will occasionally get out of shape. It's an easy thing to do. Something happens, and you can't work out for an extended period of time. Your muscles grow weak and you gain some excess weight. Eventually when you're able to start exercising again, you'll notice the muscles become fit more quickly. This is explained by the phenomenon of muscle memory. Your muscles actually have memory. They remember what it was like to be in shape, and therefore gain their form back much more quickly.

The same phenomenon is true with happiness muscles. The pain and suffering you experience along the way simply stresses your happiness muscles. If you've ever been happy before, the "muscle memory" will remember what it was that got you there. In that way, it's far easier to return to the state of happiness. You don't have to go out of your way to find suffering. Struggle and pain will automatically be presented to you. They will come. The key is in not denying, repressing, or running from adversity. Face up to your struggles. Learn from them. You will be far happier as a result. *That which does not destroy you really does make you stronger.*

Life is a series of experiences, each one of which makes us bigger, even though sometimes it is hard to realize this. For the world was built to develop character, and we must learn that the setbacks and griefs which we endure help us in our marching onward.
—Henry Ford

That Which Does Not Destroy You
Really Does Make You Stronger

THE biggest problem is, if you don't suffer occasionally you may begin to think life is easy. Having such an expectation can be disastrous. If you don't struggle periodically, you will never develop emotional endurance. You won't be "in shape." By attempting to avoid suffering, you actually become weaker.

People who face no adversity develop an expectation that life *should* be easy. They assume they should be taken care of. They come to believe that things will simply come to them because they are in some mysterious way "gifted." Rather than becoming a self-fulfilling prophecy that leads to pleasure, it becomes a disastrous expectation and leads to massive pain. Someone with this expectation, grows to feel *entitled* to the easy way. And when things don't come easily, these people simply give up. They decide "it just wasn't meant to be." Some people even begin to think they have failed or they're immoral or in some way simply because things didn't come easily. I have seen this lead to drug use, rage, and even suicide attempts.

A friend of mine gave his daughter the used family car for her sixteenth birthday. The car was six years old and admittedly had high mileage on it. Yet for a sixteenth birthday present, I thought it was splendid! He did too. Boy, were we wrong! Instead of being grateful his daughter was incensed. She wanted a brand new luxury car instead of the old family car. She acted insulted by her father's gesture. He and I had a long talk about it, and then he finally confronted his daughter. She had developed an expectation of entitlement. She not only wanted a brand new sports car, but thought she deserved it. This sense of entitlement, if carried on into adulthood, could ultimately have been disastrous. As I suggested to my friend, "How would you like to marry someone with those expectations? What would be required of you to make her happy?" It's not suffering that's wrong. It's the lack of suffering that leads to difficulty.

I exhort you also to take part in the great combat, which is the combat of life, and greater than every other earthly conflict.
—Plato

That Which Does Not Destroy You
Really Does Make You Stronger

IF you live a normal life expectancy, there will be ample opportunity to suffer. It's supposed to be that way. The best strategy is to learn from it and refine yourself. By facing struggle you'll become a better person. You'll become stronger. Failing to deal with adversity can only make consequences worse. Denying they exist is down right suicidal.

Avoidance leads to emotional atrophy. Your happiness muscles will weaken. Ultimately you'll suffer what amounts to emotional stagnation and an unfulfilling life. These are people who later describe their lives as filled with despair. And they're filled with despair because they've tried to avoid the one thing they needed to prosper—suffering. J. W. Sullivan said, *To be willing to suffer in order to create is one thing; to realize that one's creation necessitates suffering, that suffering is one of the greatest of God's gifts, is almost to reach a mystical solution to the problem of evil . . . .*

Undoubtedly the happiest people I know are those who've gone through tremendous pain. They didn't go out of their way to find it. God gave it to them and they accepted it. They simply lived life to its fullest, and as a result faced their pain instead of running from it. They experienced short-term discomfort, but long-term peace. And it really did make them stronger. Suffering clarifies and crystallizes who you are. It helps determine what you really believe. As a result, you become both figuratively and literally stronger. But you don't have to go out of your way to find pain. Live fully and intensely and experience whatever comes your way. You will legitimately be presented sufficient opportunity to struggle. Grit your teeth and sweat through it. It's simply a work-out. It's a training session. It'll be over soon. And you'll be far stronger as a result. That which does not destroy you really does make you stronger. It's a baby step on the journey to happiness.

A failure is man who has blundered, but is not able to cash in on the experience.

—Elbert Hubbard

That Which Does Not Destroy You
Really Does Make You Stronger

THAT which does not destroy you makes you stronger. It really depends on how you react to the significant emotional experience. If you hide, deny it, or cover it up, you can be destroyed. Yet if you face it and learn from it, you can become far stronger. For some people it's difficult to overcome emotional trauma. Significant emotional experiences are tattooed on your consciousness and can deeply influence personality.

If you were born anytime before 1958, it's likely you remember exactly where you were and what you were doing the moment you heard President Kennedy was assassinated. As a society, we have experienced tremendous difficulty overcoming President Kennedy's assassination. It was a significant emotional experience for our nation as a whole. People who were alive when Pearl Harbor was attacked have a similar crystal-clear memory of that event. Some people have a similar awareness when they heard the space shuttle Challenger exploded. You may not remember the day before, or the day after. However you can recall in unbelievable detail what you were doing, who you were with, and maybe even what you were wearing, when you heard the president had been assassinated.

You actually *need* significant emotional experiences to help develop your personality. They give you depth. Think about the significant experiences you have undergone. What strengths have they developed in your life? List them. Express your gratitude for these learning opportunities and recognize their positive influence in your life. In this baby step we encourage you to face obstacles. You will be far better to go through significant emotional experiences. Sometimes the greatest gift you can give yourself is learning to cope with struggle. It will not destroy you. It really will make you stronger.

For with much wisdom comes much sorrow; the more knowledge, the more grief.

—Ecclesiastes 1:18 NIV

5

Accepting Responsibility
For
Your Happiness

The Response You Get Is the
Meaning of the Message You Send—Part 1

THIS was one of the first and most important baby steps I took in my personal life. It's also one of the most easily misunderstood. It's so important, there are two parts. It's been suggested an entire book could be based on this baby step. A few people have adapted it as their philosophy of life. Like many of the baby steps it's beautiful in it's simplicity, but deep in application.

The response you get is the meaning of the message you send. The idea is not original. I first heard it in October 1979 from Monsignor Neil Tobin. Father Tobin said it sounded like something Marshall McLuhan would say, but no one has located it in McLuhan's writing. John Talbird, an Episcopal priest I discussed it with later, said he'd heard it at a seminar. He also thought it sounded like McLuhan, but like the rest of us, has not been able to find the source.

The response you get is the meaning of the message you send. By response we mean "results." By message we mean any stimuli you send out, intentionally or unintentionally, that receives results, whether intentional or unintentional. As it applies to interpersonal communication, the response can be a scowl on your listener's face. The message could be an insult. On a more dramatic scale the response can be a divorce. The message could have been lack of attention. But this idea has many other applications. The response can be obesity. The message can be overeating. A response can be unhappiness. The message can be emotional laziness. A response can be financial difficulty. The message can be poor planning. The response you get is the meaning of the message you send. The concept sounds quite simple. However it's easily misunderstood. Before you begin to think about how it works, first understand how it doesn't work.

An obvious fact about negative feelings is often overlooked. They are caused by us, not by exterior happenings. An outside event presents the challenge, but we react to it. So we must attend to the way we take things, not to the things themselves.

—Vernon Howard

The Response You Get Is the
Meaning of the Message You Send—Part 1

THE *response you get is the meaning of the message you send.* This baby step is not about 100% determining your own reality. No one can determine her reality 100% of the time. People who think they can are either naive or arrogant. No one will ever convince me that the victims of the Oklahoma City bombing sent any messages resulting in the response of their deaths or injuries. One crazed man can create that response without any message leading to it whatever. Simply because people were in a building does not mean they were sending messages that contributed to their deaths.

Another example that hits even more closely to home was a good friend of mine named Jeff Wolfe. Jeff, a young karate instructor, was senselessly murdered by four juvenile carjackers. One almost sarcastic side bar to the story is, Jeff had spent his life working with kids similar to the murderer. In fact, he had been the karate instructor for one of the carjacker's cousins. And, he had taught him without pay. No one will ever convince me that Jeff's response—the murder—was a result of messages he had sent. It was a senseless unnatural disaster and Jeff had very little to do with it.

Tragedies occur that have nothing to do with messages sent. Women get raped without sending messages resulting in that response. Tornadoes, floods, and earthquakes happen that are totally unrelated to messages sent. You can send messages to your body that result in poor health. But other medical responses are totally removed from your messages. Accidents do happen. Your messages, regardless of what you believe, did not create the response of California earthquakes. Yet when it comes to your personal life, and the things over which you have some sense of control, it's true. The response you get is the meaning of the message you send. If you don't like your responses, don't complain about it. Change your messages.

Experience is not what happens to a man; it is what a man does with what happens to him.

—Aldous Huxley

The Response You Get Is the
Meaning of the Message You Send—Part 1

A lady once came to see me after receiving divorce papers from her physician-husband. He had left her for his scrub nurse. Certainly not a novel idea. However this one was extreme. "I am nothing without my husband," she reported in between sobs. "My entire life has been wrapped up in being a doctor's wife." She was right. She even had a vanity license plate proclaiming, "MD WIFE."

During the marriage she had introduced herself as, "Dr. Jones's wife" instead of using her own first name. She was president of the medical auxiliary, and had not worked outside of the home since her marriage. She described telling him on multiple occasions, "I'm worthless without you." Unfortunately, people who send "worthless" messages, are often treated worthlessly. They get "worthless" responses. He left her. And when he did, he took not only his belongings, but also her identity. She said it, better than I could even attempt. "Everything that I was, is gone. I am nothing." That's exactly how she felt. She was so close to suicide we had very little time to waste. In this case there was nothing we could do to change *him*, so we began to focus on her.

It was a long painstaking process, but slowly she began to list the messages she had sent that contributed to her current response. She later looked at other unhappy responses in her life and began to evaluate her messages contributing to them. It was tough, but she was able to gain control over the things she legitimately could. She's better now, by the way. She has a new car, a new sense of humor, and a new vanity license plate. This one reads, "XMDWFE." And he's paying for the car! The response he gets is the meaning of the messages he sends as well.

You may be dead broke and that's a reality, but in spirit you may be brimming over with optimism, joy, and energy. The reality of your life may result from many outside factors, none of which you can control. Your attitudes, however, reflect the ways in which you evaluate what is happening.

—H. Stanley Judd

The Response You Get Is the
Meaning of the Message You Send—Part 1

THE response you get is the meaning of the message you send. It could be the most important step you can take. It's also the most easily misunderstood. It's not complex, but it is easy to apply incorrectly. Many people who suffer from serious illness struggle with this. I've heard cancer patients ask, "What did I do to deserve this?" Victims of tragic accidents have asked the same question. While there could have been certain messages you sent that resulted in these situations, it's usually not the case. People mistakenly think *If I was good enough I wouldn't be sick . . . If I had just eaten the right foods or prayed enough, none of this would have ever happened . . . .* In those cases these people miss the point.

There are a few circumstances when you do have control. Most of them have to do with your personal life. You can control the way you respond to tragedy. But you can't always control whether or not a tragedy occurs. It takes two people to have a good marriage. Yet one person can create a divorce. What *do* you have control over? Simply yourself. Yet far too many people obsess about what they can't control and give up on the one thing they can control—themselves. The response *you* get is the meaning of the message *you* send. Once you understand this particular baby step and begin to apply it, you will change your life.

There are other responses in your life over which you have no control but behave as if you do. These usually include other people, such as your spouse, boss, or mother-in-law. They can also include responses many people moan about frequently—like the weather or world events. List these responses and keep them handy as you read the next baby step. And oh, by the way. Do you have responses in you life—over which you have control—that you're not satisfied with? List them now and get ready to change your messages. When you begin to change your messages, magic occurs. I didn't used to believe in magic. Then I learned about this baby step.

Life is, for the most part, the way we see it. So, when life's not fair—it may be time to check your focus. Change your seeing to change your scene.

—Robert H. Schuller

The Response You Get Is the
Meaning of the Message You Send—Part 2

ON the way to happiness, there are many obstacles. The first and possibly biggest, is refusing to recognize your own responsibility. This is especially true in modern American society where Lorena Bobbitt, the Menendez brothers and Michael Faye (of Singapore caning fame) are media heroes. Each of these people has achieved fame by denying responsibility for their behavior. To hear them tell it, their responses had nothing to do with *their* messages.

Recently I was sitting in a barber shop reading magazines scattered in the lobby while waiting my turn. One of my sons laughed as he gestured and handed me a dog-eared issue of an old *Time Magazine.* "Infidelity—" the cover blared, "It's in the genes!" I shook my head in disbelief. "Just think, Dad," he said. "Pretty soon we won't have to be responsible for anything!" This trend has gotten so extreme that a lady was awarded $4 million because she spilled her hot coffee in her lap, while driving her car. Yet McDonald's® didn't make her buy it. Spilling was the response. Driving while holding a cup of hot coffee between her legs was the message. A young man is suing the University of Miami for ten million dollars because he didn't get to start as quarterback. His lawsuit failed to mention he warmed the bench behind Heisman trophy winner Gino Torretta.

The response you get is the meaning of the message you send. If your response is getting so angry you could maim, kill, or vandalize, then change the *rage-filled* messages you're sending. If your response is boiling away and scalding you emotionally, then take a look at the *careless* messages you're sending. If your response is warming the bench in life, then take a look at the *second-string* messages you're sending. This is a major step. It empowers *you.* It gives *you* the power rather than other people. Contemplate it. Practice it. Understand it. But most of all act on it.

———————————————————

America has no-fault automobile accidents, no-fault divorces, and it is moving with the aid of modern philosophy towards no-fault choices.
—Allan Bloom

The Response You Get Is the
Meaning of the Message You Send—Part 2

THE response you get is the meaning of the message you send. Change your responses by changing your messages. It's not that difficult to understand. But understanding and actually applying the principle are two different things. Understanding and fifty cents will buy you a diet coke. Understanding and application of knowledge will help you change your life.

The change can be positive or negative. The principles work both ways. Never send a message if you don't want to accept the response. Think about the responses you really want in life. These are the messages you need to be sending. Some people never "get it." Instead, they do just the opposite. One lady told a boyfriend over the phone, "If you don't get here by six o'clock the engagement's off." He didn't arrive by 6:00 p.m. and the engagement was off. But not because of her. He canceled it. A man kept challenging his wife: "Just leave if you don't like the way I treat you. Just get out." Eventually she did. Another lady kept sending her husband a similar message. Commenting on his sexual problems she sarcastically suggested, "If you were a real man, you wouldn't have a problem getting it up." He followed her advise, after a fashion. He got up and left.

Each of these individuals consulted with me in therapy. They were still unhappy with the response, even though their messages were partially responsible. If you don't want the response, don't send the message. If you can't live with it, don't ask for it. The response you get is the meaning of the message you send. If you want love, send loving messages. If you want friends, send friendly messages. If you want happiness, send happy messages. The responses will take care of themselves.

Man must cease attributing his problems to his environment, and learn again to exercise his will—his personal responsibility.
                                                        —Albert Schweitzer

The Response You Get Is the
Meaning of the Message You Send—Part 2

SEVERAL years ago I saw a friend and his family in psychotherapy. One of the things he and his wife were concerned about was his eight-year-old daughter's behavior at school. For the previous several weeks, his daughter, Sonia, had perpetually been bringing home notes from her teacher reporting what the teacher described as, "acting-out behavior." Specifically, Sonia was getting in trouble for playing "chase."

"It's not my fault," Sonia declared with her hands planted firmly on her hips. "Why do I get in trouble? The boys are the ones chasing me. All I do is run away from them." Pretty good rationalization for an eight-year-old, I thought. After listening to Sonia and her parents for a few minutes, I interrupted. "What happens if you don't run?" I asked. "I mean, some boy comes up to you and says, 'boo!' or whatever it is the boys do. What would happen if you just stared at him. If you don't run, there's no chase." The response you get is the meaning of the message you send. You send messages that say, "I'll play chase," and the response is you get in trouble. In life when you change your messages and refuse to play chase—or the adult equivalent—your responses change as well. By ultimately changing her message, Sonia was able to successfully alter her response.

"I don't want to play chase any more," Sonia told her tormentor. "It's a dumb game. It's for kids!" And as simply as that, it was over. Sonia was either naive or trusting enough to be easily persuaded. As adults we sometimes have difficulty believing change *is* that easy. The way to happiness is not as difficult as it may seem. It's not as complex as we make it either. The first and most necessary step is taking control of your responses in life by changing the messages you send.

For whatsoever a man soweth, that shall he also reap.
                                                    —**Galatians** 6:7 KJV

The Response You Get Is the
Meaning of the Message You Send—Part 2

THE moment you begin to practice this baby step you can change your life. Once you accept that the response you get is the meaning of the message you send, you can turn your life around. If you never accept it, change is unlikely. After reading this baby step take a break from reading, and begin writing. Make an exhaustive list of every single response you're unsatisfied with. Regardless of the response, if you're unhappy with it, write it down.

If you're dissatisfied with the way your automobile runs, write that down on your list. If you're not happy with the way your yard looks, list it too. It doesn't have to be a "human" response to qualify. Write them all down. After you've made this list, record each response at the top of a separate piece of paper. One person wrote at the top of one of his pages, "I don't like my job." Underneath that, he listed numerically from one to ten, how various messages had resulted in that response. Among them he included, ". . . got a degree in college related to this job . . . applied for it . . . have stayed here eleven years without relocating . . . have failed to get other job training . . . have not sought further education . . . have not investigated other options for employment . . ."

The next step is to generate ideas for new messages. How could you change your messages to result in the possibility of more job satisfaction? What messages could you send that would increase your current level of happiness? The same man was able to list thirty-five new messages that might change his response. They did. At first he was promoted within his company. Later he was offered a job with a different company. When you change your messages, your responses begin to change as well. The response you get is the meaning of the message you send. If you're unhappy with your responses, change your messages. The responses will take care of themselves.

Each is responsible for his own actions.

—H.L. Hunt

You're Not Who They Think You Are . . .

YOU'RE not who they think you are. You're not the thoughts, opinions, or categories others use to describe you. You're not your reputation or your job. You're not your ethnic group, body type, or hair color. Not all accountants are obsessive. Not all Italians are overly emotional. Not all mesomorph football players are dumb. And not all redheads have tempers! You're not your "sign," temperament, or the car you are driving.

People who categorize others think it helps them. But what it really does is limit both. I've heard physicians refer to patients as my "gallbladder in 308," or the "hip replacement in 402." I've heard psychiatrists identify patients as—"my three o'clock schizophrenic." Attorneys call you "plaintiff" or "defendant" instead of your name. This categorizing dehumanizes you. You become less of an individual and more of a label. It's easy to understand a diagnosis. I can look in a book and figure out what schizophrenics are supposed to do. But it's much more difficult, challenging, and *fair*, to understand you.

People who do such categorizing are making life easy for themselves. By placing you in a file they can relate to you in a pre-determined way. You become the category. Never mind if you don't fit all the characteristics. You're stuck. Don't let anyone place their label on your life. Smile and say, "No thanks." Don't be a category. Be yourself.

If a man does not keep pace with his companions, perhaps it is because he hears a different drummer. Let him step to the music which he hears, however measured or far away.
—**Henry David Thoreau,** *Walden*

You're Not Who They Think You Are . . .

YOU'RE *not who they think you are*. Many years ago I saw this illustrated in a way that made an incredible impact on me. A friend of mine had a high school-aged son who was doing extremely well in school. They tested him so they could measure his potential. I suggested against it, but they went ahead and did it anyway.

When receiving the results, what they "heard" was their son had a 96 IQ. What the diagnostician actually said was their son scored in the 96th percentile. That would have made his IQ in the range of 130. However the parents believed their son had a 96 IQ, which is a little below average. Interestingly, he began accommodating them. His grades dropped to C's and D's. Later we clarified the situation and their son's grades rose back up to A's. Labeling can not only limit you but define your performance on many levels. Another powerful example was an adult friend of mine who described himself as dyslexic. In fact he did suffer from dyslexia and had severe letter and word reversal problems. This unfortunate malady had followed him into adulthood. He had accommodated his learning style, gone on with his life, and achieved despite the difficulties. But he still suffered emotional damage from this disability.

Finally when we were discussing this, I suggested he quit referring to himself as a dyslexic. "You are not a dyslexic," I told him. "That's just the way you learn. You are you. Dyslexia is the way you learn. They are two different things." There were a few moments of emotion-filled silence. Finally he asked me to say it again. I repeated the comment five separate times before he finally burst out crying. "I've always thought of myself as defective," he exclaimed. "I've thought of myself as a dyslexic. I never thought I was a person who simply learned in a dyslexic style. I thought I *was* dsylexic." I reassured him, as I reassure you. *You are not who they think you are.*

No one can make you feel inferior without your consent.
                                                            —Eleanor Roosevelt

You're Not Who They Think You Are . . .

MANY years ago a friend and I were in business together. He decided we needed to part ways for reasons of his own. It was very difficult for me, as I imagine it was for him. Several days after I left, he began calling mutual friends and making claims about our business split which were not only ridiculous, but untrue. The friends he called immediately turned around and called me.

My first reaction was to call him. For whatever reason he didn't return my messages. The calls continued. Within a few days I began to grow quite troubled. It occurred to me that I was being slandered by my former partner and possibly judged by others for things that weren't true. I began to obsess about what this might do to my reputation. The more I thought about it, however, the more peaceful I became. I realized that I wasn't what they thought of me. And I definitely wasn't what my former business partner claimed. I recognized I had no control over what others thought. It was at this time the idea for this baby step really hit me.

In my personal life this was a significant baby step. You are not what someone else thinks you are. You are not your reputation. Your reputation is what they think about you. You are something totally different. Your reputation is an internal process *within someone else's mind*. You have no control over their thoughts. You can spend a lot of time obsessing about what others think of you. Many people do. But in the end you are still you. And you only have control over what you think. When you begin to take this baby step it's a transition process towards optimal functioning.

Don't let anyone look down on you . . . set an example . . . in speech, in life, in love, in faith, and in purity.

—1 Timothy 4:12 NIV

You're Not Who They Think You Are . . .

YOU'RE not the label others place on you. You're not your reputation. You're not your job. You're not the denomination you belong to, or somebody's wife or husband. You're not ADD, PMS, OCP, or whatever alphabet soup label your doctor gives you. So—if you are not any of those, then what are you?

What you are has to do with your beliefs, your values, and your inner-most soul. You are a sum product of the choices you have made. Those choices were based on internal qualities. And as you'll find out later, you are not even your thoughts. You literally don't have control over them. But you can control your choices. Others will fight you in this process of resisting their labels and being yourself. It's easier for them to put you in a category and interact with you according to that designation. They claim to "know" you if they can categorize, label, or put you in their file cabinet. It is even more convenient if you provide them with a label for yourself. In fact, that is the socially-accepted behavior of choice. That way other people do not have to go to the trouble of labeling you. You have made it easy for them. If you defy description, they will often try to pull you back in line. You will be making life difficult for them. Do not be conned. Be yourself.

You're not what they think you are. You are a product of your choices. Focus on your own internal processes rather than accommodating those who label you. Do not let the opinions or expectations of others determine the path of your life. Any time you give in to the stereotypes others place on you, they are not only defining your happiness, they are limiting it as well. Avoid labels. Examine those you provide for others. How do you introduce yourself? When you are asked what "you do" what is your response? Consider not providing labels for yourself. As an experiment, for a month beware of using them for others. *You are not what they think you are.* Never let anyone convince you otherwise.

Reputation is an idle and most false imposition; oft got without merit, and lost without deserving.

—Shakespeare, *Othello*

. . . But You're Not What You Think Either

THIS step is best understood if you've read the previous step first. In that baby step we said, "You're not who they think you are . . ." In this step we add to the mixture by injecting, . . . *but you are not what you think either.* This is probably confusing on the surface level. But stay with me on this one—it will make sense. On one level this baby step says, you are not your thoughts. Some people would disagree. At one time in my life I believed that *all* you really were, was the sum total of your thoughts. But I was wrong.

You are not your thoughts. You are not even responsible for all your thoughts. And most of all, you *cannot* control your thoughts. Thoughts come from many places. Some of your thoughts are generated from your own cerebral cortex. Others are reactions to the environment around you. Still others are critical memories composed of voices from your past. The voices could be that of your parents, previous spouse, school teacher, or any authority figure. They remain stored away permanently, and can be recalled consciously or unconsciously. The most powerful thoughts are those that pop up from seemingly nowhere. But they're right where you stored them. Their unconscious nature is what makes them so unexpectedly profound.

These thoughts are so powerful many of them can intrude on your consciousness and totally disrupt your concentration. I don't think you can control them. In fact, I suggest not even trying. Why set yourself up for failure? You aren't what you think. You are not your thoughts. You can't control your thoughts. It's best not to struggle with them. However there is an answer, and it's one that will work—especially with the critical recordings in your head.

We all have voices in our heads which talk to us on an almost constant basis. Our voices give us messages continually, and what they say to us affects us . . . .

—Juliene Berk

. . . But You're Not What You Think Either

IN 1994 *Forrest Gump* swept the box offices, the nation's conscious-ness, and the Oscars. Gump said his mother suggested, "Stupid is as stupid does." According to Mother Gump, if you do stupid, you are stupid. I believe everybody—especially me—has occasional stupid thoughts. I define that as normal. It's not having stupid thoughts that makes you stupid. It's whether or not you act on them. In order to get into trouble, you must continue obsessing about them. Then you must believe the thoughts. After that you finally must act on them.

Some people mistakenly react as if all their thoughts are telling the truth. You probably allow your own thoughts to get away with things you'd slap someone else for. In all likelihood, a majority of your thoughts are lies. Tell them they are. Don't let your own thoughts get away with abusing you. Some thoughts can lead to success, happiness, or joy. Others generate absolute havoc. And at times these dichotomous thoughts can hit within milliseconds of each other. One extreme of thought can be your absolute best friend. It can be supportive, friendly, and helpful. Other thoughts want nothing more than to kick you around. They take pleasure in defeating you. Unfortunately you can't control those either.

Here's the key. I don't think you can be in control of whether or not you have either extreme of thoughts. However I do believe you have control over which thoughts you decide to focus. It's not the thoughts that determine your happiness. It's the ones you focus on that will make the difference. When you concentrate on supportive thoughts you have found the key that unlocks this baby step.

One comes to believe whatever one repeats to oneself sufficiently often, whether the statement be true or false. It comes to be the dominating thought in one's mind.

—Robert Collier

. . . But You're Not What You Think Either

YOU'RE not what you think. You're not your thoughts. Each of us is capable of thinking homicidally angry thoughts. Less than seconds later we're also capable of altruistically cherubic thought. But the thoughts make us neither a murderer nor a saint. Thought is powerful. At times it's seductive.

People can get so caught up in thought, they forget to live. They shuffle, trance-like through life, like an emotional zombie from *Night of the Living Dead.* Some people spend their entire lives like this. These people usually end up having to be taken care of in a hospital. They can be dangerous to themselves or others. Others get lost playing and replaying critical thoughts until they become obsessed with their fears and immobilized. It is easy to get lost in thought. It's happened to me when driving. I've missed my exit while lost in thought. After "waking up" I was surprised. I didn't even know I was lost.

I suggest that if you want to get lost in thought, get lost in one that's going to be a friend to you. If you're going to obsess, latch on to something warm and fuzzy. Treat your thoughts like money. If you've got a hundred-dollar bill, what are you going to do with it? You can use it as a sweat rag. You can use it as cigarette rolling paper. You could waste it in some other way. Or you could take the money and use it wisely. The same is true with thought. It's the most powerful force in the universe. It's more powerful than a locomotive, faster than a speeding bullet, and able to leap tall buildings in a single bound. And it's yours.

Whatsoever things are true, whatsoever things are honest, whatsoever things are just, whatsoever things are pure, whatsoever things are lovely, whatsoever things are of good report; if there be any virtue, and if there be any praise, think on these things.
—Phillipians 4:8

. . . But You're Not What You Think Either

AS a child I remember watching Snagglepuss the cartoon character. When he was ready to get out of nasty situation he would curl up his lip and snarl ". . . exit—stage left . . ." Then he was out of there before he got in trouble. This is what I suggest you do with unwanted thoughts. If you fight them you'll lose. Tell them to exit—stage left. Everybody has terrible thoughts. The key is in letting them exit the same way they entered. Remember, you are only going to get into trouble if you believe the thoughts and then act as if they're real.

If you have a negative thought don't believe it. Tell it to get out. You can say it silently. For the more intrusive thoughts you may have to say it out loud. Tell the thought to get out, and that you don't need it. Visualize it coming at you like a bull in a ring. There you are, the gallant matador. You raise the cape, the bull charges past, except this time he continues out the gate and out of the arena. The fans roar their approval. In acknowledgment you tip your hat and bow.

I think it's equally important to nurture positive thoughts. Plant them, fertilize them, cultivate them, and get them growing. Set aside a designated period each day—even if it's only five minutes—where you make time for positive thoughts and visualizations. Read them aloud or listen to inspirational tapes. Do this for a week and observe the results. The negative thoughts—? Don't worry about those, they'll come on their own. Don't wrestle with them. Become Snagglepuss in a bullring. Tell them to *Exit!—Stage left!* . . . . And let them go out of your life. It's an important baby step on your journey to happiness.

We cannot always control our thoughts, but we can control our words, and repetition impresses the subconscious, and we are then master of the situation.

—Florence Scovel Shinn

6

Beginning to Think
Like a HAP

Normal Does Not Necessarily Mean Healthy

I enjoy comedy. The more I laugh, usually the better I feel. Few people have made me laugh over the years more than Mel Brooks. Both as an actor and a writer, his material has been extremely entertaining. In his movie *Young Frankenstein*, Igor mistakenly gets a brain from the royal brain repository that he thought belonged to Abbey Normal. Of course the joke was, it was an abnormal brain, and the Frankenstein that resulted was a bit "different." However, being "Abbey Normal" may not be such a bad deal. It really depends on how you define "normal."

Unfortunately we have come to define normal as more or less average. Scientifically, normal is whatever falls within the standard distribution of the bell curve. Anything outside the standard distribution—the top and bottom small percentages—are defined as abnormal. Therefore by scientific definition, mediocre is normal. To be happier than the rest of the population would be considered "Abbey Normal." Therefore I would prefer to fall on Abbey's side.

In our society normal and healthy are vastly different. Normal is unhappy. Normal is dysfunctional. Normal is under-achieving, blaming, and avoiding responsibility. Me? I don't want to be normal. I'd rather be Abbey Normal and happy. If you're happy, you will be outside the normal distribution. You will be considered "different" and perhaps a little strange. Good. If what I see in the news and on television is normal, then I'd rather be "Abbey."

In my opinion, we are in danger of developing a cult of the Common Man, which means a cult of mediocrity.

—**Herbert Hoover**

Normal Does Not Necessarily Mean Healthy

THERE are four signature beliefs happy people have which "normals" don't. These beliefs actually distinguish normal from happy.
Normal people believe good things can't last. Those who are happy
disagree. Their stance is yes, good things *can* last. And you can make
good things happen. As a result they develop an optimism and
confidence that things are going to be okay.

"Normals" believe people are out to get them. They believe the
system works against good people, and it's all a big conspiracy.
Happy people disagree again. They think most people are actually
okay. They know most people aren't out to get them. Frankly, most
people don't even have the time or the concern, to care that much.
Conspiracy theory? Nah! Happy people realize others are so self-
absorbed they couldn't cooperate enough to conspire.

"Normals" believe nothing really matters anyway. Happy people
have a different belief. They believe life is important in general and
their life specifically is valuable. As a result, life is filled with
meaning and they live it more fully. Finally, "normals" believe the
universe is out of control. They believe the world is going downhill
and we are all just along for the ride. On this belief happy people
disagree to a point. The universe may be out of control, yet HAPs
believe they've got *self control.* It's the only control that counts.
HAPs are not normal. But normal doesn't mean happy anyway.
They're Abbey Normal. Choose happiness. It will make your journey through life far more rewarding.

---

*I am wondering what would have happened to me if some fluent
talker had converted me to the theory of the eight-hour day and
convinced me that it was not fair to my fellow workers to put forth
my best efforts in my work. I am glad that the eight-hour day had not
been invented when I was a young man. If my life had been made up
of eight-hour days, I don't believe I could have accomplished a great
deal . . .*

—Thomas Edison

Normal Does Not Necessarily Mean Healthy

TO me there is big difference between normal and healthy. It's healthy to play with the hand you're dealt. In any game of cards the goal is to make the most of your cards. If you can replace them, go ahead and do so. If you can't, organize your cards, keep your wits, and make the most of it. In no card game is it customary to tip your hand by complaining about the dealer. Yet in life that's normal. In life, far more people complain about their cards than exchange them or ask for a new deal. They just whine. That's normal.

When it comes to happiness, it's far more important how you regard your cards, than what you do with them, or who the dealer is. By accepting your cards and making the most out of them, you remove uncertainty. Uncertainty always brings with it worry and anxiety. These qualities make the problem worse. Why test it? You really don't need these added discomforts. Make the most out of what you have and remove the uncertainty and worry.

You can do this by focusing on the few things over which you have control. Start with yourself. Choose some positive friends. Join a functional social network. Spend some time working on your family life. Improve your relationship with your spouse and children to whatever degree possible. Do your best to become happy with your career or change direction. Spend some time on personal development. Do what you need to do to feel better about yourself and your achievements. Improve your life. Focus on continual improvement. Each morning when you plan your day ask yourself, "What can I do to improve my life?" It's not normal to do this. What's normal is more likely to whine. That's why we suggest don't worry about being normal, worry about being healthy.

Great spirits have always found violent opposition from mediocrities.
—Albert Einstein

Normal Does Not Necessarily Mean Healthy

IF you are normal you think happiness comes from one of, or a combination of the following:

Money	A car	Religion
Sex	Drugs	Prozac
Alcohol	Your psychiatrist	Marriage
New Age philosophy	Divorce	The stars
Re-marriage	Another person	A new job

Healthy people believe something different. They believe happiness comes from taking *baby steps* and gradually gaining control of their life. Once you accomplish that, to a small degree you'll be in transition. This transition is an important one. You can begin to make this transition by making continual progress toward improvement. Do this by listing your answers to the following: "What can I do to improve my life?"

Your answer can include such things as listening to good music, practicing a new skill, contacting a good friend, or spending time with a child. Your list might also include baby step concepts such as simplifying, finding a reason to get out of bed, learning to drive your own bus, etc. Eventually you'll begin to measure your own progress in baby steps, rather than chasing after the approval of others. But it's not normal. In fact it's Abbey Normal. But it is healthy. And it's a baby step onward to happiness.

So I tell you this, and insist on it in the Lord, that you must no longer live as the Gentiles do, in the futility of their thinking.
—**Ephesians 4:17** NIV

Life Is Not a Collection, It's a Celebration

MANY years ago I visited with a young man who was at the end of a hormonally-intoxicated late adolescence. We had developed a close relationship and apparently a great deal of trust. Midway through the course of therapy he told me he had found the perfect woman. I asked him how he knew for sure this was "the one." "Oh, it's easy," he responded sincerely. "She's got her own car, stereo, and apartment." We both ended up laughing over his analytical assessment.

Unfortunately there are those who use people as objects, and objects as people. An object can be controlled. You can possess a thing. You can manipulate, replace, or save it. Once you own an object, it's yours. People, on the other hand, are different. You may think you own them, but about the time you grow comfortable, reality shatters your illusion. Consequently there are many who end up surrounding themselves with things. Sometimes they try to make people things. You can buy, rent, or hire people. They're called employees or consultants. You own them to a certain extent, during the hours they're employed. Yet people are still unpredictable.

Therefore inanimate objects are often more attractive. People may fall in love with cars, money, or jewelry, rather than your *soul*. Sometimes they may fall in love with your image, rather than who you are. It all works out the same. With these people it's not the person that's important but the object. They become obsessed with rings, things, and ceremonies. To them people are always expendable. It's a very sick approach to life. On this baby step it's very important to learn that life is not a collection. You can't collect life, put it in a bottle, set it on a shelf, and dust it off once a week. You can only experience it. And it is best experienced celebrating one moment at a time.

I don't want to get to the end of my life and find that I just lived the length of it. I want to have lived the width of it as well.
—**Diane Ackerman**

Life Is Not a Collection, It's a Celebration

PEOPLE collect various things. Some collect stamps. My sons collect football jerseys. Others collect expensive, antique cars. Some invest tremendous money in their collections while ignoring their families. The difference is you can control a stamp. But you can't control people. Some collect genealogy. They surround themselves with endless files of data about the dead, while ignoring the living. You can control, catalog and manipulate records of the dead, but not flesh-and-blood relatives. It's all a collection, and it's a way to ignore the celebration of life.

Other people collect less observable phenomenon such as negative emotions. They spend many hours cataloging their ills, ensuring you know what they are. They hang on to them as if they were priceless antiques. They're antiques all right, though certainly not precious. In fact, the opposite is true. Collected negative emotions from the past fill the emotional cupboards of all unhappy people. Another group of people store negative emotions in their body. They collect unwanted and unnecessary pain. They become sick and haul the extra baggage through life stored in their bodies and their minds. Eventually, what started out as an emotional disorder becomes a physical one as well.

Whether you store your "treasures" in the closets of your house, the attics of your brain, or in a spare tire around your waist, you would be better off discarding them. It takes emotional and physical energy to store, maintain and transport your collections. Owners of large retail department store chains have found it more cost effective to take another approach. They discard in-store Christmas decorations rather than pack, store, and reassemble them each year. While the practice may not be environmentally friendly, we would do well to learn from their example. Life is not a collection. It's a celebration. It's not something to hold on to. It's something to live. Try this approach. It's a baby step in the right direction.

There is no cure for birth and death save to enjoy the interval.
—George Santayana

Life Is Not a Collection, It's a Celebration

HAPPINESS is not collectible. It is to be celebrated, experienced, and lived. In fact it's impossible to collect. You can't save and cash it in later. It's there to be celebrated one moment at a time. Happiness can't be invested in things either. If you don't celebrate it at the moment, you lose it forever. Happiness has nothing to do with external qualities. Age doesn't matter. You can experience it at any point in life, regardless of gender, skin color or national origin. Happiness is an equal-opportunity phenomenon. There is no price on it. It can't be bought or owned.

Many years ago I witnessed a person demonstrate this very graphically. I was accompanying a high-ranking Japanese Jiu Jitsu master as he toured various schools. At one stop, a lower-ranking instructor was making quite a fuss about the senior master's new Rolex. I knew for a fact the expensive watch had been a gift from his students. In fact I had contributed to the fund. The younger instructor was attempting to give the master a compliment. Instead, he got a valuable learning experience. After a few moments the master took off the expensive watch and tossed to it to his junior instructor. *The watch is worth nothing.* The master grunted. *It's 'the way' that's important.*

I interpreted the transaction from several different angles. On one level the master was trying to teach "things" are irrelevant. He was saying Jiu Jitsu—"the way of gentleness"—was important. However the deeper lesson for me was the power of being detached from things. Happiness is not about things. The watch was worth a minimum of several thousand dollars. And, as far as I know, the master teacher liked it. But he was completely detached from it. Happiness is not in things. Life is not a collection. The truth is if you celebrate each moment of life along the way "things" will come to you. And incidentally, his Rolex came back to him as well.

Life is a process of becoming, a combination of states we have to go through. Where people fail is that they wish to elect a state and remain in it. This is a kind of death.

—Anais Nin

Life Is Not a Collection, It's a Celebration

LIFE is for living, experiencing and celebrating. It's active. Collecting is about accumulating, storing and controlling. It's passive. Celebration doesn't accumulate dust or cobwebs. Collections do. One of my friends lives across the country from her mother. She has invited her mom on many occasions to visit. Money is not a problem. The response for years has been the same. Her mother explained she can't leave because someone might steal her belongings.

When you avoid getting attached to things you are by definition, more independent. It gives you more freedom. Anything you're attached to, by definition, is also attached to you. The idea is not to take a vow of poverty. In fact it seems the opposite occurs. The less you're attached to things, the more you get. I heard singer and background vocalist for Elvis Presley, J. D. Summer, state Elvis had given away one billion dollars by the time of his death. He had earned more than two billion dollars. The more he gave away, the more it came back to him. There is power in being detached from things.

Some people can eventually let go of "things," but have tremendous difficulty handling disapproval. They are crushed by it. If you work on it, *approval* eventually becomes irrelevant. When it does, *disapproval* will also be irrelevant. An even higher level of achievement is being detached from results. At this level the *process* is more important than the results. When you live in the moment as intensely as possible, the results always take care of themselves. Practice this baby step, by choosing a room in your house and giving away belongings you no longer find useful. Consider getting rid of anything you haven't used in a year. Put those items in a box and date the contents. After a year is up, without going through it again, give the box of stuff away or throw it out. Don't attach yourself to collectibles. There's an incredible freedom in detaching yourself from things, people, and results. Happiness is not collectible. It can't be stored, filed, or e-mailed. Make your life a celebration and you'll find far more happiness.

It is for freedom that Christ has set us free. Stand firm, then, and do not let yourselves be burdened again by a yoke of slavery.
—Galations 5:1 NIV

Theory and Reality Are Seldom the Same

THEORY and reality are seldom the same. Theory deals with speculation. It deals with the "should's, ought's, and supposed to's" of life. Theory is in a laboratory. Reality is what goes on in your life. The two things are often quite different. It has been theoretically proven in laboratory settings that bumble bees can't fly. Theoretically, attorney James Garrison claimed in the Kennedy assassination hearing, an elephant can hang over the edge of a cliff with his trunk wrapped around a daisy stem. And of course the biggest theoretical blunders of all time include, "the world is flat," and "man will never fly."

In its early days the M-16 rifle was theorized to be a revolutionary and advanced infantry weapon. Indeed it was, in the laboratory. But in the jungles of Vietnam where it was hot, humid, and dirty, theory and reality weren't the same. Soldiers who had the opportunity would go to the "black market" and purchase other weapons with their own money. They would continue to go back and purchase ammunition, rather than depend on the theoretically advanced M-16s. Much to the manufacturer's credit the mistakes were eventually rectified. But in my opinion the problems could have been responsible for a number of young Americans' lives. In theory it was a great rifle. In the reality of the jungle, it didn't work.

Theories usually embrace traditional thinking. People who disagree with theory are often seen as dangerously unconventional, and punished. Marconi was institutionalized for believing he could send messages through the air. The inventor of the steamboat, Robert Fulton, suffered the same treatment for his unconventional and anti-theoretical ideas. Henry Ford faced a court struggle and was forced to prove his sanity through the justice system. Einstein and Edison were described by more conventional theorists as retarded. Theory is speculation. Reality is what you cope with on a daily basis. Occasionally they coincide. But it's very rare. Theory and reality are seldom the same.

Hear now this, O foolish people, and without understanding; which have eyes, and see not; which have ears, and hear not . . . .
—Jeremiah 5:21

Theory and Reality Are Seldom the Same

PEOPLE are filled with ideas about how things "should" be. This is especially true when it comes to such conventional arenas as relationships, careers, and religion. Most of these ideas, like most theory is different from reality. It's frustrating. In fact much of the anger and disappointment of "Generation X" is because theory didn't work. *The theory of how things should be today* is vastly different today than how things are. Theory and reality don't even come close to meshing.

When one person's theory becomes collective theory, people react to it. They compare their reality to speculated theory, and depending on the gap can become vastly disappointed. The disillusionment of many occurs as a result of theory failing to even come close to matching reality. The severity of reaction usually correlates with the depth of belief in the theory. Some have actually committed suicide when they realized the disparity they faced. Others end up in psychiatric hospitals for the same reason. When people are true believers in theory, they may be setting themselves up for an incredible fall. Sometimes the fall can be deadly.

A better course is to be open to what comes your way. There's no problem with believing in theory as long as you test it with reality. Most theory works at least part of the time. But your reality may differ from the laboratory where the theory was conceived. Ultimately theory needs to revolve around your own measured experience. What works for one person will not necessarily work for you. And what works in a laboratory will rarely work in everyone's life. Theory and reality are rarely the same. If you want to live in a laboratory depend on theory. If you want to live in the real world, filter theory through the prism of experience.

There is no reality except the one contained within us. That is why so many people live such an unreal life. They take the images outside them for reality and never allow the world within to assert itself.
                                        —F. Herman Hesse, *Demian*

Theory and Reality Are Seldom the Same

THEORY *and reality are seldom the same.* There's probably no part of life where this is more accurately illustrated than in marriage, especially a first marriage. We live in a society where one marriage is often viewed as boot camp for the next. Some people are more in touch with reality by the time the second, third, or fourth comes around. Yet reality still eludes many.

Marriage is a tradition which funnels a dramatic number of mystical theories into one reality. First is the religious theory. Most denominations consider marriage one of the holy sacraments. Clergy take marriage both as a ceremony and ritual very seriously. There's also the legal theory of marriage which binds two people together as a mini-corporation with serious legal ramifications. And there's the fairy tale theory. "Happily ever after" still exists in the minds of many. Whether it's discussed in an out-of-date fairy tale or an up-to-date movie is irrelevant. The fantasies are perpetuated. As a result, people enter these relationships with various confusing concepts. Reality often slams a door in the face of most of these. Yet that learning doesn't seem to be passed on to future generations.

People entering marriage today, even some for the third or fourth time, still have confused theories about the reality of such an intense relationship. As a marriage counselor I believe their flawed theories are often the reason they get divorced to begin with. It's not only that theory contributes to divorce it's often the cause of it. This is not to encourage people to believe that divorce is the answer. The case of both marriage and divorce is frankly part of the problem. People need to have more realistic theories about the reality of marriage. It's an intense relationship. There are going to be intense highs—and intense lows. The lows will often seem unbearable and the highs will be unbelievable. But our society still hangs onto the fantasy-theory of marriage. Don't lie or deceive yourself about this theory. Reality will knock you out if you do. Theory and reality are seldom the same.

Facts as facts do not always create a spirit of reality, because reality is a spirit.

—G.K. Chesterton

Theory and Reality Are Seldom the Same

IF reality is not theory, then what is it? Generally speaking, it's your own unique and individual experience. You are an experiment of one. Your one-person reality will probably never coincide with anyone else's theory of what you are supposed to do. Actually it would be a lot more comfortable if you could depend on theory. Then there would be an explanation for everything you experience. But life does not work that way.

People often telephone me to help make a decision about whether or not they want to enter psychotherapy. On virtually all occasions they'll ask what my theoretical background is. They ask if I'm like *Dr. Katz*, or *Frasier*! Others ask if I'm psychoanalytic, client-centered, or Gestalt. My response generally depends on the nature of the call. I may joke about it and tell them I'm a "Marine Corps Therapist" or I believe in "Boot Camp Theory." On other occasions I say I'm a "Nike" Therapist. I explain that I don't care about "the why" of understanding. I focus more on "the how" of change. I tell them I believe in "just do it" therapy. For more serious calls I tell them I have no theory. I explain that each person brings her own theory into the office. And to limit someone by forcing her to match my theory is the worst kind of cheating. I suggest if she goes to another therapist who forces a label on her to say, "Thanks but no thanks," and get up and leave.

There is no theory that will ever be capable of explaining the complexities of your individual life. Your individual theory is a totally subjective phenomenon. Theory is fine so long as you look on it as a guide. Take this baby step by examining your life for theories which you've embraced as truth yet aren't working for you. Many have their roots in maxims taught in childhood—marrying the "right" person will make marriage easy; life should be effortless if you're doing the "right thing;" etc. Write them down. Experiment by rejecting one for a week. If you reject theory, you probably won't be well-liked. However, I'd rather be in the group with Marconi, Fulton, and Henry Ford. People will tell you you're crazy, but they said the same of Einstein, Edison, and even Thoreau. It's your decision.

Theories are private property, but truth is common stock.
                                                    —Charles Caleb Colton

See the Forest As Well As the Trees

IT has always been fascinating to me that HAPs are described by various researchers as having an inherent distrust of beauracracies. It's an easy characteristic to misunderstand and one that deserves some explanation. First of all, happy people are not anti-authority or anti-government. This is not a commentary about patriotism. What HAPs discover is some bureaucracies are in place more to serve the bureaucracy's needs, than the people they're supposed to help.

It seems over time bureaucracies can become self-serving. Members of these organizations are required to spend inordinate energy justifying their existence. Perpetuating the bureaucracy can become the goal, not serving people. HAPs have tremendous difficulty with this. In many large organizations, policies, procedures, and documentation take over. People become secondary and are used to serve procedure rather than vice versa. The true purpose of the organization becomes lost and is replaced by perpetuating the system, "covering your rear," and keeping your job. In summary, larger organizations rarely serve their original purposes.

HAPs do appear to have a superior perception of reality. They can see the forest *and* the trees. HAPs respect rules, but not those without a functional reason for existing other than perpetuating themselves. On the other hand, HAPs are not good at pretending or playing games. Therefore they simply don't fit into most bureaucracies. They ask questions which have no concise answers in large organizations or institutions. These questions not only aren't appreciated but are often resented by beauracracies. As a result HAPs sometimes are labeled as "troublemakers" or accused of being disloyal. They're not. They just see the forest as well as the trees.

Bureaucracy, the rule of no one, has become the modern form of despotism.

—**Mary McCarthy**

See the Forest As Well As the Trees

SEVERAL years ago I saw a couple for their fourth therapy visit. They described themselves as experiencing "communication problems." It didn't take long to understand what their communication problems were. Early into the session the husband located a "run" in his wife's hosiery. He seemed hypnotized by the run and spent most of the session berating her. He seemed unable to discuss anything else during the session. He forgot about his wife. He forgot about me. He forgot about why they had come to therapy. He became obsessed with the flaw. He was unable to see the forest for the trees.

It's easy for some people to get bogged down in small details and lose the big picture. One question I often find myself asking in therapy is, "What's really important in this situation?" As an example, on three different occasions I asked the husband, "What's important here? The quality of you wife's hosiery, or the quality of your marriage? What's really important? The run, or your wife's sensitivity?" Not only did he ignore the answer, he apparently didn't even hear the question. Before the session was over, the lady got up from her chair, and stomped out slamming the door behind her. The husband turned to me, shrugged his shoulders and said, "See what I mean?" I answered, "No! I totally missed the point. Maybe you did too!"

Some people simply lose perspective. They become so obsessed with the thorns, they fail to appreciate the rose. They are so mesmerized by one small flaw in the tree, they miss the beauty of the forest. It's a dangerous tendency, and one you need to avoid at all costs. A better approach is to focus on what's right about a situation. Though it's easy to become obsessed with what's *wrong,* it's also very dangerous. This overemphasis on the negative can result in you actually becoming negative. It's a dangerous and prominent tendency. My suggestion is to do the opposite. Focus on the beauty of the rose. It is seasonal. It will fade tomorrow. The thorns will always be there.

If the doors of perception were cleansed everything would appear to man as it is, infinite.

—William Blake

See the Forest As Well As the Trees

ONE of my favorite writers is American poet Nicki Giovanni. Her essay entitled, "The Time Machine" is about a comic book she read as a child. I heard her tell this story many years ago, so I beg Nicki's pardon if I do not have the details correct.

The story was based in the twenty-first century. One evening a man walks into a doctor's office and is waiting to be seen. No one is there, yet there is a card at a table beside a machine. The sign reads, "Fill out the card and insert it into the machine." The man completes the card and follows the instructions. The machine begins rumbling and humming, and after a few seconds prints out a response which says, "You will be struck by lightning and killed tomorrow morning." The man looks up at the machine and notices a button which reads, "Death Averted." He pushes the button and the machine begins gestating again. This time it prints out another card. "You will survive the lightning strike, but three years from now your business will fail, and you will commit suicide." The man decides to push the "Death Averted" button again and the machine repeats the cycle. This time the printout reads, "You will survive the business failure, but you and your family will be killed while traveling to a vacation site."

The man becomes obsessed with the machine. He continues to play late into the night pushing the "Death Averted" button over and over. He ignores the wind blowing through the windows and the clouds gathering in the sky. He misses the thunder as it begins to rumble in the distance. And at two minutes after midnight, he's killed by lightning while pushing the "Death Averted" button. Sometimes we are just like this man. We get so caught up in the process of playing the game, we miss what's really important. See the forest for the trees. Sometimes it's important just to step back, view life from a different angle, and get a new perspective. Viewing the forest will help you see the big picture. As a result of this you can look at what's ahead. It will help you gain perspective and remain healthy.

Now we see but a poor reflection as in a mirror; then we shall see face to face. Now I know in part; then I shall know fully, even as I am fully known.

—1 Corinthians 13:12 NIV

See the Forest As Well As the Trees

IT'S important to see the forest as well as the trees. People who seem to have the most difficulty with this are Type A personalities. When Type A's go after a task they become obsessed. At times they tend to become like lab rats on a treadmill. They *run* but don't get very far. These people can accomplish a great deal but they run the risk of burning out quickly.

It's been suggested that muppet creator Jim Henson died from what was a simple bronchial infection that went untreated till he was at death's door. It wasn't that people didn't notice. Apparently a number of people noticed and brought it to his attention. He simply wouldn't submit himself to medical treatment. His condition could have been treated by four days of antibiotics. Perhaps he thought he was too busy to see a doctor. Unfortunately, he's no longer busy doing anything. He's at rest. The same was true for author and running commentator Jim Fixx. His father and brother had both died from heart problems in their forties. Yet Fixx ignored the pain in his chest and arm. He died while jogging at the young age of forty-eight. He had reportedly been having symptoms for weeks before his death. A cardiologist told me problems like Fixx had usually aren't fatal if treated promptly. Both these men were wonderfully creative. The world misses their contributions tremendously. I don't think Jim Henson or Jim Fixx chose to die. But they didn't see the forest for the trees.

Viewing the forest means you do occasionally stop and smell the roses. Sometimes when you do this the prick of a thorn acts as a reality check. To me it would seem important to pay attention when we get these reality checks. I miss the creativity of Jim Henson and the narratives of Jim Fixx. Hopefully, we can all learn from their mistake. Ask yourself, "What is the big picture in this situation?" Do this whenever you face a decision or confrontation. Try it for a week. Remind yourself of this question often. Put it on a card and post it where you will see it often. By practicing this *baby step* you will be able to back up far enough from a problem so you can *see the forest as well as the trees*. We will all be glad you did.

Your range of available choices—right now—is limitless.
                                                        —Carl Frederick

7

Learning to Control
Your Own Happiness

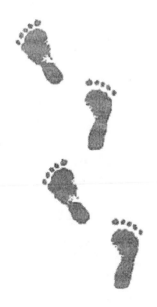

No One Can Offend You Without Your Permission

NO one can offend you without your permission. To some, this is an old concept. People have spoken about it for years. Eleanor Roosevelt expressed a similar sentiment back in the forties. Jimmy Buffet said as much in his song *Margaritaville.* *"Someone says there's a woman to blame, but I know it's my own darn fault."* To other people, however, this kind of thinking requires a radical stretch of consciousness. "What do you mean?" they demand. "I'd never give anyone permission to offend me." Yes you do—and you probably do it regularly.

I've said it often during talk shows and speaking engagements. I've been criticized for it, misunderstood, and even abused a couple of times. But I stand by it. *No one can offend you without your permission.* It takes two people to create an insult. It takes two people to play guilty. I'd even say it takes two people to develop alcoholism, depression, or virtually any other negative emotion. This is no radically-new concept. It probably has more to do with philosophy than anything else. However, it is extremely practical. To feel a negative emotion of any kind you must cooperate. Unhappiness requires two people. As an example, to feel guilt, one person has to dish it out. The other needs to accept it. If someone tries to send guilt your way and you don't accept it, there's simply no guilt. There's nothing but dead air. If you cooperate, on the other hand, there's a negative emotion.

Pain is a two-person dance. One leads, the other follows. Before long, it's tough to figure out who's following and who's leading. Sometimes the partners even switch roles. But a two-person dance requires both people to cooperate. One dancer reacts and flows with the other. *No one can offend you without your permission.* No one can hurt you without your cooperation. The lesson in this baby step is to quit issuing permission slips. Once you do that, you've got it made.

No one can make you feel inferior without your consent.
—**Eleanor Roosevelt**

No One Can Offend You Without Your Permission

DO YOU remember permission slips? You used to get them from your teacher. They meant you had permission to be in the hall on the way to the bathroom. My kids have to get them signed to take field trips. Permission slips mean that this trip—to the bathroom or the museum—is authorized. People give permission slips for pain as well. They do them in the strangest ways. And they come up in the most unusual circumstances.

I speak at a lot of churches. Almost without exception, there will be a supper or luncheon accompanying my seminar. In the South, at least, these are often of the pot-luck variety. Each person brings a dish and the meals usually turn out to be elegant. In fact, I have spoken for my supper literally hundreds of times. One occasion stands out where I observed a lady issuing a permission slip allowing someone to offer her guilt. She was supposed to bring dessert and instead brought salad. This resulted in some good-natured teasing from one of the men in her group. When the man went to bring in another load of food from his car I pulled her aside.

I explained that no one could make her feel guilty without her permission. At first she was puzzled but I continued to explain. "It takes two people to feel guilty," I told her. "One has to offer the guilt, and the other person needs to accept it. Tell him you don't want his guilt and you're tired of cooperating. Tell him you're tired of playing 'guilt.' Take your permission slip back." She proceeded to do just that. He didn't understand. But she didn't feel any more guilt. Be careful who you give permission slips to. It takes two people to offend. One person has to issue the permission slip. The other has to act on it. But you can stop it on your own. Don't be afraid to take back the slips. You handed them out—they're yours to revoke. Better yet, stop giving them out at all. On the road to happiness you really don't have time to stop and play "guilt."

No one on earth can hurt you, unless you accept the hurt in your own mind . . . The problem is not other people; it is your reaction.
—**Vernon Howard**

No One Can Offend You Without Your Permission

THIS is an important and pragmatic baby step. Once you accept it, you are on the journey to happiness. It helps you accept responsibility for your pain and pleasure. You can change it, but only if you are willing to accept responsibility for both. No one can offend you without your permission. You are the one who gives permission or withdraws it. At this point along the journey to happiness you can begin to blend some of the various baby steps together. As an example, you could blend this baby step with Snagglepuss. If someone attempts to offend you, you can tell them to *exit—stage left* . . . . In all honesty, if you did that, a lot of people would laugh. They might even think you're weird. But they'd most likely leave you alone.

With others you can do what the church lady did. Just say, "No thanks, I don't want to cooperate," and ignore their attempts. If you do this people will probably wonder. But you'll be fine. The main key is an understanding that no one can make you do anything without your permission. If someone says you're wrong, it doesn't make you wrong. If someone says you're right, it also doesn't make you right. To the degree you invest in others' opinions, you empower them. Strength comes from being totally independent of others' opinions, approval or disapproval.

No one can make you cry. No one can make you unhappy. No one can make you feel pain. No one can make you feel guilt. No one can make you angry. No one can make you anything without your cooperation. Certainly, people will try. In the past you have probably given permission slips to a variety of people in your life. You've given them permission to make you feel a lot of things. Now is the time to realize your mistakes and take ownership of those permission slips. By doing this you will have made major strides on the journey to happiness.

Do everything in love.

—1 Corinthians 16:14 NIV

No One Can Offend You Without Your Permission

ONCE you accept the truth of this baby step you're well on the way to happiness. The truth is you're one hundred percent responsible for the emotions you experience. Once you accept no one can make you feel anything without your permission you have made tremendous progress.

There's another truth that's equally important. And in the same way, once you accept this, you're also going to make significant strides. With this baby step, as well as the others, you're going to blow it, goof up and make mistakes. You're going to backslide and re-issue permission slips. You're going to mess up. Accept your own fallibility. Welcome to the human race. So you're not perfect! Once you accept your imperfection, you don't have to maintain a facade. So! Deal with it. You don't have to pretend anymore. I don't want to disillusion you. But you don't have to be perfect—even at being imperfect! Learning this baby step is just like learning all the others. It's going to take some practice to make it a habit.

Have you issued permission slips you'd like to recall? Do you feel guilty because of mistakes you've made and what others might think? Those are areas where you have given others permission to offend you. Identify and make a list of those people. Stop playing "guilt." Tell them you don't want to cooperate. There's absolutely no reason to feel bad, guilty, or dense, because of your mistakes. Welcome to the human race. We're all messed up to one degree or another. You will fall short. You will get offended. Don't worry about it. Try it for a week. People will continue to dump on you. I suggest welcoming them to the human race as well. Then tell them to "exit—stage left." And while they're on their way out, take back your permission slip.

Most successes have been built on failures, not on one failure alone but on several. A majority of the great historic accomplishments of the past have been the final result of a persistent struggle against discouragement and failure. A man is never beaten until he thinks he is.
—Charles Gow

Return To Sender

ONE of the most idolized figures in the history of popular music and entertainment is Elvis Presley. There was no one before or since who made such an impact on the entertainment world. In his later years, he obviously developed multiple problems. But his impact on our society was phenomenal. One of his early major hits was the ballad, *Return to Sender*. In this song he laments the loss of a relationship. He grieves the fact that she wrote on his letter *Return to sender*.

Elvis was probably better off without her. You don't need a love in your life who doesn't really want to be there. By returning to sender, she probably hurt her suitor temporarily. But in the long run, it was best. Occasionally it may be important for you to *return to sender*. A "gift" may not be a gift at all. In the song, since she actually didn't care for the guy anyway, the relationship would have never survived. This way he was free to find someone who would really like him. He was far better off without the gift of this person in his life.

You will be offered many gifts during your life. You may be offered drugs, get-rich-quick schemes, or other something-for-nothing promises. A friend of mine who is a TV anchorman, was offered $500 by an intoxicated man he met in a bar to give the man's wife a birthday present. The suggested birthday present was the anchorman, in bed with the drunk's wife. "Come on," the drunk slobbered. "She loves you. She watches you every night on TV." The man even offered to bring a picture of his wife to prove she wasn't ugly. And trust me, my friend needed the $500. But this wasn't a gift he accepted. And it truly wasn't a gift this man's wife needed. My friend quickly exited the bar and said, "No thanks." He returned the $500 to sender. There are many things you need to return to sender. $500 is not always a gift. Waking up next to your local anchorman is not necessarily a gift either. Say, *Return to sender*, and you will end up taking a major baby step on the way to happiness.

Men often applaud an imitation and hiss the real thing.

—Aesop

Return To Sender

A gift may be something wrapped up in a box with bows. It can also be somebody's presence in your life. It can be a compliment. A gift can be virtually anything. But it's never yours unless you accept it. It's important to evaluate all things that come your way to determine whether or not they are truly gifts. Some givers have good intentions. Frankly, some don't. People who want to hurt you would like to give you things. If you accept the gift, then it's yours. If you don't, the giver has to cope with it.

Relationships will come your way. Compliments will come your way. People will definitely be attracted to you if you're really happy. They are not necessarily gifts. Some of them will be your enemies. A giver can have good intentions and still give you something that will be bad for you. Evaluate your gifts very closely. If you're happy, peaceful, or successful, many things will come your way. To some of them you will probably need to say, "No thanks." And *return to sender.*

The classical example of this is from an Asian folk story. According to the story, an elderly monk was meditating very peacefully. He was deep into his meditation when a younger monk approached him and attempted to interrupt the master. Whatever the message was, the young monk thought it was very important. He persisted in attempting to break the master's concentration. Finally in exasperation he sat down and waited. After what apparently was quite some time, the senior monk stopped his meditation and prepared to leave. The younger monk began to question him as to why the master didn't respond earlier. Without blinking, the senior monk responded, *When someone offers you a gift, it's not yours unless you accept it.* Apparently the younger monk was confused by the response, as I was at first. But eventually I realized the importance of the metaphor. A gift is not necessarily a gift at all. *Return to sender,* and you'll be better off.

And thou shalt take no gift: for the gift blindeth the wise, and perverteth the words of the righteous.
                                                                —Exodus 23:8

Return To Sender

ONE couple illustrated *return to sender* in a dramatic way. Both had been in previous marriages and came from a strict religious denomination that didn't approve of remarriage after divorce. Yet this couple's commitment to each other was so strong they went against denominational tradition and married. They were very happy, with few problems. The problems they did have came from those who perpetually criticized the young couple, creating a great deal of guilt.

They had spent their entire lives in this particular denomination, and deep down inside believed in it. Yet they had married anyway. Dissolving the relationship would not have made their guilt any less. I attempt to reach people on various levels. Just as with various baby steps, sometimes I'll say something five or six different ways. But it may turn out to take the final way to reach understanding. It was the same with this couple. I had unsuccessfully attempted to reach them on multiple occasions. Finally, I both amused them, and succeeded in communicating. I directed my remarks to the lady, however, both were present.

I asked if I got two slices of cheap white bread, spread each one with anchovies and Muenster cheese and offered it to her as a sandwich, would she eat it. She turned up her nose and shook her head, "No!" Her husband chuckled in the background. I asked if we spiced it up with mayonnaise, peanut butter, and sardines, if she would reconsider. This time she laughed and assured me absolutely not. I continued asking again, making it worse each time. Finally she asked in exasperation, "Why are you talking about this? It's nasty!" My response finally broke through. "I can offer you disgusting food all night long. Whether or not you eat it is up to you. I can offer you shame for the rest of your life. Whether or not you consume it is up to you. No one is going to force you to eat this sandwich. In the same way, no one can force you to digest shame or guilt. If you don't want the sandwich, return it to sender and let him eat it. Do the same with shame. Return it to sender and let them deal with it." By the end of the session we finally communicated. With both of them, their guilt went away and at our next session they brought some grotesque-looking sandwiches!

The prompter the refusal, the less the disappointment.
—Publilius

Return To Sender

THERE are many occasions when a gift is not a gift. The Trojans discovered this by accepting what they thought was a gift horse. In all reality, few gifts come with no strings attached. You can learn this as a baby step or as the Trojans did. Just because something, or someone looks good does not mean it's necessarily true.

If you analyze gifts, you realize there are very few that don't have strings attached. What appears at first to be a gift is usually no gift at all. Literally if it seems too good to be true, it usually is. And most Trojan horses do look too good to be true. In many cases people accept gifts out of guilt. If somebody gives you something, you feel obligated to keep it. From a sense of duty, you can clutter your lives, physically and emotionally, with things you really didn't want to begin with. This is another case when a very polite "No thanks," and *return to sender* would have been better.

Don't waste your time with unwanted gifts. Whether they are literal or figurative gifts is irrelevant. Wasting your life cleaning, organizing and rearranging things you really didn't want to begin with, is not the way to happiness. Instead, return to sender. If you can't locate the sender, give them away to someone else. Remember a gift is not yours unless you accept it. If you want and really need it, accept it. Rest assured there will be many gifts offered. You will be the recipient of a wide variety of offerings. There will be criticisms, accusations, and derogatory remarks galore. This week, practice this baby step by disregarding devastating or critical remarks you receive. Determine they have more to do with the sender's needs. It's up to you, but I suggest *return to sender* . . . . Increase your awareness of this idea by listing "gifts" you've received lately. Examples include friends who gossip in the belief they are "defending" you, comments by bossy relatives or "news" from nosy neighbors. Decide which ones to return and follow through. You'll be far more successful on the road to happiness.

I fear the Greeks, even when they bring gifts.

—Vergil

Live One Moment At a Time

LIVE "in" the moment, not "for" the moment. This is not the philosophy of "Eat, drink, and be merry for tomorrow we die." In my seminars this step has been occasionally confused for the Bohemian approach. Living "for" the moment is quite dangerous. Living "in" the moment however, is an important baby step toward happiness.

Living in the moment means appreciating and savoring every moment of your life. It's experiencing intensely what you are doing, at the moment you are doing it. When you are in the moment, you focus all available energy into what you are doing—NOW. You block out extraneous thoughts and distractions and become absorbed in the present. HAPs who accomplish this often get so caught up in the moment that they lose track of time. They become absorbed in meaningful projects, ignore their surroundings and others who are present. Some people may describe HAPs as oblivious. But they are not. They are deeply involved and sometimes enmeshed in their project. They are not lost in thought. It's the "doing" that intrigues them.

These people are often described as absent-minded, eccentric, or even a bit "flaky." Several years ago I served in a behavioral science study task force for the government. During one of our meetings I shared a room with a brilliant American researcher. I won't mention his name to save him any embarrassment. This man typified the description of the "absent-minded professor." And apparently, that's what he was. The morning after we checked into our room I got a phone call from his wife. In an extremely polite way she asked if I would remind her husband to take a shower and brush his teeth. *He gets so caught up in what he's doing at times he forgets to take care of himself . . . .* I found out later she was exactly right. But he was a man who had mastered living in the moment. You may not want to go to that extreme! But living one moment at a time will speed your journey toward happiness.

I never did a day's work in my life. It was all fun.
—Thomas Edison

Live One Moment At a Time

PEOPLE who live in the moment don't get stuck in the past. At times it's fascinating to talk with people who live intensely in the moment. You ask them about what happened three years ago and they simply don't remember. In many ways the past is a different life to them. They are free of regrets, ghosts, and resentments. It's not because they are in denial. They deal with the moment as it's presented to them. Living in the moment means coping with the moment. Cope with what's given to you at the time it's presented. As a result you won't have to worry about regrets from the past, or anxiety about the future.

A fixation with tomorrow is avoided by HAPs. Living in the moment means you are in the here and now. That excludes both the past and the future. HAPs learn from the past. They look to the future. But they live in the present moment. This does not exclude goal orientation. HAPs have goals. They use goals to give them direction. Goals guide them. But they don't live in the future of the goals. They are far too busy with now. To HAPs, life is nothing more than a finite series of moments. Each moment is presented to you separately. What you do with it is up to you. You are programmed by advertisers and marketing experts to think in terms of the future. You will be happy *when* you buy this car. You will be cool *when* you smoke this cigarette. You will be a better athlete *when* you buy these running shoes. Too many people lose the moment. They are so busy waiting for the future that they never experience "now." And life ends up passing most of them by.

Don't allow this to happen in your life. Live one moment at a time. When your mind begins to wander—as it will—take a break. Shake it off. Focus somewhere else in that "here and now" moment. Then focus back on your important task. Just do it one moment at a time, and you will be happier on your journey.

Let us endeavor so to live that when we come to die even the undertaker will be sorry.

—Mark Twain

Live One Moment At a Time

I always felt like I grew up in Asia. I arrived in Vietnam when I was nineteen-year-old boy, and left as a young twenty-two-year-old man. I've always described those years as the most learning-filled and powerful of my life. After my tour in Vietnam I spent years studying martial arts and traveling throughout Asia. During these times I learned to appreciate our cultural differences.

I've always been amazed by Japanese rituals surrounding what westerners consider mundane or artless tasks. To a Japanese Kendo expert the sword is a piece of art, a way of life, and yes—also a weapon! The Japanese garden is a similar ritual-filled study. Yes, it's a garden. But it's far more. It becomes an art form all it's own. The Japanese tea ceremony is an equally-hypnotic study of living in the moment. It has to do with far more than tea consumption. Yes—at a tea ceremony you do consume tea; but it is more than that. All of these rituals have to do with experiencing the moment fully and intensely. Each of these processes is a way to learn appreciation for the moment. "Now" becomes an art form. Regardless of what you are doing *now* you become totally absorbed in it. It's appreciating the moment given to you.

In a similar way if you look at Japanese martial arts, you'll discover they're about far more than fighting, sparring, or combat skills. The study of Japanese Aikido, jujitsu, and Judo are prime examples. The language of these particular martial arts are filled with words such as "blending," "joining with the person," "becoming one with their energy." Watching or interacting with true masters of these arts is a similar way of appreciating the moment. Live one moment at a time. Never take it for granted. In my family we have a system of rules. Among those listed rules include the following. When you eat; eat intensely. When you study; study intensely. When you play; play intensely. When you sleep; sleep intensely. The idea is to teach my children from a very early age to live intensely in the moment. Live one moment at a time. If you do so, you will live a life of few regrets.

There is a time for everything, and a season for every activity under heaven.

—Ecclesiastes 3:1

Live One Moment At a Time

LIVING one moment at a time is giving yourself and others a generous present. This is what most people miss. The greatest gift you can give to yourself is your own presence. Being in touch with what you're thinking, feeling, and experiencing is a characteristic many people have lost. Welcome moments of solitude and contemplation. Give such time to yourself on a daily basis. During these brief seconds, be with yourself. Think. Listen. Learn.

The power of the present moment is also a valuable gift in a relationship. Actually, being with another person in all of your intensity is a most priceless gifts. Focusing on another person, looking and listening patiently without expectation, is something that rarely happens. Your attention, exclusively and energetically focused on another individual, is an incredible investment. I used to help one of my babies get to sleep in a way that emphasized the power of the moment. I would take off my shirt and lay him on my chest. Then I would simply breathe in and out with him matching his pace. After a few moments of this—if I didn't pass out first—I would slow my breathing. He would follow and slow his as well. Finally, I would take a long deep sighing breath. He would mirror that. Within a few moments he would be asleep. The power of the moment relaxed this child to the point that he was ultimately able to go to sleep.

Living in the moment is a way of focusing on what you are doing. If the moment is for you, it is a precious one. If the moment is for another, it is equally precious. Either way, it's a gift. Decide to give yourself or someone else the gift of being in the moment at least once a day. Choose a relationship that would benefit from your complete attention. Nurture and enjoy it, *one moment at a time.*

Is not this the true romantic feeling—not the desire to escape life, but to prevent life from escaping you?
—Thomas Clayton Wolfe

Know Your Plimsoll Line

BEFORE I introduce you to your Plimsoll Line let me tell you what it means. The Plimsoll Line is a concept first articulated by Admiral Plimsoll of the British Royal Navy many years ago. He noticed a large number of ships were sinking because they were over-loaded. He required ships to have a line painted around their hull. If the line was visible on all sides, the boat was loaded properly. If the cargo's weight caused the boat to ride so deeply that the line was covered by water, the boat was over-loaded. In time, this became known as the Plimsoll Line.

People have Plimsoll Lines also. You, specifically, have a line beyond which you shouldn't be loaded. And the fact is, if you take on too much you can sink as well. Knowing your Plimsoll Line means knowing when to say, "I've got all I can handle . . ." By doing this you can avoid becoming overloaded and sinking. Several years ago USA Today had a fascinating article about a lady who had gone way beyond her Plimsoll Line. She had become so stressed she entered a coma-like state for several months. She had taken on too much and couldn't say no. After recovering, she wrote a book about her experience and several doctors were debating her book's merits based on whether or not it was by definition a "textbook" coma. To me this was stupid. The woman had over-worked herself to the point her entire system shut down and took a break for several months. Whether it was a technical coma or not is irrelevant. Frighteningly, the same reaction could happen to you. You can go so far beyond your Plimsoll Line it would be hard to come back.

Knowing your Plimsoll Line means respecting your limits. It means knowing when you have had enough. It's not dishonorable or disloyal to say you need a break. In fact it's intelligent. Know your Plimsoll Line. Don't let it take a coma or a near-death experience to "wake you up." Decide what your maximum load is and don't go beyond it. You'll be better off in the long run.

Men don't seem to jump off the bridge for the big reasons; they usually do so for little ones.

—W. H. Ferry

Know Your Plimsoll Line

THERE are some things in this world worth fighting for. How-ever, when you think about it there are few. Part of knowing your Plimsoll Line is knowing what are your physical limits. The other part is to choose your battles wisely. There are things worth fighting for. But it is important not to fight too often. If you draw lines in the sand too frequently you'll either wear yourself out, or no one will listen to you. If you do it too rarely, you'll get taken advantage of frequently.

Even though World War II was a noble war, you would have difficulty convincing someone who didn't know, that the Americans were victorious. Other than speaking English, the evidence would be that Germany and Japan won. Much of the U.S. economy is dominated by Japanese and German influences. "American" cars, appliances, and electronics are rarely "made in the U.S.A." It is interesting to consider the long-term consequences of most wars. The Vietnam War made very little difference. And not much has changed since the Gulf War. The same power structure still exists in Somalia and Panama. Politically, the landscape changes little. It just gets fertilized with the bodies of dead soldiers.

But there are times when you must fight. And if you chose your battles wisely you come out ahead. The strategy of Generals Powell and Schwarzkoff was a brilliant one. Their preparation time for the Gulf War lasted far longer than the actual conflict. When the fighting began, it was over within a matter of days. But the preparation had been going on for months. It was inevitable a battle was going to occur. Yet they chose to fight it on their terms and avoided being suckered into a losing proposition. That's choosing your battles wisely. It's also important to fight for a cause, not just for the sake of a fight. If you stand *for* a cause, your energy level will be much higher. If you are just there for the theatrics, you'll give up quickly. Choose your battles wisely. There are causes worth fighting for, but only a few. If you find yourself doing battle frequently, evaluate carefully. You're probably way beyond your Plimsoll Line.

What counts is not necessarily the size of the dog in the fight—it's the size of the fight in the fog.

—Dwight D. Eisenhower

Know Your Plimsoll Line

KNOWING your Plimsoll Line means knowing where to draw limits. Sometimes the limit is just saying, "Thanks, but no thanks. I'm over-committed already. Any more and I will sink." It's also knowing when to say you've had enough. It means knowing when to say, "I quit." It also means knowing when to let go.

Sometimes the cargo you're carrying is out of date, or unnecessary. You can lighten your load simply by dumping some of this old baggage overboard. Occasionally, your ship of life has everything it needs to make the journey. The engines are fine. Your sails are sturdy. Your navigation equipment is reliable and your rudder is pointing you in the right direction. The winds are at your back and you're ready to go. You are simply riding below your Plimsoll Line. You are over-loaded. Once you begin to unload some of the unwanted baggage you'll feel lighter. You move through the water faster. The wind fills your sails and you're off to your destination. Your Plimsoll Line is evident. You're carrying the proper load. And most of the time, you didn't need the old baggage anyway.

There are things in life you need to cast overboard. There are likely old destructive habits that have kept you from achieving your dreams. It may be people who constantly remind you of their low opinion of you. It could be resentments or grudges from the past which haunt you emotionally and exhaust your supply of energy. This kind of old cargo is not only a burden, but unnecessary. Let go of it. Get rid of the stuff. As your Plimsoll Line rises higher in the water you'll make better speed toward achieving your goals. Know your Plimsoll Line. Then rid yourself of your excess weight. If you are like most people, you already have all the equipment you need to achieve your dreams. It's the extra cargo you are carrying that prevents you from moving.

Every man shall give as he is able, according to the blessing of the Lord thy God which he hath given thee.
—Deuteronomy 16:17

Know Your Plimsoll Line

HONORING your Plimsoll Line is not attacking or hurting other people. It's the process of knowing your limits and then politely saying "No" to being over-committed. Some people think the only alternative is to attack others. They either let people run over them, or they run over other people. One extreme is just as bad as the other. The art form is being able to say "no" and help the other person feel good about it.

I learned to do this through trial and error. It's probably one of the most important things I've mastered. There was a point in my life when I was speaking at PTA meetings or churches three nights a week for free. It was taking a great deal of time, energy, and was affecting my business adversely. My earnings had dropped and even worse my effectiveness as a therapist had diminished. People were complaining, which had never happened before. I realized the problem, but simply had difficulty saying, "No." I made it a goal to assert my Plimsoll Line. I mentally practiced and visualized myself tactfully asserting my Plimsoll Line. It took weeks but the results were phenomenal.

Several weeks later a lady called and asked me to speak at a local PTA meeting. She told me I had spoken at her sister's church in a nearby community several months earlier. According to her sister I was better than *three Abraham Lincolns.* This is the kind of stuff my ego likes to hear. Normally I'm a sucker for it, as she'd probably already been informed. But I stuck with my plan. After thanking her for the compliment, I politely told her I was going to have to decline. I explained I was approaching my Plimsoll Line, and even suggested an alternate speaker. At the end of my speech she stuttered, apparently unsure of what to say. It was probably the first time she had ever felt good about a negative response. It was almost humorous. Try this approach a week for yourself. Say "no" and explain the Plimsoll Line to three other people. They'll probably thank you. Know your Plimsoll Line. Enforce it assertively. It will speed you along as you sail toward happiness.

We always have time enough, if we will but use it aright.
—Johann Wolfgang Von Goethe

The Best Revenge Is Happiness

SOME people think that if they mind their business others will leave them alone. Unfortunately, that's not quite the case. You can follow Thoreau's model and move to Walden. Or you can join some isolationist cult and try to get away. But people will find you. Someone will decide his primary responsibility in life is to make you feel as unhappy as he is. In this case, the mistake you made was attempting to ignore others and live your life. For some that may be the greatest sin.

In actuality, most people aren't out to get you. But occasionally someone is. When this occurs, your temptation may be to ask, "What did I do wrong?" You don't necessarily have to do anything wrong. You were just there! It may be, regardless of what you do, there will be those who see it as their task to make you as unhappy as they are. Other times it may seem people are out to get you, when in fact, they are out to get anyone! It's not uncommon for people to "go postal" today. Unfortunately it happens. One person I saw in therapy was being stalked by a former high school friend. This high school associate was upset about something that happened twenty-five years earlier when they were teenagers.

For whatever reason, there will be people in your life who want to hurt you. It may be for something you actually did, or something you symbolize. It may be simply that you are happy and they are not. In any case, the best revenge is getting even. And the best way to get even is to continue to be happy in spite of it all. The best "revenge" is not hurting the other person. The best revenge is happiness. Try it out as an experiment. You'll be impressed with the results and you'll be taking a major baby step along the way.

In doing this you will heap burning coals on his head . . . .
—**Proverbs 25:22** NIV

The Best Revenge Is Happiness

I have a very close friend who spent most of his adult life doing undercover police work. He conducted deep-cover operations as both a narcotics and vice detective. We once laughed that a police department psychological inventory had pronounced him paranoid. When the tester reviewed the questions which indicated he was paranoid we laughed even more vigorously. When people really are trying to shoot you, it's not paranoia at all. It's reality.

Face it. There is no reason to be naive. There will be occasions when people want nothing more than to hurt you. It can be for a variety of reasons. What do you do? You want to get even, but you are baby-stepping your way through life. In my research I've found that the best response is to be unaffected. If you let go of any need to get even, you will in fact *get even*. If you continue to be unaffected, they will not be able to stand it. Maintain your control. Usually what these people want is their sense of control over you, handed back to them.

The only winning solution is to be happy. I know. It's difficult to be happy when people are sniping at you. I've been there. If you are trying to keep the bullets from hitting you, it's difficult to think about baby steps. Be smart. Dodge the bullets. Don't waste your energy shooting back. The best revenge is to forget about it as soon as possible, and resume baby stepping. Focus on what you really can control. The other person has already proved they don't have control over you. Now learn from their mistakes. You don't have control over them either. Let go of it and focus on yourself. Go to this baby step, or whichever one you need to work on and start at that point. Be happy. It's the best revenge of all.

To strive with difficulties, and to conquer them, is the highest human felicity.

—Samuel Johnson

The Best Revenge Is Happiness

MANY years ago I was taking several children to school in a large van. One of my children was strapped in an infant-carrier in the back seat. Unfortunately, on the return trip I had a flat tire on a very busy interstate. It was during morning rush hour and had been raining. It was winter, rather cold, and still somewhat dark. I've had my share of flats on the journey, so this was no tragedy. I grabbed the proper tools and began to change the tire.

To mount the jack I had to crawl underneath the van. I was laying on my back looking behind me in the direction of oncoming traffic, far off the highway shoulder. As I busied myself I heard the long intimidating moan of a diesel air horn. I looked down the interstate and to my horror saw a tractor trailer approaching full speed about a mile away. It was on a direct collision course with my van! I scrambled out and jumped inside the van to extract my son. As I looked up the diesel continued on the collision course at full speed. Probably due to my own anxiety, I had difficulty unlatching the car seat. It was stuck. Literally at the last moment I freed it and dove out of the van. At the last possible moment the driver swerved and barely missed us. The force was so great however, it knocked the van off the jack. By this time, my child and I were laying on the shoulder. He was upset from being awakened so rudely, and I was upset for other obvious reasons. Several cars stopped who had witnessed the events. We changed the tire, comforted the baby, and then called the police.

Several things happened later. One of the more tragic was that the same truck repeated the game thirty miles up the interstate. A child and one adult were killed when the driver failed to swerve in time. I discovered later the truck driver was on amphetamines and playing a game. It was stupid. He only frightened us. He killed the others. I thought about writing him a letter and letting him know how I felt. But I decided instead to focus the same intensity toward my children, but in a positive way. The best revenge is happiness. It works for me and it will work for you.

Cherish all your happy moments: They make a fine cushion for old age.
—**Christopher Morley**

The Best Revenge Is Happiness

IN graduate school I did a lot of things to make money. One of the most enjoyable was swimming "shotgun" on spear fishing trips. Frankly, I don't consider spear fishing a sport. Playing with sharks—now that's sport! "Shotgun" means you're there to chase sharks away. You carry a bang stick with a dart on the end of it. The dart is supercharged with a .375 magnum bullet. If you hit the shark at the right spot, at minimum, his day is ruined.

At one point I was talking about this to a girl I was dating. We were walking along the beach when we saw a crowd of people gathered around two beached shark puppies. The pups were probably not more than several months old, and apparently had become disoriented. She looked at me and said, *Well, go get 'em Sharkey.* I realized then she probably didn't believe me. As the others watched, I carefully picked up one puppy and held him so she could rub him. I then waded out into the water and let him swim away. As the others cringed, I picked up the second one and repeated the act. One person started to touch the shark's nose and I warned against it. Even pups have razor sharp teeth. The sharks had a happy ending by the way. My dating relationship did not.

A shark's goal in life is not to ruin your day. Sharks simply do what they do. They swim. They eat. They sleep. That's their job. If you're kicking the water, making any movement similar to a flailing fish, you're inviting a shark to lunch. That's what sharks do. I don't have a fear of sharks. The problem is some people—including the girl I was dating—act like sharks. I do have a natural fear of them. You will meet people in life who are predators. Try not to take it personally. And don't worry about getting revenge. They're doing what they do. Make a list of predators in your life and decide to get out of their way. Interact with them only as necessary. Limit damage as much as you can. For instance, if they attack you on the phone write letters instead. Protect yourself, and be happy. A shark is just doing what a shark does. These people are the ones who are really dangerous. Focus on your own happiness. It's the best revenge.

Let us not look back in anger or forward in fear, but around in awareness.

—James Thurber

8

Staying On the Path
of
Happiness

Would You Rather Be Right or Happy?

WOULD you rather be right, or happy? I frankly don't remember where I first heard this question. It was probably in graduate school. Though not original, it is one of my favorite questions. I ask it of someone at least daily. Occasionally my staff or children ask it of me. It's an important idea and one of those baby steps that helps you clarify life. At first glance, most people say they'd like to be both. It may be possible, but it's highly unlikely. The real question is, what's your priority? Is it more important for you to be right? Or is it more important for you to be happy? You can't answer both ways.

Needing to be right—translated *perfect*—usually originates from growing up in a home where love was based on performance. If you felt conditionally accepted as a child you may have difficulty, as an adult, in needing to be right. As a result, therapists' offices are often filled with people who think they have to be *right* or they're never going to be loved. It's not only one of the biggest causes of emotional problems, but according to physicians, one of the biggest causes of illness in general. You can be right. You can win the arguments and lose your marriage. You can win contests but lose your friends. You can be perfectly right and get fired by alienating your employer or boss. In fact, some of the most miserable people I know are those who are *right* most often.

Several years ago I was bringing a carload of teenagers home from a wrestling tournament. I was driving on the interstate, going the proper direction and observing the speed limit. I was *right*. As I looked up from the steering wheel I noticed a car in my lane coming straight toward me at full speed. That driver was wrong. I was right. Regardless, I pulled off to the side of the road, turned around and watched this car eventually swerve into the median after side-swiping several other cars. I was right. I had the right-of-way. I was observing the law. I could have also been dead right. Nah, I think I'd rather be happy.

The most savage controversies are those about matters as to which there is no good evidence either way.
—Bertrand Russell, *Unpopular Essays*

Would You Rather Be Right or Happy?

ONE of the bigger problems with the need to be right is that it's automatically a set up for self-defeating beliefs. One of the first beliefs people preoccupied with being right seem to develop is, *If I achieve second, I am therefore second-rate* . . . . And to most of these people who think in "black or white" terms, second-rate is failure.

An accompanying belief is that *people will think less of me if I'm occasionally wrong* . . . . Those obsessed with being right will defend their thoughts and actions to irrational extremes. They believe that if they are mistaken they are less of a person. As a result, they are unusually aggressive and occasionally take violent stands on what appear to be illogical issues. An additional series of beliefs have to do with their need for mastery. These people believe that if they can't do something skillfully—or master it—they simply won't do it at all. Consequently, they take few risks. They fear becoming less of a person by displaying weaknesses and end up shying away from new experiences where they may appear unskilled. They also believe that less than perfect is immoral.

People with a need to be right confuse morality with many issues. They are unable to distinguish between a simple mistake and failure. Failure is immoral. What's a simple mistake to someone else has monumental consequences to those with a need to be right. They feel diminished as people. Finally, they believe that admitting error makes them look stupid. And to admit error twice makes them doubly stupid. They overlook that a baseball player who gets a hit only three times out of ten at bat is probably going to make a several million-dollar annual salary. They also overlook the fact that Babe Ruth and Hank Aaron led in home runs and strike outs. They weren't making mistakes. They were swinging the bat. You can only hit the ball if you swing. Sure, you may strike out. But you may also hit a home run. You never know unless you try. You can't always be right. But you don't need to be. Just be happy.

But the meek will inherit the land and enjoy great peace.
                                                        —Psalms 37:11 NIV

Would You Rather Be Right or Happy?

THERE are various reasons I would never encourage you to worry too much about being right. It creates too many problems. If you are preoccupied with being right, someone else always has to be wrong. Even people whose first priority is being happy, don't enjoy being wrong *all* the time. If you are obsessed with being right, your relationships will be destroyed. No one will enjoy being around you.

Another problem with this orientation is that by definition it's self-defeating. Nothing will ever be perfect. Therefore, you automatically set yourself up for frustration. Insisting on perfection will lead to an over-emphasis on control. You'll become a control freak and strive to appear perfect. Yet, since you can't control others, you'll be *perfectly* frustrated. This orientation leads to tremendous pain. People obsessed with being right have more health problems than others. They experience less happiness, fewer satisfying relationships, and lower earnings. To me, the results speak for themselves. You have a choice to make. It is very clear. You can be *right* or you can be happy. If for no other reason, make the decision on the basis of actuarial science. Be like an insurance actuary. Figure the probability of risk. Which option makes more sense? Ascertain the odds. But before you do, factor in the following paragraph.

People obsessed with being right will be plagued by loneliness and helplessness. Since nobody wants to be around them they will usually end up suffering from severe depression and ultimately become involved in self-destructive behavior, including suicide, with far more frequency others. Would you rather be right or happy? I don't know about you, but I'd rather be wrong occasionally and happy. Choose happiness.

The wise man realistically accepts failures as a part of life and builds a philosophy to meet them and make the most of them. He lives on the principle of "nothing attempted, nothing gained" and is resolved that if he fails he is going to fail while trying to succeed.
—Wilferd A. Peterson

Would You Rather Be Right or Happy?

IF you are obsessed with being right, how do you start to overcome it? First, decide what's really important to you. What is it you want to do extremely well? Choose one or two important things, then prioritize everything else. Commit most of your time and energy to the highest priority on your list. Then learn to accept less-than-perfect in other areas.

Many people say, "That sounds easy, but how do you actually do it?" I suggest you begin by visualizing yourself getting a report card. See the two most important items listed first on your report card. On these you get A's and A+'s—but there can only be two! On those that are less important, see yourself getting B's and maybe even a C, and being satisfied. As you begin to visualize this you will have obvious difficulty at first. Someone who needs to be right will have difficulty seeing herself enjoying anything less than an A. Yet if you practice it, you ultimately will grow more accepting. The next thing to do is to "fix" where these beliefs came from. Most perfectionism, as mentioned earlier, comes from troubled relationships with parents or other authority figures. I suggest if you struggle with this repeatedly, to see a therapist and work on these old relationships. The good news is this usually doesn't require the cooperation of the authority figure. You can do it on your own.

The final suggestion is to enlist others to help you. Ask friends you trust to begin reinforcing your less-than-perfect performance. Get people to write notes, and give you verbal compliments that they are proud of you for doing less-than-perfect. If you invest a lot of confidence in these people it will have surprisingly positive results. Good luck! I know it's difficult. Stay at it. For me, I'd rather be happy.

No one that ever lived has ever had enough power, prestige, or knowledge to overcome the basic condition of all life—you win some and you lose some.

—Ken Keyes, Jr.

Misery Doesn't Love Company—
It Loves Miserable Company

IT was a story that grabbed national attention and has inspired countless jokes ever since the fall of 1993. Lorena Bobbitt committed her crime. Then she rode around with the evidence in the passenger seat for thirty minutes. Eventually, she threw it out the window and littered a suburban Maryland lawn. And society loved it!

Before and after Bobbitt, there was Tanya Harding, then Michael Jackson. Afterwards it was the wealthy Menendez brothers. Fascination peaked as millions watched the pathetic forty-mile-per-hour caravan on a Los Angeles freeway as O. J. Simpson began to face subsequent murder charges. As a society, we are mesmerized by misery. And it's even better when it's someone famous. Our own misery is not enough. We watch it on soap operas, talk shows, and tabloid TV news programs. We pay to read about it in magazines and newspapers. Misery sells. It's as if by becoming absorbed in other's misery, we are distracted from our own. Misery loves miserable company.

It's comfortable, familiar, and powerfully cozy. The collective mass of misery wants you to join. Whether you do or not, may be a surprisingly difficult choice. Misery loves miserable company. Most people are miserable. You can join them or leave them behind. Misery seems to be the common denominator which draws people to a mutually unhappy status quo. It has a magnetic quality. It's hypnotic. If it's not to be your destiny, take a baby step away from misery. You may be lonely at first. But there is an entirely different approach awaiting you. Misery loves miserable company. Similarly, happiness loves happy company. You can't have both. Face the initial loneliness. Happy company will soon find you.

Men who are unhappy, like men who sleep badly, are always proud of the fact.

—Bertrand Russell

Misery Doesn't Love Company—
It Loves Miserable Company

MISERY *loves* miserable company. It can become familiar, and predictably comfortable, and survive as long as everyone co-operates. When people change, misery changes as well. But the status quo has an attraction all its own. My favorite example of this comes from a good friend who saw me for counseling. She'd been improving her life and becoming more functional. I had cautioned her ahead of time that happiness could be "hazardous to her health." She didn't understand at the moment. Later, however, she did.

She had invited her husband into therapy with her, but he refused. She continued, and as she did, his control over her decreased. She grew more self-confident and less intimidated by her husband. The entire process became threatening to him. Although she was paying her own way, he ordered her not to continue therapy. It didn't work. So he escalated. The marriage had been troubled from the beginning. It was based around his control and her weakness. The attraction provided a sick security and mutual misery for both. He needed power, and he got it. She needed security and she got it. Then she broke the rules. She began to get healthy.

After feeling his control slipping, he applied more pressure. It didn't work. Finally in an act of brazen manipulation, he walked into the bedroom one morning and calmly made an eerie announcement. If she didn't go back to being the way she was, he would either divorce or kill her. Wisely, she remained calm and friendly. Without any further discussion, she filed for divorce and left him the very same day. Today she's divorced. And she's not quite as secure. But she's happy. He has almost everything he wanted. He's got control, power, and his familiar misery. But he doesn't have her. Misery loves miserable company. He will find someone else to share his misery. His former wife has taken several baby steps toward happiness.

The secret to being miserable is to have leisure to bother about whether you are happy or not. The cure for it is occupation.
—George Bernard Shaw

Misery Doesn't Love Company— It Loves Miserable Company

MISERY also *seeks* miserable company. One of my favorite hobbies over the past ten years or so has been guesting on radio and TV talk shows. I especially enjoy the live call-in variety. My appearances have led to a lot of fun, and on a few occasions, some upset callers. One such caller was less-than-pleased with my suggestion that he could overcome his agoraphobia. Inspired by this, his wife began putting a bit more pressure on him. He blamed me. After our conversation, I began getting threatening phone calls from this very dissatisfied phobic who suggested it was a good thing he couldn't leave home or he would beat me up!

With some people, misery becomes their "red badge of courage." William Faulkner said, "If I had to choose between pain and nothing. I would always choose pain . . . ." Misery has that sick appeal. It can fill up a rather dull and empty void and give you an identity. Being an agoraphobic is better than being nothing. But it's still misery. The caller's wife later told me her husband had said at first it was his job that made him miserable. When he lost that, he blamed his early family life. Then it was his first wife, then his doctor, then the government. Then he got around to blaming me for suggesting he could improve. If I took away his identity as an agoraphobic, he would have been nobody. Or even worse, he would have to get well and go on with life.

Misery isn't any of the above. It's not in jobs, doctors, or the government. It's definitely not in the weather. It's also not in your marriage. Misery, is inside of you. Or it's not. You are free to join the club. Membership is non-discriminating and open. Most people belong, because misery loves miserable company. Or you can risk the insecurity of leaving your misery behind. If you do, people may walk away from you. They will exclude you. Some will avoid you. There is a price to pay. Misery loves miserable company. You can join that company or not. It's entirely your choice.

Envy is the tax which all distinction must pay.
—Ralph Waldo Emerson

Misery Doesn't Love Company—
It Loves Miserable Company

MISERY has an investment in your remaining miserable. One of the most felonious violations of this baby step occurs when someone succeeds. There seems to be an unwritten rule perpetuating and standardizing mediocrity. Mediocrity itself becomes the rule. Achieving above that level can be a major violation. When the people from *Sixty Minutes* or *Nightline* are knocking on your door to call you a fraud, don't hide. Consider yourself a success. It means you have broken the rules. You have probably achieved.

At times its almost comical to observe society's reaction to those who achieve beyond the status quo. When someone succeeds, bad news follows—often within days. Happy people aren't popular. They're not miserable. In some cases, it's more socially acceptable "not" to succeed. On Monday Jane Doe is mediocre. On Wednesday, she is famous. On Friday, Ted Koppel accuses her of being a fraud. The equation is repeated over and over. Jane *is* a fraud. By society's standards it's fraudulent to achieve. Nobody identifies the mediocre as being fraudulent. Society has always had a love-hate relationship with those who rise above mediocrity. From King David to the frenzy surrounding O. J. Simpson society has a sick fascination with its fallen heroes.

It may be safer to remain miserable. Mediocrity and misery go together. They form the collective mass. It's a cesspool called the status quo. Once you begin to rise above it, you'll be the enemy of the moment. If you become mired in the cesspool, however, they'll accept you once again. And Ted Koppel will leave you alone. Take a baby step away from misery. It may lead to short-term difficulty. Consider it a prelude to massive happiness which will follow. Take this baby step by describing one example of something you've done in the last twenty-four hours to perpetuate misery in your life. Make a commitment to avoid the same behavior for the next twenty-four hours. It's a baby step on the journey to happiness.

. . . men loved darkness instead of light because their deeds were evil.
—John 3:21 NIV

If I'm So Successful, Why Am I Miserable?

IT was a Kodak moment! I wish I had it on videotape. I was speechless. My friend, sitting across from me, was successful in all measurable terms, and had accepted society's definition of success. He had become obsessed with his career and the three R's that went along with it. Each had been acquired—respect, recognition, and remuneration. But like many others, he had paid a price. "Success" had cost him three marriages, five alienated children, alcoholism, open-heart surgery, and severe ulcers. But by all measures he had achieved the "American dream." He had earned all the money he would ever need.

He leaned over with his piercing blue eyes fixed at a point on the wall above my shoulder. Finally, he looked at me. "Tell me this John," he began. "You're supposed to be so smart. Explain it to me. If I'm so successful, then why am I miserable? How on earth could I be miserable? I've got everything I could ever want. I've got money, homes, cars, a plane. You name it. I've got it. And if I don't have it, I can get it. So tell me, 'Doctor John.' If I'm so darned successful, why am I miserable?"

After a few moments of silence, my friend began rambling again, which gave me time to think. The more I thought about his question, the more I realized how brilliant it was. Like many other highly successful people, he had become obsessed with the wrong thing. He was hypnotized by the quest for success. He accepted the great American dream and discovered it to be the great American myth. Success may be the three R's. But happiness is not. Asking how much money it takes to be happy is the wrong approach. Thinking if you had the right car, right person, or right job, is focusing on the wrong thing. Happiness can never be defined by measurements outside of yourself. My friend was successful but miserable for one basic reason. He had never made happiness a priority. The moment he began to do so, was the moment he began to change. It was a major baby step for him, and it can be for you too.

There is a time when a man distinguishes the idea of felicity from the idea of wealth; it is the beginning of wisdom.
—Ralph Waldo Emerson

If I'm So Successful, Why Am I Miserable?

THE unfortunate reality is you don't always have control over money, career, or general success. To the degree other people are involved in these arenas, your achievement can be limited. You do not have control over other people. If you are like most people, your success can be limited by the bureaucratic requirements of your employer. Earnings can be limited as well. But no one can limit your happiness. Your happiness is controlled by you alone. Success and money are *externally* controlled. Happiness is *internally* controlled.

Yet most people think it's the other way around. Most people think they have total control over things they don't, and no control over that which they really do. So, what do you have control over anyway? Children? Spouse? Weather? Employer? Job? The government? Forget it. You don't have control over any of these things. But you do have complete control over yourself. In fact, science has demonstrated you can control things you probably never imagined. You can influence your blood pressure, heart rate, skin temperature, anxiety level, and many other internal responses. And in probably ninety-five percent of cases you also have complete control of your weight. But most of us blame others for those dilemmas. That way we get to avoid responsibility.

Avoid the temptation. It will only detract from your happiness. Get a grip! Grab onto this reality. *You can control your own happiness.* Make it a priority. Ask yourself daily, "What do I need to do to be happy today?" Don't use the three R's as answers to this question. Happiness is not found in the 3 R's. Then give honest replies. It is deciding that you are tired of pain, and reacting to the truly important priorities. When you do what it takes to make you happy, you will be well on your way to happiness.

Anyone who claims to be in the light but hates his brother is still in darkness.

—1 John 2:9 NIV

If I'm So Successful, Why Am I Miserable?

IF you are like the rest of us, you've been lied to. You were told that if you pursue remuneration, respect, and recognition, you will be happy. Some well-intentioned soul simply misled you. They said if you got enough things, happiness would follow. You were told once you were successful, you'd be happy. Once you got that promotion you'd be happy. Once you got married you'd be happy. Once you had children you'd be happy. Once you got divorced you'd be happy. Once you got re-married you'd be happy. They were all lies.

You've been convinced that happiness is in a car, a person, or a job. Those are lies as well. The next time somebody hints that you find happiness outside yourself don't argue with them. You can't convince them anyway. Just nod your head. Say, "thanks for the advice," and keep on walking. The truth is just the opposite. The key to happiness is inside you. It's not the key to a new automobile or a new relationship. If you want happiness you simply have to make it a priority in your life. But don't look for it outside of you. At it's best happiness is an attitude. It is the way you approach life, including the difficult times. If you pursue it as anything else you will always miss the mark.

Make happiness a priority and you will ask a different question than my friend did. He said, "If I'm so successful then why am I miserable?" You'll be asking a different question. Perhaps it'll be this. "If I'm so happy, why aren't others?" It's because they didn't make it a priority and you did. And then success will follow you just as happiness has. That's the key that fits the ignition to start a happy life. "If I'm so successful then why am I miserable?" It's real simple. You didn't make it a priority. Make happiness a priority and you will experience it.

One might think that the money value of an invention constitutes its reward to the man who loves his work. But, speaking for myself, I can honestly say this is not so . . . I continue to find my greatest pleasure, and so my reward, in the work that precedes what the world calls success.

—Thomas A. Edison

If I'm So Successful, Why Am I Miserable?

THE big problem is, many people define success, money, and happiness synonymously. They're wrong. Success and money can occasionally mean the same thing, but not necessarily. You can inherit wealth or win the lottery and still not be successful. At the same time, you can be wealthy and successful, but not happy. Unless you make happiness a priority you probably will not experience it.

As an example, you can decide you are going to be successful in your career. Or you can decide you are going to be a successful wife or mother. Or, you can decide you are going to be rich and become obsessed with money. But in the final analysis, unless you make happiness a priority you will still be miserable. And this misery will occur regardless of circumstances, people, or the number of things surrounding you. When I discuss this at seminars people think I'm kidding. People privately whisper, *Really now—you don't think people can be happy without money do you?* Of course I do! In fact, in some ways I think it's probably easier. For the sake of review, in its absence, money is like a lack of oxygen. It can create serious problems. But in its presence, money is like oxygen as well. Just because you breathe doesn't mean you're happy. Just because you have money doesn't mean you're happy either. The kind of focus required for happiness is vastly different.

"If I'm so successful, then why am I miserable?" It's an ingenious question. The answer is simple. You must make happiness a priority, not success or money. What is standing in the way of you and happiness this very moment? Once you honestly answer that question, you'll be taking baby steps in the right direction. But think of it deeply. At first impulse most people give the wrong answer. To be fair with yourself, list ten things you must *do* to achieve happiness. If money is your first one, then focus on your second and third. Usually, if you live a happy life you'll solve your financial problems along the way. "If I'm so successful, then why am I miserable?" Because you haven't made happiness a priority.

Joy comes from using your potential.
—Will Schultz

Love Is Not a Biscuit

LOVE is not a biscuit. My father died when I was ten years old. For a long time afterward I lived with my grandparents. My Granny was the iron lady head of the house. To Granny, love was expressed with food. Every meal was a feast. She expressed her affection by the way she cooked, and you expressed your appreciation by the way you ate. Food was not only something you consumed, but an emotional experience as well.

There was a point in my early childhood where I can remember people asking me what I was going to be when I grew up. My response was, "I am going to be a preacher and eat fried chicken!" I'm not sure what eating fried chicken had to do with being a preacher. But in my mind I was planning not only my vocation but eating style! Eating had become confused in all aspects of my very young life. It's easy to get one commodity confused with the other. In the same ways it's easy to get the past confused with the future. As an example, in my past, food and emotions were very closely aligned. But that does not have to be the way it is, in the present or future. It's normal to modify certain behaviors as a child to please your parents. But it could be very unhealthy to continue those as an adult.

The past does not equal the present. And the present does not equal the future. Your past is a part of you. Appreciate it. Learn from it. But don't live in it. I have loving memories about Granny. She was one of the most accepting people I've ever known. It wasn't just dough in those biscuits. There was a lot of love in them as well. But love is not a biscuit. And overeating as an adult does not necessarily honor my Grandparents. Your past does not equal your present. Your present does not equal your future either. Once you act on this you'll be taking a major step on the road to happiness.

The past can be a rudder that guides you or an anchor that hinders you. Leave your mistakes with God and look to the future by faith.
—**Warren Wiersbe**

Love Is Not a Biscuit

IN too many people's lives the scars of the emotional past dictate the unstable present. This decides the course of their future. Thirty years later many people are still fighting battles they should have left behind. Love is not a biscuit. It's not a traffic jam. It's not a combat zone. But to some people it seems to be.

One Vietnam veteran described sitting in a traffic jam and feeling himself beginning to boil over. His wife asked a very important question. "What happens when you're not on time?" Apparently he answered without blinking or pausing. "If you're not on time, people die." He went on to describe an experience that occurred in Vietnam which resulted in a friend's death. His patrol got lost and ended up straying into a free-fire zone. Other Americans began opening fire and several people were mistakenly killed as a result. This traumatic learning had left a powerful impact on the combat veteran. When his wife told him this was a traffic jam, not a combat zone, he responded appropriately but sincerely. "I know that in my head," he responded. "But I still have trouble knowing it in my heart."

Traumatic learning from the past leaves an extremely powerful impression. Though the intellectual reality may be different, emotions are often so powerful they win. Love is not a biscuit. War is not a traffic jam. And people aren't going to die if you're not on time. On an intellectual level you know it's true. But emotional truth can be quite different. The problem is, people don't know how to heal those old emotional wounds. You are not your past. The past does not equal the present or determine the future. Love is not a biscuit—*though there may be love in biscuits*—they're not the same thing. It may be necessary to ritualistically say good-bye to overcome this connection. When the veteran said good-bye to that particular struggle, he began to heal. The same thing will work for you.

We have to do with the past only as we can make it useful to the present and the future.

—Frederick Douglass

Love Is Not a Biscuit

AT one time or another you likely have thought love was a biscuit. This confusion can occur as a result of what I call a "4F feeling." 4F stands for your "Favorite Familiar Fouled-up Feeling." It's the negative feeling you most frequently identify with when you feel emotionally "yucky." I have a "4-f-er" I call Brady Lambert. Brady lived across the street from my grandparents when I was a child. We were boyhood partners and got in all sorts of trouble together. He was a year younger, a lot smarter, and probably more in charge of our escapades. I merely liberated him so we could get into trouble.

One summer day I was pushing my bicycle up to Brady's house, poised to rescue him. This was before air-conditioning and it was a sweltering southern August day. Through the open windows and screen door I overheard a tremendous argument. Brady's parents were telling him he couldn't play with me, and Brady was protesting. "Why not?" he asked defiantly. Finally in what sounded like exasperation, his mother explained, ". . . because he's dirty. He stinks. He doesn't take baths . . ." As she spat out those words, I internalized the 4F's—of not being worthy enough, clean enough, or good enough to play with her child. I was inadequate to play with her child. I hunched over as each word hit me like a bullet. Finally, in absolute shame, I turned and pushed my bicycle home. Of course, an hour later, Brady escaped and was waiting for me. We proceeded to get in trouble again. The discussion with his parents was never mentioned.

That experience had a profound impact on my life. To this day it has defined my 4F feeling. You've likely had at least one experience that led to a 4F feeling in the past. It could be responsible for most of the depression and emotional suffering you experience today. I still experience my 4F feelings today. But now it lasts a few seconds or less. I simply ask myself, "Is this something that's going on today or is it a Brady Lambert feeling?" If it's part of present reality I deal with it. If it's a Brady Lambert feeling I put it where it belongs. *Love is not a biscuit,* but you sure can get confused.

Shut out all your past except that which will help you weather your tomorrows.

—Sir William Osler

Love Is Not a Biscuit

LOVE is not a biscuit. Just because something was one way in the past, does not mean it still is that way today. The past can be very powerful, and you can let it control your life. But it doesn't necessarily have to be the case. Figuring this out is like putting a jigsaw puzzle together. There are 500 pieces, and you are trying to figure out how they all fit together. You turn them over, and try to match them up. Eventually, you succeed and it begins to make a little sense.

As you gain more clarity, you can distinguish whether it's love or a biscuit. But at first, it will take a lot of work. It will take far more time and work than it does to put a real jigsaw puzzle together. With time, however, it grows easier. You will ultimately need to take the "chicken test." The chicken test is not about food, just like this baby step is not about food. The chicken test is a hard-core reality check. It's a test manufacturers of high-performance aircraft use to ascertain whether or not a jet engine is going to survive. After the engine has passed all of the quality-control procedures, engineers take a cannon and fire broilers into the engine. If it continues to run, the manufacturers assume it will not get clogged up if a bird were to fly into the engine. It passes the "chicken test."

There will be plenty of chicken tests in your life. You won't have to arrange for them. They will be sent to you. And you'll keep on getting tested until you've learned what you need to learn. Love is not a biscuit. Brady Lambert's parents no longer worry about my hygiene. Life is not a combat zone. The more quickly you learn these things the healthier you'll be. The past does not equal the present, and the present does not equal the future. Unless you allow it to. Love is not a biscuit unless you want it to be. It's a baby step toward happiness. Take this baby step today. Choose three "Brady Lamberts" in your life. Identify the "4-f-er" that goes along with each. Describe on paper how it has disrupted your life. Then pledge to change your behavior.

Make it a rule of life never to regret and never to look back. Regret is an appalling waste of energy; you can't build on it; it's only good for wallowing in.

—Katherine Mansfield

9

Being Happy With Others

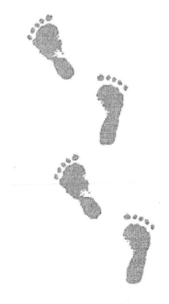

Choose Your Friends Wisely

CHOOSE *your friends wisely.* One of the most important decisions you will ever make is your choice of friends. The closer they are, the more important they become. The boundaries of friendship eventually become blurred. You influence your friends and they influence you. The total becomes more than the sum of its parts. Friends are necessary. But the truth is you can't appreciate them if you don't appreciate yourself.

You can't love someone else if you don't love yourself. You can *need* someone else. You can *want* them. But you really can't love another person unless you love yourself first. You cannot give away that which you don't own. I can't give away five dollars if I don't own it. I may want to, in the most sincere of ways. I really may want to give you five dollars. But if I don't own it, I can't give it to you. I can give you two dollars—because that's all I have. If you don't own it first, you can't give it away. The same is true with love, respect, and happiness. If you don't own it, you can't give it away. The only way to love someone else is to love yourself first. The only way to love yourself is to own it. If I own love for myself, I can then give it to others.

Choose you friends wisely. It's one of the most important decisions you'll ever make. However, it's no more important than the decision to choose yourself as a friend and then treat yourself as one. Love your friends. But love yourself as well. *The New Testament* (Mark 12:31) *says, love your neighbor as yourself* . . . . If you don't love yourself, you won't be a very good friend to your neighbors. *Choose your friends wisely*, but choose the way you feel about yourself wisely as well. Be a friend to yourself. It will free you to truly be a friend to someone else.

Do not be misled: Bad company corrupts good character.
                                                —I Corinthians 15:33 NIV

Choose Your Friends Wisely

IN the spring of 1969 I was eating lunch in a bar outside Camp LeJeune, North Carolina. Kenny Rogers and the First Edition were singing *Ruby Don't Take Your Love to Town* on the jukebox. *It wasn't me who started that old crazy Asian war. But I was proud to go and do my patriotic chore . . . .* Two kinds of people were having lunch that day. There were marines who were getting ready to go to that old crazy Asian war. And there was a motorcycle gang.

I sat and watched a fascinating interaction between one of the bikers and his girlfriend. Back in those days we would have probably called her a hippie or flower child. She was anemically thin and had a stringy blond ponytail hanging down her back. On three separate occasions she walked up behind the biker, took his head in her hands, and whispered something in his ear. He seemed irritated and told her to leave him alone. He was playing cards with a group of friends and obviously didn't want to be aggravated. Finally she wrapped her arms around him and whispered for the fourth time. His face turned red. He balled up his fist and while standing up, angrily backhanded her with his forearm. She sprawled against the wall and fell limply to the floor. He turned and stood over her with his back to us. The other marines and I stood up and got prepared. We figured a fight was ahead. Rather than kicking her however, he loomed over her, *Love you! Love you!? Woman! I love my dawg, I love my brother, I love my Harley. But I sure don't love you!*

Love is not always a many-splendored thing. In fact it can be quite confusing. I had never considered love for my dog or motorcycle as the same as love for my girlfriend. But for the biker, it was tough to separate. As relationships grow more intimate—hopefully those with people, not motorcycles—they become more complex. It gives added reason to choose your friends wisely. Your best bet for love, is someone you are first friends with anyway. *Choose your friends wisely.* Teach them how to treat you. And then watch love grow. Ignore the traditional attractors. *Choose your friends wisely*—not physically—and you'll be on the road to happiness. Who knows. Maybe you'll travel on a Harley!

Go often to the house of thy friend; for weeds soon choke up the unused path.

—Scandinavian proverb

Choose Your Friends Wisely

HAPS adopt a slogan from the Marine Corps, but apply it to relationships. They're looking for a few good men—or women. The emphasis here is on the key word "few." HAPs usually have only a few truly close friends. However the depth and bond of these relationships is often somewhat staggering. It's the close relationships that are most important. Like other people, HAPs do have acquaintances. There are usually quite a number of these. Yet the close friendships are limited and profound.

What HAPs look for in these relationships has little to do with traditional measures of attractiveness. The happier they are, the less they are attracted by such qualities as good looks, body type, clothing, or other surface qualities. Instead, HAPs focus on the three C's. They're looking for compatibility, companionship, and character. HAPs want friends, not trophies. They see things others often miss. HAPs have a way of penetrating pretense. Typical characteristics others notice are not ignored by HAPs. It's just that HAPs don't choose their friends based on qualities that have nothing to do with friendship. Compatibility, companionship, and character are "friendship qualities." Breast size, cute buns and "good looks," have to do with anatomy and physiology. Looks are obviously important. It's just that anatomy and physiology are inherited. The three C's however, are qualities you develop.

As a rule HAPs are low-tech and high touch when it comes to friends. They don't have friendships in a "chat room" via internet. They give and receive higher degrees of physical and emotional affection to real people, than do others. They are affectionate toward people and animals, and get tremendous pleasure from helping others. *Choose your friends wisely.* Teach them how to treat you in ways that will make the relationship grow. And then nurture the three C's that will make the relationship last. It's an important part of this baby step.

Be courteous to all, but intimate with few, and let those few be well tried before you give them your confidence. True friendship is a plant of slow growth, and must undergo and withstand the shocks of adversity before it is entitled to the appellation.
—George Washington

Choose Your Friends Wisely

CHOOSE *your friends wisely*. Then teach them wisely how to treat you. You teach people how to treat you in a variety of ways. One of those is how you treat them. Another is how long you allow them to mistreat you. You don't teach someone how to treat you by giving them an instruction book, though that might help. It's also not lecturing, which incidentally, never helps. The best way to teach people how to treat you, is experience.

If someone abuses you once, that can be merely a learning experience for you. Frankly, if someone abuses you twice it's because you've taught them it was okay. You taught them by allowing it to occur the second time. If the consequences had been sufficient on the first occasion, it would never have occurred twice. This doesn't mean to give up easily. It does mean, however, that you bear some responsibility. If you are not getting treated the way you deserve, then change what you are teaching. I have found that when it comes to this point, honesty is indeed the best policy.

I tell my friends to teach me how to express caring for them. And I suggest that I will do the same in return. People have different levels of pain tolerance. To one person a particular interpersonal behavior would be considered abusive. To another, it's merely an inconvenience. I never suggest to people what they should define as intolerable. However, I do encourage you to know yourself. Then teach your partner what you will and will not accept. *Choose your friends wisely*. Determine if there are friendships you wish to cultivate and take action this week. Then teach your friends wisely. Examine those friends you currently have and decide where some "education" needs to occur. Be tactful, and diplomatic, yet honest. If you accomplish this you will have wondrous and rewarding relationships. You will be well on the road to a major baby step in the journey of happiness.

Don't lead me; I may not follow. Don't walk behind me; I may not lead. Walk beside me and be my friend.
                    —**Anonymous line quoted by Jacqueline Bisset**

Never Try To Join a Club That Doesn't Want You As a Member

NEVER try to join a club that doesn't want you as a member. This is another easily-misunderstood baby step. A sense of belonging is important in life. In my opinion, community and friendship are vital to our existence. But just as it's important to choose your friends wisely, it's also important to choose your community with care. In fact, it may be more important. Some people spend far more time in community than with "just friends."

The term "community" doesn't necessarily mean where you live. It can be, but actually that's more the exception. Community is where you spend most of your time interacting and exchanging social feedback. That can be the workplace, church, or civic group. You do need community, but don't try to join one that doesn't want you as a member. One of my best friends is a minister. Several years ago it appeared the denomination he was a part of was going to split, going separate philosophical directions. My friend was lamenting this and considered himself among those who were on the "outside." He felt rejected by those who were in control, and this confused the issue more. They didn't seem to want his particular faction as a part of the denominational community. After listening to him for over an hour I asked him the question. "Why would you want to be part of a group that doesn't want you as a member? If they allow your faction to stay, what have you really gained? You won't be accepted. You won't be welcome. You'll simply be scape-goated. Why not just let it go? Never try to join a club that doesn't want you as a member."

This was the first time I'd used that particular concept but it hasn't been the last. It's an important baby step on the journey to happiness. Don't try to join a club, or relationship, that doesn't want you as a member. You won't gain anything. And you may lose a great deal in the process. Belonging is important. It's very important. But you can never truly belong to a group that could choose to ostracize you. Don't try to join a club that doesn't want you as a member. You'll be better off on the long run.

I am part of all that I have met.

—Alfred Lord Tennyson

Never Try To Join a Club That
Doesn't Want You As a Member

NEVER try to join a club that doesn't want you as a member. Actually, most HAPs aren't "joiners" anyway. They do join occasionally, and have a strong sense of community. But it is a relatively small one. HAPs are extremely selective. The case with most HAPs is, if they can't have input into the direction of the community, they usually steer away from it. However, in a stronger sense they simply refuse to set themselves up for conflict, abuse, or discomfort.

A HAP is not going to *prove* his or her worth to anyone. They don't need the validation to feel good about themselves. So while HAPs are members of a community, they are very selective. A HAP would not try to join a club that would exclude them—or anyone else for that matter. Social network is vastly important. A strong community is like a wind gust in your sails. It can speed your journey and ease your progress along the way. We are social creatures and seek to belong. The great American philosopher Eric Fromm described the ultimate isolation of man leading to insanity. If not insanity, it as least leads to major levels of depression.

Research scientists over the years have supported this idea. Scientists from Duke University, Boston University, and Southern Methodist University, among others, have strongly demonstrated the health and sometimes life-saving benefits of social networks. You need a support group. But you need it to be accepting. You can have this but not by attempting to become part of a community that doesn't want you as a member. Find one that will be supportive of you and your goals. You will have to look, shop around, and risk. But ultimately it will be worth your effort. Do join a club, but only one that will welcome you as a member.

There can be no vulnerability without risk; there can be no community without vulnerability; there can be no peace, and ultimately no life, without community.

—M. Scott Peck

Never Try To Join a Club That Doesn't Want You As a Member

NEVER try to join a club that doesn't want you as a member. The fee will always be too high. One of the biggest problems with these kinds of clubs is they often want to keep you from growing. I saw this dramatically illustrated in a counseling case. The man was in his forties and extremely intelligent and talented. Yet he continually found himself self-destructing.

The pattern had been repeated on multiple occasions. He would get a job, advance through the ranks, and be doing extremely well. Then right before he was to get a major promotion, he would go on a drinking binge. Not only would he lose his promotion, but the job as well. Afterwards, he would pick himself up by his boot straps and start all over again. Months later he would repeat the cycle just about the time he was to get another promotion with the same result. The puzzle eventually fit together. As a child his family had moved from an urban area with a progressive school district, to a rural community. When he got to the new school, not only did he become an excellent athlete, but an excellent student as well. His grades rose from barely passing, to A's and B's. This boosted his confidence and affected the way he conducted himself. Girls flirted with him, teachers liked him, and he became quite popular. He became successful and accepted by everyone—except his peers. The "townies"—the local boys—didn't like this newcomer's notoriety and they made it known. The third time he ended up in the hospital emergency room. He had been beaten up severely and never quite forgot it.

He described it quite poetically. "Oh, I learned a lot from that! As long as I was mediocre there were no difficulties. It's only when I started doing great that I ran into problems." Mediocrity was necessary to be accepted in "the club." Many clubs require mediocrity as a condition of membership. At the very least, you are required not to rise above certain other members. These agendas are usually hidden. Yet they exist nevertheless. Remember, *never try to join a club that doesn't want you as a member.* The fees are too high.

. . . Two are better than one; because they have a good reward for their labor. For if they fall, the one will lift up his fellow: but woe to him that is alone when he falleth; for he hath not another to help him out.
—Ecclesiastes 4:9–10

Never Try To Join a Club That Doesn't Want You As a Member

THERE is no commodity in life that feels as good as acceptance. Unconditional acceptance is so rare that once it's experienced you will never be the same. In his writings, Dr. Carl Rogers called it unconditional positive regard. Others have called it unconditional love. You can call it a variety of things. But there aren't many who experience it. There are few people who can honestly recall any relationship where they felt absolutely, unconditionally, accepted.

In most relationships there are necessary conditions. Your job, as an example, is usually based on the condition of your performance. While the acceptance is conditional, it's understandable. Unconditional acceptance can't come from a relationship that by its very nature is conditional. One twisted version of this was presented by a couple I worked with. The reason they entered therapy was because the husband suspected his wife of having an affair. He suspected her because her self-esteem was increasing! In the past few months she had started losing weight, growing self-confident, and becoming happy. The husband figured if all that was happening then she must be involved with another man! As long as she was fat, unhappy, and depressed, their relationship was fine. It was only when she began improving herself that unexpected problems began. This is not the kind of club I would want to join. Nor would I recommend it for anyone else.

Never try to join a club that doesn't want you as a member. Now let's take it one step further. Never try to join a club that doesn't want you as a member—just the way you are. If they want you to get a special tattoo, learn the secret hand shake, or memorize a pass word, politely tell them, "No thanks." You only have so much energy to invest. Don't invest it in any organization that is based on the principle of exclusion. As you examine closely the organizations you are a member of, you will find that few are based on unconditional acceptance. Find one that will accept you unconditionally. Make it this week's goal. When you've found one, wrap up in the comfort of such a group.

No man is an island, entire of itself; every man is a piece of the continent.

—John Donne

To Help Yourself, Help Others

TO help yourself, help others. I first heard this attributed to Dr. Karl Menninger, the great American physician and researcher. He was probably the most renowned behavioral scientist our country has ever produced. He and other family members were responsible for the Menninger Foundation and Menninger Hospital in Topeka, Kansas. Apparently, prior to his death, Dr. Menninger was being interviewed by a reporter. One of the many questions the reporter asked was a poignant one that caused Dr. Menninger to reflect for a few minutes. The reporter asked what one thing Dr. Menninger would suggest that would be most helpful for a depressed person.

He could have said anything. He could have said, "Shock treatment." His recommendation could have been, "Come to my facility in Topeka, and we will make you better." He could have suggested major antidepressants or long term psychotherapy. He recommended none of these. Instead, after considering the question for apparently several minutes, Dr. Menninger gave his response. He explained he would tell the person to find someone more depressed than they were and help them.

That's incredible commentary. Coming from a scientist like Dr. Menninger, that comment should be in USA Today, CNN, and before a Senate subcommittee. *Find someone more depressed than you are and help him.* Not Prozac. Not hospitalization. Not fix the mythical chemical imbalance. Dr. Menninger is suggesting if you want to get healthy, focus away from yourself and on to others. I later discovered Dr. Menninger was not the first to suggest such advice. Many years earlier Dr. Carl Jung had suggested a similar idea corresponding with one of his many patients. He and Dr. Menninger agree. It's an important baby step. If you want to help yourself, help others. You'll be on the road to happiness.

For it is in giving that we receive.

—Saint Francis of Assisi

To Help Yourself, Help Others

SOMETIMES it's easier to help strangers than those closest to you. Unfortunately, many people spend their lives helping others and ignoring their own friends and family. One of the saddest conversations I ever had was with a friend of mine who was a physician. He called me one afternoon and asked if he could come over and chat. He had just returned from taking his nineteen-year-old son on a two hour trip to enter the Air Force.

On his trip back home my friend not only realized he was losing his son; more importantly his son told him that this was the longest period of time they had *ever* spent—one on one—together. As a physician, he had always been so busy tending to the needs of others, he didn't have time for his own son. Since then they have both spent time working on their relationship. It's important to make time not only for business acquaintances but family and friends as well. Sometimes, it's too easy to overlook those closest to you. You can end up taking them for granted. It's easy to get so caught up with the "business" of living, you ignore life. This is especially true if the important person is by nature somewhat quiet. My friend's son had always been "the quiet child." He never complained. He didn't make any noise. He was "a good boy." Then he was gone. And his father never knew him. Their relationship will probably have a happy ending. Sadly, many others like this don't.

To help yourself, help others. This includes husbands, wives, sons, daughters, fathers, mothers, best friends, grandparents, etc. Don't make the mistake of ignoring those closest to you. Obligation can destroy your family. This is especially true as it applies to that special breed of quiet and compliant people. Ignore them long enough and they'll be gone. Don't let that happen to you.

Therefore encourage one another and build each other up.
—I Thessalonians 5:11 NIV

To Help Yourself, Help Others

TO help yourself, help others. It's an important part of all good relationships and a critical link in the puzzle of your personal happiness. The biggest obstacle to this baby step may be your own fears. People seem to have a natural fear of closeness. So do fish, incidentally. Many years ago I was scuba diving in the Florida Keys. I had been experiencing seasickness, which was ruining the trip for me. As a short-term solution, my friends decided to suit me up, tank and all, and lay me on the floor of the boat. When we got to the dive site, they picked me up, and threw me overboard!

After the air bubbles cleared, I looked around and realized I was nose-to-nose with what appeared to be, a five-foot-long barracuda. He hovered, staring at me, grinding his razor-sharp teeth back and forth. I had never read of a scuba diver being attacked by barracuda and assumed everything was going to be okay. I was nervous, but not overly frightened. Finally I reached out, slowly attempting to touch the huge fish. He inched backward very slowly and methodically just beyond arm's reach. When I lowered my arm, he came forward the same distance, still remaining just far enough away that I couldn't touch him. After a few minutes I gave up and tried to swim away. I looked behind and noticed the barracuda tracking me, still the same distance away. I stopped and started swimming toward him but he went the opposite direction, still keeping the same gap.

I expended an entire tank of air dancing on the ocean floor with this beautiful fish. But we never touched. We never embraced. And we never got any closer or further away than beyond arm's reach. Dancing back and forth with the 'cuda is a lot like life. This is what we do. It is the biggest obstacle to helping others and it is the biggest obstacle to helping yourself. To help yourself, help others. You have to overcome your fear of closeness to achieve this. There's no such thing as helping from long distance. Emotional closeness is the key to helping. By definition it's also the same key to helping yourself. Take a baby step in the right direction. You will definitely find happiness.

Nothing that you have not given away will ever be really yours.
—C.S. Lewis

To Help Yourself, Help Others

TO help yourself, help others. How do you do it? Not by creating dependencies, or need-based relationships. The goal of all helping is to allow the other person to thrive and prosper on their own, regardless of the kind of relationship. The goal is to free yourself and others to prosper independently. This is the result of all truly "helping relationships."

It's important to empower others. It makes both of you stronger. You can't do this by carrying the other person on your shoulders through life. The goal is to help a person gain strength and become independent. This is the only way you can help somebody on a long-term basis. If you want to help, begin by simply listening. It is a lost and unappreciated art, but an invaluable one. The kind of listening that is truly helpful lets the other person know you're there. It means taking the initiative, reaching out to someone, and letting her know you care. And it means doing it no matter how busy you are.

I have a close friend who is an extremely successful businessman. During the time he was building one of his companies, I ended up going through one of the most difficult periods of my life. One day he called and said he had heard about what I was going through. He insisted on taking me to supper and spent most of the time listening. I felt so self-conscious of his busy schedule that I kept attempting to cut the conversation short. But he wouldn't let me. By his mere presence, he forced me to talk, which was the healthiest thing I could have done. It was the most vulnerable time of my life, and few others even knew what I was experiencing. To this day, I have no idea how he discovered it. He won't tell me. But he was very helpful. Later on he explained his motives were not altogether altruistic. He suggested it made him feel good to help me. This was primarily because on another occasion I had done the same thing for him. That's the way it works. Take this baby step today. Make a list of three people you can help next week. List the names of the people and how you intend to help them. Then actually follow through and offer assistance without expecting anything in return. You'll be amazed at the results.

Nature does not give to those who will not spend . . .
—R. J. Braughan

Forget About Understanding,
"Let's Be Stupid Together."

I wish I could honestly say I created all these baby steps. This is one of my favorites and I actually got the idea from a friend's testosterone-poisoned adolescent son. He and his girlfriend were "love drunk" and having enormous arguments. They had gotten engaged, run away from home, broken up, gotten back together, and gotten re-engaged over a dozen occasions in half as many months. Finally, in sheer exasperation he blurted out *Can't we forget about all this understanding stuff and be stupid together?*

The three of us burst out laughing. But it has become one of my favorite metaphors. I've actually used this baby step with other couples on multiple occasions. With many people the need to understand is a struggle which goes on indefinitely. They become obsessed with *why*, but ignore the more important question of *how*. Instead of asking how do I change, they get stuck on *why* can't I? On most occasions it becomes an absolute cop-out. Since there is no objective way to measure the validity of the answer to *why*, there is no accompanying responsibility to change. Skipping why, and focusing on the *how* of creating change necessitates action. Frankly, some people don't wait to create change. It's work. So instead they commiserate about why. They'd be far better off just being stupid together!

People grow so busy trying to *understand*, they actually never *live*. They obsess about the unanswerable and ignore the achievable. It's a tremendous waste. Learning to accept without completely understanding is healthier. Acceptance without understanding may be the beginning of health. This is true whether you're discussing relationships, or life. Forget about completely understanding another person. It will never happen. And most of the time you can forget about understanding life. If philosophers can't do it, neither will you. Learn to accept without understanding. Just be stupid together. It's the beginning of healthy change.

Perfect understanding will sometimes almost extinguish pleasure.
—A. E. Housman

Forget About Understanding, "Let's Be Stupid Together."

MANY years ago I taught at a small, but academically elite college. The school took pride in their selectiveness and had an excellent academic reputation. I was hired to *teach*. That was an important distinction that was made clear by the academic dean when he hired me. He said he had enough geniuses on campus. He wanted someone who could teach. I wasn't sure if it was an insult, compliment, or challenge, but I figured it really didn't matter anyway! I was happy to be working.

It didn't take long to recognize he was telling the truth. The faculty was composed of scientists, researchers, and laboratory junkies. I seemed to attract the most disturbed of them for some reason, and I don't mean students. Other faculty began hanging around my office. Since I'm not a scientist, I didn't feel the necessity to compete with any of them. I guess that helped them relax around me. Most of these brilliant people had terrible interpersonal skills. They were great in a lab, or on a computer, but interpersonally remote! One, a biochemist, was probably the worst and for some reason he decided to spend his free time with me. He was the world's leading expert on lentils, or blackbeans, or something like that. He was a militant vegetarian, extremely thin, and totally obnoxious. He had tremendous understanding, but no acceptance.

On one occasion we were eating lunch together. I was having my usual—a diet Coke®, ham sandwich, and potato chips. I don't recall what was on his menu, but I'll never forget his reaction. As I was turning up the diet Coke to wash down the sandwich and chips he reached up and grabbed my wrist. "Don't you know what that's doing to your body?" he asked. "How can you put that poison in your system?" I told him I didn't know what it did to my body, and I really didn't want to. "You destroy your relationships by being obnoxious," I told him. "I destroy my stomach by drinking diet Coke. Don't tell me what it does. I already know too much anyway. At least I can enjoy them. You don't enjoy anything . . . !" Later he agreed. Forget about understanding. Just be stupid together.

Bear with each other and forgive whatever grievances you may have against one another. Forgive as the Lord forgave you.
                                                                —Colossians 3:13 NIV

Forget About Understanding, "Let's Be Stupid Together."

FORGET *about understanding. Let's be stupid together.* At times it seems impossible. Most of us have been led to believe understanding is power. Frankly, you probably have been misled. Having proper perspective may be the equivalent of power. But understanding is useless unless it's applied. Perspective is *how* you look at things. By changing perspective you can redefine a tragedy into an inconvenience. Understanding alone can be torture. Perspective helps determine how you will apply the understanding.

Don't get me wrong. Understanding is nice. It's also a luxury few people are equipped to handle. Like most baby steps this one is progressive. The first step is beginning to let go of the need to understand and simply experience life instead. The true beginning of understanding is living instead of looking for answers to the "big questions." Acceptance without understanding is definitely one of the keys to happiness. Too many people put *understanding* first, *acceptance* second, and *living* far down the list.

As a result of living, you can gain more understanding. As a result of living life passionately with another person you can begin to understand them. As a result of living life passionately on your own, you can begin to understand yourself. And with this living, you eventually gain wisdom. Just because you don't understand something doesn't mean it isn't real. Just because you don't understand computers, for example, doesn't mean they don't work. Just because you don't understand another person's feelings doesn't mean they don't work for that person. Your approval and understanding is irrelevant. I like the other approach. Just accept and live. Be stupid together. Understanding will take care of itself.

I have known it for a long time but I have only just experienced it. Now I know it not only with my intellect, but with my eyes, with my heart, with my stomach.

—**Hermann Hesse**

Forget About Understanding, "Let's Be Stupid Together."

UNDERSTANDING another person can seem impossible at times. Yet we claim to be searching for it. I have grown to believe it is not understanding people want. It's the acceptance they think will come with understanding. In reality, understanding does not lead to acceptance at all. Love leads to acceptance. The beginning of acceptance is empathy. Empathy comes from the German word, "einfuhling," literally translated as "in feeling." To empathize with another person is to attempt to feel the way they feel. Empathy is not feeling sorry for someone. That's sympathy. Empathy is identifying with the way they feel.

I first experienced empathy when I was driving up the Pacific Coast Highway with a lady I was dating in graduate school. She was trying to explain something, and I was having difficulty understanding. Then, in frustration she threw up her hands. She said talking to me was like trying to talk to a steam roller. I was hurt by her description and I pulled the car over to give her my full attention. I persuaded her to try again. She began by describing her feelings. I responded by saying, "What I hear you say is . . ." and then repeated what she said. Afterwards I asked if I had understood her correctly. I didn't editorialize, interpret, or comment. I simply said it back to her. She was pleasantly surprised and told me I had heard correctly. She continued talking. Whenever I answered her, I did it the same way using the prefix, "What I heard you say . . ." and the suffix, ". . . Did I hear you correctly?"

We continued this process for over an hour. When it was done she said it was the first time she had ever been completely heard. Empathy brought us much closer together. I didn't totally understand my girlfriend. But I did accept her. Try the same technique with your spouse, boss, friend, or child. Use "What I heard you say . . ." and the suffix, ". . . Did I hear you correctly?" Be non-judgmental in your language. Acceptance without understanding is very powerful. It will make your journey to happiness far more joyous. And by the way, we did get stupid together. It was nice!

All, everything that I understand, I understand only because I love.
—Leo Tolstoy

10

Let Your Emotions Propel You
Toward Happiness

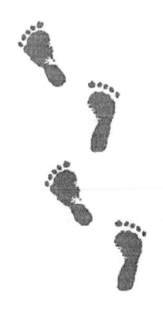

Deal With Your Feelings or Become Them

DEAL with your feelings or become them. Too many people do the opposite. They ignore feelings until they become them. And it's happening at an alarming rate. While this is predominately true for men, it's unfortunately becoming more common for women as well. Modern society has the highest homicide, violent crime, and spouse abuse rates in world history. Some people attribute it to a better reporting system. But I doubt it.

Feelings destroy lives. Marriages and families have been destroyed. Wars have been pointlessly fought. Businesses have been ruined. At the same time feelings have been responsible for virtually all creativity, heroic effort, and acts of unselfish sacrifice. All of these dichotomous experiences come from the same supply of emotional energy. It's not your feelings that are the problem. It's how you deal with them. Most people actually handle big disasters quite well. It's the minor squabbles that bog them down. I have a friend who is an extremely skilled surgeon. He handles life-and-death situations daily and has few observable problems. But on several occasions he's "lost it" in traffic.

He once got out of his car and challenged another driver to a fight in the middle of a traffic jam. When the other driver drove away, my friend actually ran after the speeding car on foot! Like most of us, he rises to the occasion in big tragedies. In fact he grows quite calm in the midst of medical emergencies. It's the small things that cause him to "flip out." In reality it's not the driver or the traffic jam that leads to his outbursts. Due to the stressful nature of his work, he's forced to keep a tight lid on his feelings during surgery. Later, when he begins to relax, which happens to be while driving, he loses control. But it's neither the driver, the car, nor the traffic jam that leads to his outburst. The center for emotional control is in your brain, not in someone else's behavior. It's not only a scientific fact, but an important awareness to accept. You can deal with your feelings. Or you can become them. These are the only two options. The choice is yours.

Above all else, guard your heart, for it is the wellspring of life.
—**Proverbs 4:23** NIV

Deal With Your Feelings or Become Them

I picture feelings, with a limited daily capacity, being carried in a container. How you use it is up to you. You can use your supply of emotional energy in a positive or destructive way. But once you've exhausted the daily supply, it's gone. The next day you have a new supply of emotional energy with new decisions to make. You can deal with your feelings then—or become them.

In combat I saw the crippling effects of becoming one's feelings. On a particular patrol a friend and I were walking point. We came around a bend on an extremely narrow jungle trail and ended up bumping "nose-to-nose" into several North Vietnamese soldiers who were approaching from the opposite direction. We were not the only ones shocked! They turned and ran one direction. I hit the dirt. My friend turned in the opposite direction and ran away screaming. He didn't stop. We never found him. Another American patrol located him two days later. He was returned to the states and treated for emotional problems. My friend, God bless him, *became* his fear.

To over-simplify, he didn't deal with his feelings. Instead, he became them. He was literally "carried away" by his emotions. The results of not dealing with your feelings can be devastating—even deadly. Physicians say eighty-five percent of all illness, and virtually all headaches, ulcers, and backaches are feeling-based. There is even a link between feelings and cancer. Stuffed feelings can destroy the T and L lymphocytes of the body. These are the body's natural cancer-fighting hormones. I've worked with several people in counseling who attributed their cancer to internalized negative feelings. Each day you carry a limited supply of emotional energy. You can exhaust that energy on fear, anger, and rage. Or, you can spend it on love, happiness, and joy. If you invest in unhealthy feelings they will ultimately control your life. If you use the same energy in positive directions it can save your life. I suggest dealing with your feelings instead of becoming them.

You don't get ulcers from what you eat. You get ulcers from what's eating you.

—Vicki Baum

Deal With Your Feelings or Become Them

I have never met actor and director Michael Douglas, but I would like to. I think he's probably done more for the American family, men in particular, than any so-called expert. He has used his art form more brilliantly than any self-help author could imagine. Three of his movies follow a similar formula making brilliant behavioral statements. *Fatal Attraction, The War of the Roses,* and *Falling Down,* are in my opinion masterpieces. They are obviously drama, and stretch the point to make the point, but he's not far off the mark.

Falling Down paints the picture of a man who has lost control. He's lost his job, family, and dignity. Finally, he can take the pain no more and begins to retaliate. Some would say he has had a breakdown. And perhaps that's where the title originated. The bottom line for the man, portrayed brilliantly by Douglas, is he's lost control of everything but his own life. He implodes with rage until he can no longer survive. Then he explodes. If you haven't seen the movie, please do. It should be required viewing considering our social climate today, especially for men. In the movie the character's feelings were all he had left. Everything else had been stripped from him. Like a drug, his feelings gave him power and influence. They reminded him that he was alive. In fact, they were ultimately his only reason for existing. When faced with the loss of influence his feelings had provided, the character poetically arranged his own death. It was a sad and artful punctuation to a dreary story. But again, Douglas was prophetic.

Since this movie, real life appears to be reflecting Douglas' predictions. People are beginning to embrace an almost vigilante mind set. The collective negative feelings in our society are intoxicating and seem almost contagious. However, there's still a choice. Don't join the club. Don't sink to the status quo. Negative feelings are a drug you cannot afford. Deal with your feelings. Don't become them. It's no more difficult. In fact, considering the consequences, it's far easier. Take a baby step away from the effects of negative feelings. You'll be happy you did.

Never apologize for showing feeling. When you do so, you apologize for truth.

—Benjamin Disraeli

Deal With Your Feelings or Become Them

A feeling is a profound awareness accompanied by a biochemical change. There are many chemical reactions that can occur within your body to heighten this awareness. It could be an adrenaline surge, an endorphin reaction, a flush of seratonin, testosterone, progesterone, or one of dozens of chemicals your body can produce. Regardless, the injection of chemicals increase the awareness and intensity associated with an experience. The chemical change is usually jump-started as a result of sensory stimulation. As the intensity level increases, so does the power of that feeling. You can get into emotional trouble if you fail to resolve these feelings. Unexpressed, they can be damaging to yourself or others.

Expression is the opposite of depression. Though these two words look similar, their Latin derivations are the exact opposite. Expression means "out with pressure." Depression means "under pressure." You can't do both at the same time. Any negative feeling—anger, depression, fear—can be dealt with by expression. Expressing feelings is different than becoming them. Expressing is talking, writing, singing, dancing, painting, throwing pencils at the ceiling, etc. "Expression" is not screaming or hitting. That's "becoming your feelings." These are two different reactions.

I believe the source of most problems in our society today is the same. Whether it is an emotional problem, marriage problem, or crime, the root source is consistent. Your feelings can destroy your happiness. Today choose two active ways to deal with your feelings such as jogging, or dancing. Then choose two passive ways such as journaling or talking to a friend. Spend an entire week utilizing one active and one passive strategy per day. You'll be far happier.

It has long been my belief that in times of great stress, such as a four-day vacation, the thin veneer of family wears off almost at once, and we are revealed in our true personalities.

—Shirley Jackson

Motion Controls Emotion

LIKE the other baby steps, this one has a variety of meanings. At one level, it simply means you can change the way you feel by vigorously moving the large muscle groups of your body. At another level it has deeper meanings. Anyone who doesn't believe motion controls emotion has never been seasick. Motion sickness definitely affects you emotionally. It's not only the dizziness, disorientation, and nausea that gets you down, but it has a profound emotional impact on your psyche. Motion sickness will convince you once and for all that *motion controls emotion*, even if you have doubts about it at first.

Similar to other baby steps, this one is not an original concept. I first heard the phrase when explaining to someone in counseling that you can change the way you feel by changing what you do with your body. I gave examples of running or jogging. In turn, he responded, "You mean, motion can control emotion." I liked it and have used it since then. I've heard other people use similar ideas in their discussions of feelings. More importantly, I have also come to believe motion can change emotion. However, many people have the opposite idea and let their emotions—*such as depression*—control their motions. They allow their feelings to immobilize them.

The truth is, you can jump-start yourself out of a depression or any other emotional slump through movement. Generally speaking, by aerobically exercising the large muscle groups of the body you can jump-start yourself out of any dark mood. It may not happen the first time you walk rapidly, jog, or get on a cross-country ski machine. But usually, with two or three attempts, many people can begin experiencing an endorphine-induced mood lift, as well as an incredible change in perspective. Motion can control emotion. It's totally up to you. It's a baby step on the road to happiness.

Be joyful always; pray continually; give thanks in all circumstances . . . .

—1 Thessalonians 5:16–18 NIV

Motion Controls Emotion

THERE are several forms of healing based on the philosophy of this baby step. The idea that motion controls emotions has influenced counseling, physical therapy, orthopedics, chiropractic medicine, osteopathic medicine, and other healing professions. Entire treatment approaches in these various healing arts have been based around this baby step.

It's fairly well-accepted that emotional memories can be stored in the body. By manipulating the body in various ways, these neurologically-stored memory patterns are often brought back to conscious-awareness, then released. Working further with the muscular skeletal system, some advanced healers can not only release emotion but alter the nature of it. Many years ago I was walking through a local mall with my children. It was several weeks before Christmas and the mall was crowded with shoppers. A man and his son stopped me in the hallway. He said he recognized me from television, hesitated, then suddenly hunched over in a standing fetal position. *The pains are coming back. They're hurting me . . . .* He moaned as he explained that memories were trying to overwhelm him. I took him to a relatively-quiet spot in the mall where we sat and began discussing his problems.

He explained how childhood memories had been intruding during the Christmas period. I noticed that as he began to describe these he went into a fetal position and started moaning. Suddenly, in my best Marine Corps fashion I told him to stand up. Startled, he followed orders and the pains went away. I explained to him that as long as he remained erect, and didn't look down, the memories would not return. I accompanied him to find his wife. We telephoned a local psychiatrist and he was given an emergency appointment. In this particular case, motion defined emotion. Each time he resumed the infantile posture, old memories returned. By merely straightening out his posture and continuing to move, he temporarily controlled the flashbacks. It was not a cure, but it made his symptoms go away. The same can be true for you. *Motion controls emotion.*

Use it or lose it.

—Jimmy Connors

Motion Controls Emotion

ONE important form of motion is aerobic exercise. I consider it the most valuable anti-depressant in the world today. It is also the most overlooked. By exercise, I don't necessarily mean backbreaking or torturing degrees of physical self abuse. Rapid walking, slow jogging, and step training are all good forms of aerobics. As little as twenty to thirty minutes a day of such movement can change the way you feel and give you a happier mood.

Most people who discuss exercise suggest it as a way of conditioning the body. There are obvious reasons for this that really don't need to be discussed here. More important is the impact of exercise on your mind, emotions, and happiness. It creates a mood lift due to the injection of endorphins during periods of physical exercise. It also oxygenates the brain which can result in an even more intense "rush." However, there's another benefit that also occurs during exercise. By sweating, and burning fat, you are actually disposing of toxins. In my opinion, this frees negative emotions as well as poisonous body fluids and wastes, thereby increasing the benefits of exercise, especially when it's done out of doors. Furthermore, there's the added scientific benefit that indicates you get a two-to-one ratio of return in time spent in exercise to increased life expectancy. As an example, for each thirty minutes you spend in exercise, scientists tell us you get an additional hour in life expectancy. That's an incredible investment.

Best-selling author, Covert Bailey, suggests that if the benefits of exercise could be put into a pill it would be the most widely-prescribed form of medication in history. In fact, the pill already is available—it takes thirty minutes to swallow—it's called *exercise! Motion controls emotion.* Start moving immediately and you'll know why.

If we could give every individual the right amount of nourishment and exercise, not too little and not too much, we would have found the safest way to health.

—**Hippocrates**

Motion Controls Emotion

AS a child I can remember my grandfather telling me to do my homework. I would often respond that I really didn't feel like it. He would quickly reply, *"I didn't ask how you felt. I said, go do your homework."* This interaction began to be quite a joke between family members and we laugh about it, even today.

Later, as a Marine Corps parachutist, there were many occasions when, staring down from ten thousand feet, I really didn't feel like jumping. Yet, once I exited the aircraft and my parachute popped open, I enjoyed the ride. The same phenomenon was true when I was in combat . When rappelling into enemy territory there were many times I didn't *feel* like going—I was frightened. But, realizing that it was my responsibility, I went ahead and did my job. Today as an adult, there are many mornings when I don't *feel* like getting out of bed. There are other times when I don't feel like going to work. But I make the right choice and get started with my day. Once rolling, I realize that it's not so bad after all. In fact, I have fun. But a few hours earlier I didn't even want to get out of bed. Sometimes we let our feelings control our behavior. We give in to negative feelings. But the truth is, we don't have to. We can change our emotions by following this baby step.

You can change the way you feel by changing what you do. The opposite is also true. But you can decide what you want to be true for you. Motion can control emotion. Emotion cannot only control motion but success or failure as well. Don't let emotions destroy you. Use this week as an experiment. When you feel like staying in bed, get up and go for a walk or exercise instead. When you find yourself avoiding a task, clear your desk and work on it for fifteen minutes. When you feel depressed, exercise—even if you are confined to a chair. Focus on motion and the emotions will follow.

We are under-exercised as a nation. We look instead of play. We ride instead of walk. Our existence deprives us of the minimum of physical activity essential for healthy living.
—John F. Kennedy

Reject Dependence In Any Form

WHEN I think of dependency, my mind casts several images. One is from an old WWII poster. I recall seeing a picture of a ghostly-looking skeleton with the motto: *Loose Lips Sink Ships.* I guess it was someone's attempt to convince people that secrecy was important. To me, dependency creates a similar association. I visualize the Grim Reaper asking the question: "Dependency Anyone?" The concept of dependency is a frightening one to me. I hope it will be to you.

When thinking of dependency, it is easy to discuss the obvious ones. Without question, most people accept alcoholism and other drug addictions as a form of dependency. But there are others probably even more dangerous due to their benign-looking nature. Many of these dependencies are socially acceptable. The reality is, you can become dependent on a number of things. You can become dependent on your parents, spouse, or children. You can become equally dependent on money, gambling, sex, food, excitement, and even fear. They all have one thing in common—they are crippling.

Dependency sidetracks you from the pathway of happiness. The purpose of taking baby steps is to gradually and methodically help you take control of your life. Dependency does just the opposite—it is crippling. It gives control of your happiness to something or someone other than yourself. It will handicap you. Reject dependence in any form. From the obvious to the more subtle, dependency will destroy your happiness. Don't risk it.

Every form of addiction is bad, no matter whether the narcotic be alcohol, morphine or idealism.

—Carl Jung

Reject Dependence In Any Form

IN the early 1980's First Lady Nancy Reagan initiated a major anti-drug campaign. It is one I would like to continue. When it comes to dependency, "Just Say No." I visualize the word "dependency" in bold, pulsating, dayglo orange print. "Just Say No" is written diagonally across it. Happy people don't have room in their life for dependency of any kind.

One of the basic reasons for this is there's no such thing as dependency without hostility. If you are dependent on something, you are going to be angry at yourself and the object of your dependency. In the same way, if you allow someone to be dependent on you, they too will experience hostility. You probably expect them to be grateful. In a way they are. But they are also angry. There's no such thing as dependency without accompanying hostility. Dependency weakens the person who experiences it and ultimately creates a high level of resentment. This is so common that "hostile-dependency" has become a relatively hackneyed term in the helping professions. This is true whether the dependency is on a person or a substance. There is no dependency without hostility. And the hostility will increase or decrease based on the intensity level of the dependency.

The best approach is to have nothing to do with it. Reject dependency in any form. Make it your goal to be independently healthy. This does not mean living alone or becoming arrogant. Certainly, you love others. You just don't need to depend on them. And you don't allow them to need you in the same manner. The biggest gift you can give someone is independence. Then they are free to love you as an equal. *Reject dependence in any form.* You'll be glad you did.

What is dangerous about the tranquilizers is that whatever peace of mind they bring is a packaged peace of mind. When you buy a pill and buy peace with it, you get conditioned to cheap solutions instead of deep ones.

—Max Lerner

Reject Dependence In Any Form

DEPENDENCY is a seductive concept. When we say reject dependency in any form, that's exactly what we mean. This includes allowing others to be dependent on you. You may think it's a problem only if you are dependent. Allowing your spouse or children to be dependent on you can actually feel good—temporarily. That's the seductive part. You feel needed. You rationalize the situation by believing you are only helping them. But you're not.

Another seduction is that some dependencies have become not only legalized, but socially desirable. Alcohol as an example, occupies a very important place in our society today. It represents Christ's blood at celebration of Holy Communion in many church services worldwide. That's an extremely-powerful symbol. The "toast" is given as a traditional ritual of celebration. Being "old enough to drink" is a rite of passage in our society. It is considered a macho compliment to describe someone as being able to "hold his liquor like a man." It's not only socially acceptable to drink, it can be socially unacceptable to abstain. Yet alcohol is the number one drug of abuse in our society, and probably the biggest cause of family problems and violence worldwide.

Another seduction stems from the medical community—a place where you'd least expect it. Many different people have told me their Xanax, Prozac, and Valium were not drugs. *Those aren't drugs,* they suggest defensively. *I've got a prescription for them.* Yet for many, the actual reason they came to see me in the first place was to get off these same prescription medications. Rejecting dependency in any form will help you become happy. It will also help others around you. If you are dependent on anything—to the degree of your dependency—you are a slave. If you are allowing others to be dependent, you are both enslaved. There's no such thing as a well-adjusted slave. *Reject dependence in any form.*

No one can build his security upon the nobleness of another person.
—**Willa Cather**

Reject Dependence In Any Form

OVER the years I've worked with thousands of alcoholics and other drug addicts. I have never met a single one who was happy. Many of them appear to be happy when intoxicated. Yet, when the substance is gone, or when the "high" is over—whether it is from drugs or an addicting activity—they are miserable. Interestingly enough, I've never met anyone who said their mission in life was to become an addict or become dependent. No one begins with that goal in mind. Yet, according to some experts, one out of four people in our society is dependent on something.

The word *addiction* is a fascinating one. It comes from the Latin word "addicere," which means "to give assent." An addictus was a person who had "given their assent." By Roman definition, an addictus was a *slave.* They were right. When you are dependent, that's exactly what you are—a slave. You become a slave to whatever or whomever your dependency is directed. One philosopher suggested, "There's no such thing as a well-adjusted slave . . . ." Any dependency will make a poorly-adjusted person out of you. Don't risk it. Reject dependency in any form. If you are already a slave, then free yourself. Overcome your dependency and experience the resulting freedom. It will be painful at first, but the long-term response is well worth it.

Make an experiment out of it. Give up caffeine for one week—cold turkey! Simply consume no caffeine for seven days. Trust me. It will be painful. You'll get headaches, backaches, or may feel as if you have severe PMS. But you'll survive, and walk away with an appreciation of how powerful dependency really is. You'll also be amazed at the freedom you experience when you are "detoxed." Detoxification is painful. Dependency is more painful. Avoid both. You'll be far better off on your journey to happiness.

Who of you by worrying can add a single hour to his life?
                                                —**Matthew 6:27** NIV

Depersonalize

THIS is another one of those important baby steps under-valued by others. A lot of pain is caused as a result of taking things personally. I think it's a sign of health to do just the opposite. I can remember, as an early child and throughout my life hearing, "Don't take this personally, but—" And then someone would proceed to give a tremendous insult. Naturally, I'd end up taking it personally. It was as if the warning "don't take it personally" was another way of saying "get ready for an insult." In fact, we should take their advice. Actually, few things in life *are* really personal. We suffer a lot of needless damage by "personalizing."

Personalization is an ego-centric attitude. At times it can border on narcissism. I hear people in counseling daily saying things like: "What did *I do* to deserve this? What has God got against me?" I sit back and wonder if all God has to do is think of some way to ruin this person's day. When it rains on your parade it's not God's way of getting even. Unless you've experienced the Saul of Tarsus' conversion, I doubt God has directly intervened in your life at all. God doesn't have to. We are fully capable of messing up our own lives without God's help.

It's a step of growth to come away from this attitude. There are few negative experiences in life personally directed toward you. The more quickly you depersonalize, the better off you'll be. *Depersonalize.* Few of the things that happen to you are intended to be personal. Those that are, you need to learn from and forget. There's no reason to continue berating yourself. Depersonalize. It's an important *baby step,* and will help you live longer.

Never pay attention to what critics say. Remember, a statue has never been set up in honor of a critic.

—Jean Sibelius

Depersonalize

A friend of mine used to own a radio station, where I hosted a counseling talk show. A local psychiatric hospital wanted to advertise on my show. Since my treatment philosophy is outpatient-based, I objected to using them as an advertiser. I didn't want my listeners to associate me with the hospital. I decided that if I let them on my show, it would appear I was endorsing them. My friend saw it from a different angle. He said it's just business. He told me to quit taking it personally. "If these people want to give you money, let them give it to you. This isn't about your personal credibility. This is about business."

Whether I agreed or not, to him life is about business. One of my former martial arts instructors was the same way. He suggested taking the emotion out of martial arts practice. Instead of feeling any emotion at all during practice, he suggested removing emotions from it altogether. *It's just business,* he kept repeating. *There's no room for anger. Anger destroys flow. Once you remove the emotion you can have more success with technique.* He was right. The business was the practice of martial arts. It wasn't an emotional experience at all. In fact, to him emotion destroyed it. Look on most of life as business, and remove the emotions that will confuse you.

Perhaps looking on much of life as "just business" is the best approach. Whether the business is earning an income, teaching martial arts, or being happy, the best approach may be to remove emotion and attend to business. If it helps you take the stress and worry out of everyday life, perhaps it's best for you to view most of your life that way. Being able to practice this particular baby step made me less defensive and more relaxed. My world deals predominately with other people's emotions. When I began to depersonalize, I was far better off. I realized that I could not conduct someone else's business for them. If the other person chose to be less miserable, I could show them the path. But I could not make them walk it. Depersonalizing has probably added years to my life expectancy. I think it could do the same for you.

Anger makes dull men witty, but it keeps them poor.
—Elisabeth I

Depersonalize

ON many occasions emotion can blind you. This is one good reason not to personalize things. It's a serious mistake to make a decision based exclusively on emotional reactions. I stretch this to an extreme that probably few people do. The more intensely emotional you are, the more likely the odds are of making mistakes. Don't get me wrong, I think emotions need to be considered. But if the decision is based on anything more than 25% emotion it's probably wrong.

Emotions are as intoxicating as drugs. In many cases they are probably more. They are extremely powerful, and you can't deny them. The goal is to recognize your emotional reaction, absorb it for what it is, and then let go of the intoxicating effect. The mistake too many people make is letting their emotions control situations which truly have nothing to do with emotions at all. Paying your bills is not an emotional experience. It's an accounting exercise. Driving your car is not an emotional experience. It's a way of getting from one point to the other. Being a postal worker is not an emotional experience. Unfortunately, too many people are making it that. The more you react emotionally, the greater the possibility of personalizing. You'll end up taking things personally that have absolutely nothing to do with you.

Emotions belong in your life. However, the goal is not to let them control it. Thought and emotion are vastly different. I suggest integrating emotion into your life, but at the same time let your intellect control it. If you do you'll be far more successful baby-stepping your way to happiness. If you don't, you may still find happiness. It will just take longer. By depersonalizing, you'll find a short-cut to happiness that others miss.

Seest thou a man diligent in his business? He shall stand before kings.
—**Proverbs 22:29**

Depersonalize

IN Vietnam I was wounded on two separate occasions. The first was either by a grenade or rocket. I still have fragments in my shoulder and lower leg to remind me of that experience. The second time was different. I made eye contact with the person who shot me. We were that close. It was far more difficult not to take it personally. As I look back on it today I realize it wasn't personal at all. The young man who shot me didn't even know who I was. I didn't hate him. I'd never met him. And he didn't hate me. I was probably just like him. It was warfare. His job was to shoot the enemy, just as mine was. And like the well-trained soldier he probably was, he raised his rifle and shot at the enemy. I was simply a uniform with a body in it. It was *just business*.

I find that the more I'm able to depersonalize attacks like this, the healthier I become. I will not lie to you. On occasion, I still let emotion disrupt my happiness. But it happens far less-frequently. Some things are personal. But getting shot was not. The soldier was shooting at the uniform, not me. And most of the attacks I've suffered over the years are the same thing. *They're just business.* Do you want to be happy? Practice this baby step. Very little of what goes on around you, or to you, is intended to be personal. It's mostly about business. I believe that even most divorces aren't intended to be personal. It's just one scared person thinking they are going about the business of self-protection from another scared person. In these situations people often let emotion make the decision for them. That's not personal either. It's not about you. It's about someone else's fear.

To depersonalize is to take a baby step of enormous magnitude. I don't think it will be easy. It's something you will have to practice repeatedly. Read this step again. Make index cards. Carry them in your pocket, put them in your mirror. Tape one on your dashboard. Write the word personalize. Then draw a circle around it with a diagonal line down the middle. Once you accomplish this baby step you'll be far happier. Remember *it's just business*. The business of being happy.

Emotion has taught mankind to reason.
—Marquis de Vauvenargues

Don't Worry, Be Happy

IN 1988 gifted artist Bobby McFerrin came out with his classic ditty, *Don't Worry, Be "Hoppy (Happy)."* It's a humorous and talented piece of work. McFerrin is incredible. He can produce and mimic various melodious sounds using only his voice. This particular song was done in a reggae rhythm and was quite a hit when first released. "Don't Worry," McFerin suggested, "Be Happy."

On the other hand, I have a friend who thinks it's his job to worry. His motto would be the opposite of McFerrin's. He would suggest, "Do Worry, Be Happy." In fact, he literally carries his briefcase full of worries with him. I've seen him do this on multiple occasions. Virtually everywhere he goes he carries his regular briefcase and an extra. This one is filled with old bills he can't pay, collector's notices he's received, and other such paraphernalia. After observing this for quite some time I finally asked him why he did it. He responded on a very sincere level that he carried the second briefcase so if he ran out of things to do he could pull out his bills and worry about them. This wasn't an attempt at humor or sarcasm. He was serious.

My friend believes it is his job to worry. He thinks it is a constructive activity. He worries about his bills. He worries about his aging parents. He worries about his brother's health. When I asked him about this, he responded. "If I don't worry about them, then who will?" The funny thing is, other than his worrying, he is a fairly well-adjusted individual. He's not "crazy," though he occasionally may lean in that direction. He simply believes that if you care about someone, you worry. Not only *about* them, but *for* them. His motto is if you love them, you worry about them. He and I had several discussions about the subject. We joke about his briefcase full of worries. But to this date he hasn't changed. He worries, and he's unhappy. But he thinks if he worries more, he will be happy eventually. In reality he'd be better off to take a cue from Bobby McFerrin. Don't Worry, Be "Hoppy (Happy)."

I've always believed that you can think positive just as well as you can think negative.

—Sugar Ray Robinson

Don't Worry, Be Happy

SO who's right? Is it Bobby McFerrin—*Don't Worry, Be "Hoppy (Happy)?"* Or is it my friend who says, "Worry enough and maybe you'll eventually be happy." I don't know of any philosophers who disagree with McFerrin. Nor have I been able to find any evidence in the Bible, science, or philosophy, which suggest worry is an important thing to do.

Yet when I questioned my family about this, I discovered I'm not passing on my values very well. Of eight children gathered at the table that day, six said if you really cared about someone, you'd worry about them. They thought worrying helped. Another said it depended on the situation. The eighth said, "No, worrying isn't helpful. Other people's problems are their own." Apparently most people believe if you really care about someone, you worry about them. Yet they're unable to explain its benefit. After finding out it was such a popular point of view, I thought maybe my own thinking was misguided. So I researched it further, thought about it on my own, and was still unable to figure it out. If I love somebody, is worrying going to communicate anything in a positive way?

Maybe I'm wrong; and I am open-minded about this; but to me there's another point of view. If I love somebody I need to tell them. If I'm concerned about their welfare, I need to pass that message on and do what I can to help. If I fear they're going to have travel problems, maybe I need to discuss it with them, and do what I can to ensure that they arrive safely. But to me, worrying is very selfish. If I worry, I become absorbed in my own pain and misery. It doesn't do anything positive to help the other person. Worry is becoming so absorbed in my own anxiety, that I have no room for anyone else. Worry is becoming obsessed with the negative. You may be making the situation *worse* for both of you. Worry is sending negative messages to the person you are worrying about. In addition, it is harmful to you. So why is it appropriate to worry about someone you love? I simply do not understand. As I said—I am open-minded. But I prefer the alternative. *Don't worry. Be happy.*

Therefore do not worry about tomorrow, for tomorrow will worry about itself.

—**Matthew 6:34** NIV

Don't Worry, Be Happy

MAYBE I am just brainwashed by Bobby McFerrin. Perhaps his reggae limerick sends subliminal hypnotic messages to me through the radio and distorts my brain. It could be true. The brain is a magnificent instrument. It can process thoughts at an incredible rate of approximately 700 words per minute. But it can only focus on one particular thought at a time.

If I'm focused on a worrisome thought, that doesn't leave room for anything else. If I'm obsessed about worry, I'm literally blocking out all other forms of possible stimulus. One's mind cannot entertain two contrasting thoughts simultaneously. So if I'm worrying, that's where my mind is going to stay. On the other hand, if I'm thinking positive thoughts, that's where my mind will be focused. When focusing on negative energy, your mind is like a battery that's losing it's power. Worrisome thoughts literally drain your energy. They can exhaust your power supply. Positive energy can increase your power. Negative focus can only drain it. In the absence of a positive thought, negative worries will almost always creep in. The better alternative is to focus on something positive, and quit worrying.

If you really want to help someone else, don't worry about them. It will just destroy you, and give *them* something to worry about. Instead, take care of yourself. Improve your own health—mentally and physically—by changing your negative thought patterns. Then project positive energy your friend's way by sending them prayers or meditation which can influence their life. It's a very important thing to do and may turn your life around. It could also help my buddy's briefcase full of worries. But that's up to him. I'm not going to worry about it. I've told him how I feel. Now I'll be "Hoppy (Happy)."

Worry is evidence of an ill-controlled brain; it is merely a stupid waste of time in unpleasantness. If men and women practiced mental calisthenics as they do physical calisthenics, they would purge their brains of this foolishness.

—**Arnold Bennett**

Don't Worry, Be Happy

GENERALLY speaking, people who worry obsessively are over-whelmed with fear. In my friend's case, he is afraid of his elderly parents dying, or his brother's health problems growing worse. Other people simply fear loss in general. Some hesitate to face the pain that can accompany loss. Other people, who are even more unhealthy, obsess about the loss of things. All of these underline anxiety about loneliness—a basic human condition. The inability to be alone is a major problem.

Having been in the helping profession since 1975, I've come to a few basic assumptions about human behavior. One of them is that there are two primary emotions. One is love. The other is fear. The dread of being alone is probably the most basic of all. When you finally face fear, and deal with it, you will overcome your ultimate demon. Worry then, comes from the fear of letting go. It's the horror of emptiness, loneliness, and ultimate abandonment in the universe. When my friend carries his briefcase full of worries, it's painful. When he worries about his mother and brother, it's not altruistic. He's worried about himself, not them. It's an uneasiness about facing life alone.

Deal with your fears. If you love someone, don't worry about them. Say "I love you." If you are concerned about your parents' health, discuss it with them. Send them articles about healthy eating. Buy them a Nordic Track® or an exercise bicycle. If you're worried about your bills, write your creditors a letter or talk to a financial planner. Don't worry. You will get an ulcer. Then you'll worry more. Instead, I suggest listening to Bobby McFerrin's, *Don't Worry. Be "Hoppy."*

Worry affects circulation, the heart and the glands, the whole nervous system and profoundly affects the heart. I have never known a man who died from overwork, but many who died from doubt.
—**Charles H. Mayo** (surgeon, brother of William J. Mayo)

11

Let the Breath of God Propel You
Toward Happiness

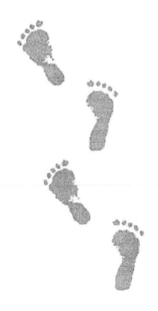

Spiritual Is As Spiritual Does

FORREST Gump changed the world. We will never be the same. "Life is like a box of chocolates," and "Stupid is as stupid does." Likely, nothing will seem quite as original as Tom Hanks in that historic role. This baby step takes a similar angle. *Spiritual is as spiritual does.* Happy people are usually deeply spiritual. They are loving, moral, and have deep religious convictions. The difference between HAPs and others is they live their beliefs. What they *do* definitely speaks louder than their words. Their spirituality is not limited to church attendance. They live it.

HAPs describe their spirituality as deep and meaningful. They passionately believe in a sense of purpose much greater than themselves. HAPs often experience their life work as a holy calling, and pursue it with unbelievable commitment and energy. Their spirituality is found in the way they work, play, and interact with others. They don't lecture. Their spirituality comes through in the way they reach out or make time for their friends who are a high priority.

Spiritual is as spiritual does. HAPs have deep religious beliefs and a profound spiritual commitment. But, most importantly, it is demonstrated by their behavior. Love is an action verb. They may not be handing out religious tracts, playing tambourines in airports, or evangelizing on street corners. But it is what they *do* that makes the difference. You see it in their everyday life. After all, *spiritual is as spiritual does.* It is a baby step on the journey to happiness.

Do not pray for easy lives. Pray to be stronger men. Do not pray for tasks equal to your powers. Pray for powers equal to your tasks. Then the doing of your work shall be no miracle, but you shall be the miracle.

—Phillips Brooks

Spiritual Is As Spiritual Does

WHEN this book was in its early stages I found myself describing it to a friend as "a very spiritual little book . . ." He asked me what I meant, and I found myself stuttering in an attempt to define terms. I eventually told him I thought the book was inspiring. But the fact I hesitated was the awakening for me.

It's very popular today to describe something as spiritual. The term itself is used and abused to the point it could be misleading. This Baby Step claims *spiritual is as spiritual does*. First, let me explain what I mean when I use the term spiritual. My dictionary defines spiritual in many ways. The definition I ascribe to is "concerned with God or affecting the soul. That which is not material or tangible." But I like to take it a step further. I have a love affair with this word. The term actually comes from two Latin words, "spiritus" and "spirare." These translate roughly to *the breath of God*. There are several other words that come from the same root including spirit, inspire, aspire, and respiration.

The implication is that to be spiritual is to inspire. It is to breathe life into another. It is to "attempt" speaking to others with the breath of God flowing through you. And the result of that speaking is to give others encouragement, or life. This is an incredible challenge. If spiritual is as spiritual does, what do you therefore *do*. You live your life in a way the that breath of God flows through you to others. There are people who live this way. But there are only a few. The closer we come to this, the more impact we will have on others. You may not see these people on television, or read about them in the paper, but they are there. It may be your friend Roy, or your buddy Butch, or your pal LA. They may be mechanics, policemen, or editors. *Spiritual is as spiritual does.* Let the breath of God flow through you.

And why call ye me, Lord, Lord, and do not do the things which I say?

—St. Luke 6:46

Spiritual Is As Spiritual Does

AS you can tell by now, I regard my grandparents with great reverence. Many of my early memories surround interactions with either grandma or grandpa. I spent most summers of my early life with them, and lived with them for extended periods of time after the death of my father. The "breath of God" flowed through each of them.

They practiced what would be considered today as an extremely unusual ritual regarding funerals. I could always tell when one of the "old souls" died. Regardless of the time of day, granny would start preparing a feast. Grandpa would begin loading his pickup truck with rocking chairs, Bible, hymnbooks, and ultimately full picnic baskets. My question was not where are we going—but who died. It was that obvious. But I looked forward to it. In many ways, it was like an extended family reunion with the dead person's body in the living room. The community would congregate at the home and for the next few days, life revolved around the deceased. The ladies would flock to the kitchen and cook. Twenty-four hours per day they would cook, sing hymns, grieve, and occasionally pass out. The old men—they all seem old when one is eleven—would sit in rocking chairs by the casket. For the next three days they "sat up with the dead." They rocked in the chairs, and told stories about the dead person around the clock. There'd be no less than four of the men all taking turns talking about the deceased. And always with great respect.

I loved it. I would crawl under the casket and listen. Several hours later, grandpa would threaten me to get me to go home. I remember having no fear or apprehension. There was none present in the room. There was compassion, empathy, sadness, reverence, and tremendous love. Fear or superstition were never around. To me it was an extremely spiritual experience—one I regret we have let pass. On those late nights, as I listened to the old women singing and the old men praying, I heard the breath of God. And I was inspired. *Spiritual is as spiritual does.* Build rituals in your life that allow the breath of God to flow through you.

Do all the good you can, In all the ways you can, In all the places you can, To all the people you can, As long as ever you can.
—*John Wesley*

Spiritual Is As Spiritual Does

SPIRITUAL is as spiritual *does*. The emphasis is on the last word of this baby step. The way you live is the true measure of your spirituality. As an example, attending AA may be helpful. But that alone does not necessarily place you "in recovery." You cannot become physically-fit by watching a football game on television. Listening to music does not make you a musician. Similarly, being in "the club," will not necessarily make you spiritual.

As both parent and therapist, I have learned many things from children. The most important thing I've learned is loving your children is not something you think. It's something you do. I adore my children. Frankly, I suspect most parents do. I have never met a parent who had "bad" intentions. Some parents make bad decisions, but I've never met one who didn't "love" their child at some level. However, I've listened to dozens of children express doubt whether or not they were loved by their parents. The children didn't experience love because their parents failed to express it in an active, effective way.

B. F. Skinner described this reaction as a result of affluence. People look at beautiful things, listen to beautiful music, and watch exciting entertainment. But the only behavior that is reinforced is looking, listening, and watching. As a population, we have become passive. Spirituality cannot grow in such an atmosphere. Spiritual is as spiritual *does*. You can't be a spiritual person without *living a life* that reflects it. It's the perpetual state of love in action that measures the true nature of a person's spirituality. Don't call yourself spiritual. *Do* spiritual. You will be a better person. And your world will be a better place. Take this baby step today. List three things you can do this week to make you more receptive to the breath of God flowing through you. Then do them. And let it flow.

Share the gospel at all times. Whenever necessary use words.
—St. Francis of Assisi

Seek Balance

TO some people, the concept of *balance* is more spiritual than emotional. Some identify balance as a "holy" word. The Japanese use the term "kuzush" to mean balance. It also means centering. I think that's what balance does. It helps us center, both physically and spiritually.

When I was approximately eight years old I went on a trip with my grandpa to the Carolina coast. This particular part of North Carolina was very swampy and the vegetation was different than what I was used to. Grandpa stopped the truck, looked around in the woods for a few minutes, then asked me to come where he was standing. I scrambled toward where he was kneeling. "What is it?" I asked. He told me to be careful because I was standing next to a man-eating plant! I jerked back and must have looked startled. Grandpa was laughing. "Don't worry about it son," he snorted. "It's really not a man-eating plant. It only eats women!" What Grandpa had found was a field of venus fly traps. This fascinating plant eats insects as a way of maintaining its growth in swampy soil lacking nitrogen. Grandpa explained this to me in the next few minutes and demonstrated how the plant worked. Naturally I wanted to take one home. Grandpa explained that it would die there. His final explanation was the real point.

"The soil is balanced . . . balance," Grandpa explained, "is everything. A little sun, a little water, good soil and you have a healthy plant. Take any of those away and it doesn't turn out right. People are the same way. They can be balanced and healthy. Or, they can become like the Venus' flytrap, a twisted version of a plant that gets its nitrogen and protein by eating other forms of life." Over the years I've learned to more deeply appreciate my grandfather's wisdom. Balance is vital to happiness. It's one of the most important baby steps and probably a life-saver.

The soul's joy lies in doing.

—Percy Shelley

Seek Balance

THERE are many elements of balance. Over the next three pages a variety of them will be discussed. They come from studies completed at Boston University, Duke University, and Harvard Medical School. I have synthesized the various studies for the purposes of this book. The principles are priceless.

The first two concepts require little explanation. The first is to eat at least one hot, balanced meal per day. The second is to get sufficient sleep to meet your needs. Your need for sleep is probably different from someone else's. Most people require somewhere between six and eight hours. A few fall below this range. Some fall above. Sleep is very important, but few require more than eight hours. The third key to balance is giving and receiving physical and emotional affection. It's a very important part of life. The fourth key is having one dependable relative nearby who lives outside your home. Nearby means within a thirty-minute drive, but the key concept is dependable. If you don't have a relative, adopt someone to act in that capacity.

The next key is exercising to the point of perspiration a minimum of three times per week. Frankly, I think it should be more, but I'm not a scientist. Others say you only need to exercise on the days you plan to eat! It's great therapy. The next key to balance is to avoid smoking. The research on this is not open to debate. Another key to balance is avoiding alcohol or mind-altering drugs. Science now tells us the maximum of one ounce of alcohol every twenty-four hours can prolong life expectancy. If you can't limit yourself to that amount, it's probably best to abstain. There are occasions when prescription mind-altering medication can be a lifesaver. Yet those are generally the exception, rather than the rule. When it comes to mind-altering drugs, I suggest avoiding them unless absolutely necessary. To me it's irrelevant if they come from a "street pusher" or a pharmacy. If it alters consciousness, you might be making a mistake using it. You may have heard that there are "wonder" drugs available. They are a wonder to me too! That's why I suggest you stay away from them.

Peace be within thy walls, and properity within thy palaces.
—Psalms 122:7

Seek Balance

THE next keys to balance on your *baby steps to happiness* involve quite subjective measures. The first is having an income adequate to meet basic needs. What your basic needs consist of is entirely up to you. This definition will vary greatly from person to person. The next key is deriving strength from your religious beliefs. Obviously, there is no scientific recommendations as to what your beliefs should be. However, this is an important element of balance and happiness as well.

Another consideration is whether or not you regularly attend club or social activities. Here's a hint. It's neither the club, nor the nature of the social activity, that's important. It's the interaction with others and the opportunity to build a social network that makes this vital. Similar consideration is given to having one or more friends in whom you confide on a regular basis. These friends are not the superficial variety. Another factor has to do with being in good physical health. The question becomes, "How is it measured?" Researchers tell us that this, too, is a subjective process. You probably know better than anyone else how you feel. If you feel energetic and like the way your body looks and feels, then you are probably in good shape. If you are fatigued or lethargic most of the time there is likely a problem.

The next two factors have to do with communication. The first one is, *do* you speak openly about your feelings? Notice the question does not read, "*Can* you speak openly about your feelings?" It's the doing that's of more importance here. This is extremely important and will be discussed in more detail in another baby step. The final factor on this page is of similar significance. Do you have regular, calm conversations with family and friends about important daily-living issues? These are small things that can lead to tremendous stress among people. Calm conversations are simply a way of lowering your anxiety level before it becomes overwhelming.

I have always made a distinction between my friends and my confidants. I enjoy the conversation of the former; from the latter I hide nothing.

—Edith Piaf

Seek Balance

THE final series of factors involve a number of things you can do to remain balanced. These are more behavioral than emotional. You can begin doing them immediately. The first suggests you do something "for fun" at least once a week. Define what's fun, but healthy for you and do it. Another key is being skilled at handling daily minor hassles. Develop a method to deal with traffic jams, phone problems, screaming children, or anything else that may be an aggravation in your life. You can come up with first-aid measures that will help you "chill out" in these situations and avoid toxicity later.

The next two factors are: Avoid consuming coffee, tea, or caffeinated beverages. And take quiet time for yourself during each day—even if only for five minutes. This is time alone when you can meditate, decompress, or simply listen. It is also important to say, "no" when necessary. There are tactful and diplomatic ways to assert yourself and to be unselfish at the same time. It is a way of avoiding over-obligation of yourself. The next factor is of a similar nature. It's being able to organize your time effectively. A simple time-management tool, such as a day planner and time spent in a seminar or with instructional tapes can help you with this baby step.

Finally, in seeking balance it is important to laugh heartily at least three times per day. Laughter, along with aerobic exercise, are under-valued ways to jump-start yourself out of a bad mood. They result in positive biochemical changes in your body and in many ways can "prime the pump" of your internal pharmacy. The last, but maybe the most important, is to learn to like yourself. How do you do that? You are in the process of doing it now. Books, tapes, seminars and counseling can help you in this particular area. Each factor mentioned is a key to balance and can be considered a small baby step on its own. This can change your life.

The most wasted day of all is that on which we have not laughed.
—Nicolas Chamfort

Diversify

OVER the years I've enjoyed reading about the fourteenth-and fifteenth-century Samurai of Japan. There is no one in modern society who compares. Though trained to be warriors, they were extremely talented in many areas. However, they weren't assassins. They actually faced their enemy, literally eye to eye. Before doing battle they would introduce themselves to their opponent and announce their number of kills. Each knew, before it was over one of them would die.

The survivor, incredibly enough, would go home and continue his artwork! You are probably thinking *martial* art work, right? Wrong! The Samurai were also poets, writers, and artists. Such was the depth of their diversity. Interestingly enough, it was the most artistically skilled who won! Or, perhaps, after surviving such incredibly stressful confrontations as warriors, the artistic skills of the Samurai flourished in the process. Regardless, some of the most victorious of Samurai contributed profusely to the tomes of art, philosophy, and culture found in Asia today. Diversity means a lot of different things. When I use the term I'm referring to having a wide range of interests. By spreading your interests, it becomes difficult to be obsessed with one particular area to the point of destruction.

With a narrow range of focus it's easy to lose perspective. But with a diverse base, people seem to have a higher quality of life. If you want to begin to diversify first develop a variety of interests. These can be hobbies, friendships, or other activities. We know very few HAPs who are narrowly focused. Those who are, diversify within their specific boundaries of interest. Diversity is a key to happiness. It's only a baby step but one that will speed you on the journey.

I have become all things to all men so that by all possible means I might save some.
                                                    —I Corinthians 9:22 N IV

Diversify
_____

TOO many people identify with their jobs. This is especially true
for men. Often when I conduct a seminar or speaking engagement
I meet with people afterwards. It never fails that most of the men
will introduce themselves, "Hi, I'm Bob from Bob's Realty." Or "Hi,
I'm Jack with Jack's Hardware." There's nothing wrong with being
proud of your job or career. But much is wrong if you identify with
it. It's the opposite of diversity.

You are not your job. You are not your career. Your identity is far
more complex than simply being "Bob the Realtor," or "Jack the
Hardware Salesman." And it's certainly far more complex than
being Bob's wife! One of the frightening things about such an
identity process is that when you lose your job, you lose your identity
as well. And it's inevitable. You'll either quit, get fired, or retire. In
some cases retirement means death. But you never die as "Jack the
Hardware Salesman." It's Jack, all by himself, facing that possibility.
Diversity means that when one component of your life is removed
there are others to take its place. Tom Landry was the only football
coach the Dallas Cowboys had up to the point of his retirement.
He retired and the team continued to excel. And so did Landry. He
became involved in a variety of other things, including teaching
Sunday School, spending time with his family, and pursuing other
business interests.

Bear Bryant was one of the greatest coaches in the history of
college football. He defined "winning" during his era. Football and
Bear Bryant were synonymous. When Bear Bryant retired from
football he died within a matter of months. Football, on the other
hand, continued. Coach Bryant didn't. That's the way it works. If
your only identity is what you do professionally, when you lose it,
there's often simply no reason to live. I suggest diversifying as an
alternative. Never identify exclusively with one person, one job, or
one interest in life. The Samurai had multiple reasons for living. So
did Tom Landry. Don't make the mistake many others have. Diversifying is a better choice.

_____

*Pray that your loneliness may spur you into finding something to
live for, great enough to die for.*

—Dag Hammarskjold

Diversify

DIVERSITY is a fascinating concept. The word itself originally comes from two Latin words. One, "versare" means "to occupy oneself with." The other, "vertere," means "to turn." A man I saw in therapy was overly-occupied with his job. As a result, his life turned inside out. When he came to me for therapy he was only thirty-five years old. He could've been forty-five or sixty-five, and the same thing could have occurred.

In actuality, it probably was a blessing that he had this experience while young. It was easier for him to bounce back. He had made the mistake of burying himself in a job over which he had no control. He described his life as having been perfect, and the company he worked for had made it so. Then the company "downsized." As a result of this experience, the young man became immobilized by depression. "I built my life around that company!" he moaned. "I can't imagine a life without my job." The conversation continued in this direction for over an hour. The feedback I gave him was difficult to hear, and probably more difficult to follow. Then the conversation turned to the subject of *diversity*.

Rebuilding his life took quite a while. In fact, he not only lost a career, but also his girlfriend and his physical health. He had not *diversified*. He had committed the almost unpardonable sin of putting all his eggs in one basket. When that basket dropped, as it inevitably does, everything was crushed. Though he did recover, he paid an enormous price. Diversity is a way of avoiding the obsessive-compulsive trap. It's difficult to be obsessive when you have a wide range of interests. Since obsessive-compulsive personalities are more prone to illness, diversifying can be a life-saving baby step. *Diversify*, for your health and happiness.

One thing life taught me: if you are interested, you never have to look for new interests. They come to you. When you are genuinely interested in one thing, it will always lead to something else.
—Eleanor Roosevelt

Diversify

I have several friends who are financial planners. Two of them have investment talk shows. I've heard them discuss the principle of having a "diversified portfolio." Here is an example of this principle.

I once worked with a man in therapy who had done just the opposite. He had inherited a large sum of money at his father's death. On several occasions he referred to "several hundred thousand dollars." Apparently, after receiving the inheritance, he quit his job and made what he thought was a wise investment. He put all the money (except ten thousand dollars cash) in the stock market. He suddenly became a walking, talking, mood-swaying indicator of the Dow Jones! He didn't wear his mood on his shirt sleeve—he wore the Dow Jones trends.

Whether you are investing money, emotional energy, or identity, *diversity* is the key. Diversification is not that difficult. Develop a wide range of interests, hobbies, and friendships. Establish diversity as a priority. Identify areas in your life where you need to be more diversified. List interests you would like to develop and make a plan to carry it out. Diversification is a baby step. And it will insure safe passage on your journey to happiness.

A great preservative against angry and mutinous thoughts and all impatience and quarreling, is to have some great business and interest in your mind, which like a sponge shall suck up your attention and keep you from brooding over what displeases you.
—Joseph Rickaby

Simplify

IT'S probably no coincidence that Forrest Gump and Rush Limbaugh have been so phenomenally successful at this particular point in world history. Both the movie and the talk show host have succeeded in simplifying extremely complex issues while entertaining millions of people along the way.

Life has grown increasingly chaotic. People are looking for answers and understanding. Albert Einstein said, *Make everything as simple as possible, but not one bit simpler.* Apparently Gump and Limbaugh have successfully mirrored Einstein's advice. Life has become so confusing that many people feel lost. Concepts such as "moral," "acceptable," and "normal" are continually being redefined. Technology changes rapidly, but emotions do not. As a result, it is important for one to learn to *simplify.* This means many things. It varies from person-to-person. To begin with, you can make a list of changes that would make your life less-cluttered. It could be that there are a number of them or perhaps only a few. Regardless of the number, each area you are able to simplify will result in removing clutter and complication from your life.

Most people agree. There is little debate. From journalists, to philosophers, to theologians, it is quite clear that chaos reigns. The goal of this baby step is to focus on where you can simplify emotional and social craziness. It's a very important baby step and one that will require some thought. Start now by listing those areas of your life that need to be simplified, or are becoming too overwhelming to handle. It may be in your social life. It may be an aspect of your career. It may be your personal life. It's time to simplify.

. . . let him do it with simplicity . . . .

—**Romans 12:8**

Simplify

DURING the baby step process it has been emphasized that self-control is literally the only control you have. So begin to simplify by looking at your own personal life. What can you do within yourself to help remove chaos? The first minor change would be to focus on being yourself. This is achieved by being consistently straightforward in all aspects of your life. Whatever you believe, do so consistently and enthusiastically. To accomplish this, you've got to know what you believe. That goal will be accomplished during your baby step journey.

The next part of this baby step is to be yourself in all relationships. It is a mistake to be one person with Jim and another person with Jane. Being yourself means consistency within, and between yourself and others. The lack of chameleon-like behavior removes confusion. Reducing emotional games helps sort out the emotional clutter. Both of these things are of vast importance.

Once you have achieved this, it's important to consistently tell the truth in a tactful way. Don't lie. It creates too much confusion. A prominent theologian once told me he would never tell a lie if someone asked him a direct question. On the other hand, he said there are many things he doesn't say—things they don't need to hear. Telling the truth, tactfully, helps you be honest without being offensive. As an example, even though I think your shoes are ugly I don't need to tell you. On the other hand, if you ask me . . . . You get the picture. Avoid confusion and chaos by knowing yourself. Afterwards, be consistent in communicating that self to others when appropriate. Be tactfully honest and straightforward. From personal experience, I know this will simplify your life.

Simplicity is the peak of civilization.

—Jessie Sampter

Simplify

ONE of the goals of simplification is to remove clutter and confusion from your surroundings. This can easily be accomplished by developing rituals and structure in your life. Similarly, planning can help you simplify. In fact, applying structure and planning in all areas of your life will save time and help clarify some of the chaos. What you do with your time is one of the few things you have control over.

I have worked with people in therapy who have applied the principle of *synergism* in many areas of their lives. They have combined activities and ended up simplifying without even being aware of the time, energy, and confusion they have saved. Using commuting time to dictate correspondence, listening to seminars on tapes, or making important phone calls is a synergistic principle. However, if you do these, please drive carefully. Logistically, you are accomplishing two or three things in the period of time you used to accomplish only one. You can virtually do the same thing while eating, folding laundry, doing the dishes, etc. While I don't believe watching the evening news during mealtime is a good principle, I do believe listening to inspirational cassettes is a powerful one. It also involves synergism. The same process applies in virtually all settings. By combining activities, you can save time and simplify your life.

It is also vastly important to never say something unless you really mean it. Talk about complications! This one can destroy all of your relationships. By letting your emotions take control and responding in anger, you are setting yourself up for disaster. Sure, you can apologize and usually the person will forgive you. But it doesn't remove the pain. Getting a divorce, losing your job, or being dropped by a best friend is a high price to pay for verbalizing anger inappropriately. It also makes things extremely complicated. The goal here is to simplify. It's an important baby step in life.

All great things are simple . . .

—**Winston Churchill**

<u>Simplify</u>

SIMPLIFY.

Be straightforward and honest with yourself and others.

Be brief.

Use synergy.

Simplify.

You'll live longer.

Determine what areas in your life need to be simplified. Examine your personal life, family environment, relationships, and career. There are many good books you can purchase, or borrow from the library, that deal with specific topics—simplifying housework, organizing daily routine, improving relationships, etc. Choose one area to simplify this week. Make a plan and follow through. Just remember to keep it simple.

———————————————

Simplicity, Simplicity, Simplicity! I say, let your affairs be as two or three, and not a hundred or a thousand; instead of a million count half a dozen, and keep your accounts on your thumbnail . . . Simplify, simplify.

—Henry David Thoreau

Life Is Precious–Handle With Prayer

LIFE is precious, handle with prayer. USA *Today* published an article in 1994 citing scientific evidence that prayer works. The evidence was based on research completed over a number of years. The scientists followed rigorous protocol to arrive at their conclusions. They used the most reliable methods available and their studies have been reviewed and replicated on multiple occasions. The conclusions stand. Prayer actually works.

Some of these studies were done in medical hospitals. Others were conducted in laboratories. In both settings prayer had positive results. As an example, in a series of controlled studies it was discovered that people who were "prayed for" recovered from illness far more quickly than those who were not. In another double-blind study, red blood cells were placed in a solution of salt water. Those cells that were "protected" through prayer showed a much lower rate of hemolysis—swelling and bursting. The same results even occurred with plants! Flowers that were prayed for became healthier than those that weren't. The scientific conclusion was that *prayer works.*

Though researchers can verify prayer is effective, they can't explain how it works. The religious orientation of the person doing the praying didn't seem to matter. It wasn't the prayers of any particular denomination that worked. It was prayer, not the theory of the person who was praying that made the difference. It's not the denomination that matters. It's not calling yourself a Christian that makes you a Christ-like. It's praying enough that the breath of God will eventually begin to flow through you. Life is precious. Handle with prayer. It's a major baby step on the journey to happiness.

Pray as if everything depended on God and work as if everything depended upon man.
—**Francis Cardinal Spellman**

Life Is Precious–Handle With Prayer

LIFE is precious, handle with prayer. There is little disagreement today, if any at all, about the benefits of prayer. From traditional theologians to the most empirical scientists the consensus is in. Prayer works miracles. Some of these are emotionally-based. Few dispute those. However, there is now evidence prayer can produce medical miracles and real-life change. The most significant point of the studies is they were conducted by skeptics, not by people who wanted to prove anything.

For some people scientific evidence is irrelevant. They have a high degree of faith, and nothing else really matters. For others the evidence is welcome, but merely proves something they already knew within themselves. There is a third group of people to whom the research is quite troubling. They had placed prayer in the same category as mysticism, magic, or shamanism. And people who believed in prayer were either considered naive on one extreme, or stupid on the other.

The studies were completed at Harvard Medical School and several other locations. Those getting prayed for, were unaware of it. The people actually doing the praying were not personally acquainted with the objects of their prayers. They also were not given instructions on how to conduct the prayer. No prescribed method or denominational orientation was suggested. Yet the results were phenonmenal. Those prayed for not only recovered more quickly, but were also far less likely to have complications and relapses. This all occurred even though they didn't know they were being prayed for at all. Prayer is helpful on an emotional and social level. It helps you feel hope, and more connected to the things around you. It makes you feel less alone. It can also help you heal and create real-life change. It's free, easy, and you don't require an appointment ahead of time. Give it a try.

If you pray for bread and bring no basket to carry it, you prove the doubting spirit which may be the only hindrance to the gift you ask.
—D. L. Moody

Life Is Precious–Handle With Prayer

FOR the past thirty years I have been fascinated with the writings of Dr. Carl Jung. He was a man who would have believed life is precious; handle with prayer. Jung was a Swiss psychoanalyst and later considered more of a philosopher. He was a gifted writer and had much written about him as well. Of all of Freud's student, Jung was the most spiritual. He lectured, wrote, and discussed this topic prolifically.

Jung formulated a concept he called the collective unconscious. He described it as a mass of extraordinary thought available to people who were able to tune into it on an intuitive level. Jung postulated the collective unconscious was not within your mind. He suggested it was "out there" in the universe. Jung's contemporaries speculated the collective unconscious to be the basis of most creative thought. Some even claimed creativity was not an internal or individual process at all. They said creativity only occurred when a person was able to tune into the collective unconscious and allow thought to flow through them. I was highly suspicious of these ideas when I first read them. But later, events caused me to wonder. I heard singer and songwriter Smoky Robinson describing to an interviewer that he never wrote a song, he just allowed them to come through him. Later I heard Steven Spielberg, composer John Williams, and author Stephen King make similar comments. Afterwards I began to think of this issue in more depth.

It is my opinion that we all come closer to God, the ultimate creator, during our most creative moments. When a song "comes through" Smoky Robinson it could very easily be the breath of God flowing through. Perhaps Smoky Robinson is just more open to that source. In a similar way, if you are intuitively in touch, an answer can come to you, or through you, in some cases immediately. The most creative people may not be those who can focus pen on paper, but those who are the most open to receiving input. Pray. And then listen. Let the breath of God flow through you.

If any of you lack wisdom, let him ask of God, that giveth to all men liberally, and upbraideth not; and it shall be given him.
—James 1:5

Life Is Precious—Handle With Prayer

I was one of the speakers recently at a conference on "spirituality and everyday life." During a question and answer period, a participant asked if I prayed. In reality, he wanted to know if I prayed the same way he did. I wasn't aware of his hidden agenda at the time. We had a strange discussion about his question, and eventually I came to several conclusions. The first, that he really had no interest in what I believed at all. The second, was he wanted validation for his own beliefs rather than an explanation of mine. The third, was I needed to grow more skilled at openly answering such questions. The questioner occupied a great deal of time and became intrusive rather than inquisitive. But he had caused me to think. That night I prayed about the discussion. And I then listened for a response.

The next day I sought the participant out at the conference center. I apologized to him and said I had not given a comprehensive answer the day before. Afterwards, I proceeded to clarify my earlier comments. In summary, I told him both prayer and meditation were vastly important to me. I explained that prayer was my way of communicating with God, and meditation was how I perceived God communicating with me. I suggested to the man that prayer and meditation both were important in my life, but not just to give my "wish list" to God. To me, the purpose was to get quiet and listen to what God had to say back to me. I suggested this was far more important than what I had to say to God.

The question had required me to clarify my thoughts and I thanked the man for asking it. He seemed befuddled by my response. However, months later he wrote to me and suggested the second discussion had profoundly changed his life. That was nice, since it had changed mine as well. Life is precious, handle with prayer. Take this baby step today. If you pray regularly, for one week double the amount of time you spend. If you don't pray regularly, spend fifteen minutes in prayer and meditation for one week. Afterwards, determine if you want to continue for an additional week.

The word meditation is rather an abused word . . . it would be much better to use the words "quiet time," in which a person shuts out the noise of the world, enters into himself and studies himself not by his press clippings, but how he stands with God.
—Bishop Fulton J. Sheen

12

Letting Go of the Past & Looking Toward a Happy Future

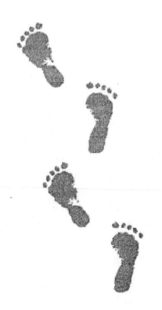

Finish Business–Part I

THIS baby step is about finishing business. It's an extremely important baby step and has several parts. Finishing business is something your mind really wants to do. It's so important that your mind attempts to do it automatically, even when you don't consciously choose to. In fact, your mind will perpetually attempt to finish business. That's part of the problem. Since *happiness is not what you are, but a series of things you do,* you must *do* something to finish business. Your mind alone cannot complete it. Obsessing—which is what your mind does when you ignore unfinished business—is the opposite. Finishing business means getting closure and letting go.

Your mind constantly seeks closure. In many ways it's like a guided missile or "smart bomb" made famous during the Gulf War. The bombs will go over, under, around, and through obstacles to reach their target. Your mind will do the same thing. Its target is always finishing business. And your mind can become like a smart bomb. It will obsess about the target—*closure*—until it locates it. If it doesn't, it will implode. But whatever happens, there will ultimately be an eruption.

A stimulus demands a response in most life situations. Anything which is incomplete seeks to be completed. Similar to the old knock-knock jokes, when someone says "Knock-knock" it's difficult not to respond—"Who's there?" The stimulus seeks a response. When you look at the telephone in your office and see the blinking lights, you want to take the people off hold. When the doorbell rings, it's asking to be answered. These are all stimuli regardless of their intrusiveness, requiring a response to be complete. Your mind works that way too. It wants to finish business. It wants to get closure. The difference is your telephone will stop ringing. The person on hold will eventually hang up. But your mind won't stop. It will replay the unfinished business until you finally accomplish a degree of closure. Get closure. It's very important and will help you find peace along the way to happiness.

Cast thy bread upon the waters: for thou shalt find it after many days.

—Ecclesiastes 11:1

Finish Business—Part I

MOST people have had this experience at least once. You are driving down the road with your radio blaring. A song—usually an oldie—is playing on the radio. It reminds you of some significant emotional memory in your past. Maybe it was popular when you were in high school. Perhaps it reminds you of a relationship you were involved in at one time. Regardless, the song is filled with memories. You arrive at your destination while the song is still playing. Maybe it's half-way or three-quarters complete. But your commute is over, and you turn off your engine. With the end of your commute, the song is over as well—or is it?

Several hours later you find yourself still humming the song. You recognize it resonating in your mind as you're trying to do other things. The melody intrudes while you are trying to make phone calls. You whistle it repeatedly and sing the few lyrics you remember. On the way home you find yourself trying to locate the song once again on the radio. Unable to find it you sing what you remember repeatedly. Finally you lie down, go to bed and hum the tune through to completion. Your mind relaxes—at last.

Some called this process the repetition compulsion. The idea is, what you fail to complete, repeats. And it will repeat ad nauseum. The repetition compulsion explains why people end up entering almost identical relationships on a repeated basis and with the same results. Since they never finished business the first time, they're destined to repeat it until they finally reach a conclusion. You must finish business. Your mind demands it. The stimulus of the event, demands the response of closure. When something has ended, it needs closure to be complete. If not, you'll repeat it continuously even to the point of destroying your life in the process. It's a better idea to simply finish business. You'll be far better off on the road to happiness.

In the carriages of the past you can't go anywhere.
                                    —**Maxim Gorky**

Finish Business–Part I

I live within a mile of Interstate Highway 75, the main North-South thoroughfare extending from Canada to Florida. I always thought it fascinating when I speak in Canada to find that most folks who attend my seminars recognize my exit! It's apparently a familiar stop for Canadians on the way to Florida.

It was also a major landmark for American soldiers caravanning on route to the Gulf War. On the way from Fort Campbell, Kentucky to Jacksonville, Florida they passed through Chattanooga which identifies itself as "America's most patriotic city." I was trying to get on the interstate at the same time a caravan was passing through. I couldn't help but notice a large number of people gathered along the highway. To Chattanooga it wasn't a caravan route. It was a parade. High school bands, cheerleaders, and radio and TV reporters lined the interstate. People held up banners and flags wishing the soldiers safety and good luck. As I trailed behind the convoy I eventually found myself becoming mesmerized by it. I began to fantasize it wasn't a parade of young soldiers going to Saudi Arabia. It was a welcome home parade for Vietnam veterans.

I got tears in my eyes, realizing this was one of the reasons the Vietnam War was so difficult for our country to overcome. The war was never really finished because there was no closure. There was no ceremony. There were no parades. There was no ritual. A stimulus demands a response. The Vietnam War was a stimulus of mammoth proportions. There was no response. Most veterans rotated from Vietnam individually. There was no welcome home. There was no celebration, banquet, or parade. Most veterans were in the jungle one day, and back home three days later. They were given a plane ticket home, a steak and egg breakfast, and not even a pat on the back. It was an anti-climactic response to an extremely powerful stimulus. That's why the war continues to be fought, even decades after it ended. There was no closure. What's true for our society is also true for you. Get closure. *Finish business.* It's a major baby step on the journey of happiness.

It is never any good dwelling on good-byes. It is not the being together that it prolongs, it is the parting.
—Elizabeth Bibesco

Finish Business—Part I

YOUR mind wants to finish business. When you have an open sore on your body it wants to be covered. Your body will take care of that problem itself by developing a scab. When the skin doesn't heal it often requires stitching or at least some sort of medical treatment. Continual pain will often be the stimulus that results in the response of your getting help.

In many ways the same metaphor applies with emotionally-unfinished business. The emotionally open wound wants to be healed or stitched. However, emotional pain is often not respected. It's considered to be insignificant, or a sign of weakness. There is no visible symptom to diagnose, so the wound is ignored. The pain is there, but you can't see anything. An emergency room won't know how to treat it. Yet it needs closure, the same way a physical wound needs sutures. Similarly, if emotional wounds go untreated you can suffer from shock. Infection—*such as depression*—can set in and kill you slowly. Either way you'll reach an unhappy ending. It's important to ascertain what remains unfinished in your life. By doing so you can get closure on emotional wounds you may have left untreated.

Divide your life into chapters. A book has various chapters, yet it's still one book. Your life is the same. There have been many chapters in your life, even though they all come under the heading of the book—your life. During each of those chapters there are probably sections still unfinished. Most of the important ones will be resentments from things that happened in the past. They'll be about people who hurt you, times you felt betrayed, and trespasses you haven't forgiven. Begin to make a list by chapter of all the things or people that need closure. After you've made the list, put it away for at least twenty-four hours and then review it again. Make sure when you've finally completed this list there is nothing in your head or heart that isn't written down. This will help as you begin Part II of finishing business.

We ought not to look back unless it is to derive useful lessons from past errors, and for the purpose of profiting by dear bought experience.
                                        —George Washington

Finish Business–Part 2

IN a previous baby step I explained that there are only two primary emotions, *love* and *fear*. All other emotions are secondary. Positive emotions result from love. Negative ones are derived from fear. By beginning to write about your fears—especially from early childhood—you can diminish their control. Write in detail the truth about what happened at that time. If it occurred when you were a child, write how you felt emotionally at that time. If it occurred in a previous marriage, recall what you experienced in that relationship. If there was a time you felt victimized, discuss what you experienced as a victim. Focus on when the event actually occurred, not on today.

After you've done this, begin to investigate the memory objectively, as though you were a detective. Interview other people who may have been involved, either as participants or observers. If the person who hurt you is now dead, write a biography of that person. Talk to others who knew him or her. Do your best to actually get to know the victimizer, even if they're deceased. After you've completed your research, put the writing away for at least seventy-two hours. Then pull it out and begin a review. See if you've missed anything. Perhaps the last few days have produced additional memories you may have overlooked. Ask yourself the questions mentioned earlier. This time, ask them from a different perspective. Begin to think about what you needed in the earlier experience—not only to survive, but to create something positive.

Design a ritual to get closure. In some cases imaginary rituals will suffice. In others you may need to conduct actual ceremonies to adequately obtain closure. I have participated in ceremonies where people dug holes in the ground and buried coffin-like shoe boxes filled with memories of the past. These often included the writings they had completed. At other times, I have found people who merely needed to imagine or visualize the ritual. There is no one proper way to do this. It's important that you do something that works for you. Closure is an important experience, and it is individualized.

Thou canst begin a new life! See but things afresh as thou used to see them; for in this consists the new life.

—Marcus Aurelius

Finish Business–Part 2

THE ritual can encompass virtually anything. But primarily it has to do with completing things that are unfinished and then letting go. What you let go of usually are negative emotions associated with the event. You are letting go of anger, resentments, grudges, and unhealthy feelings. This normally results in forgiveness. Sometimes the forgiveness is indirect. At other times it is very specific. But the ability to forgive usually is a prerequisite to complete healing and finishing business.

The ritual will work if you remember that one of the goals is to *express* whatever unfinished emotions still exist. Often this results in crying, grieving, or the occasional expression of intense anger. Some people find it difficult to verbally express their emotions. However, there are other ways to express one's emotions. You can paint your feelings, write songs, or role-play them. Others have even danced their emotions. It is not the form of expression that is important. It is *expressing* emotions that makes the difference.

In whatever form, the process always is the same. Comprehensively discuss how you felt at the time the events occurred. Compare these with how you feel now. Write letters to the people involved. Express your emotions, both as they existed as a younger person, and now. If it helps, express it verbally, as well as in writing. It usually helps to express your emotions in a variety of creative ways. The key is to release them, and the more outlets you use, the more thorough it can be. After freeing your emotions about an event, design a ritual of closure. If you are still angry about abuse from your childhood, design a ceremony to strengthen the younger you who was abused. If you are carrying around resentment toward an "ex" who hurt you, discuss how you feel. Then, design a ritual to bury the anger. If you are still grieving about the way you were treated when you returned from Vietnam, design a welcome-home party in your mind and actually experience it. In whatever form, be sure you say good-by to the negative emotions that accompanied the series of events. By doing this, you will be better off, and free yourself as you travel on the way to happiness.

This one thing I do, forgetting those things which are behind, and reaching forth unto those which are before. I press toward the mark . . .
—**Philippians** 3:13–14 NIV

Finish Business–Part 2

THE best approach to finishing business is to do it right the first time. During this book I've discussed various things I've learned from my grandfather. In his long life he taught me much. However, he taught me far more by the way he died. In November of 1974 my grandfather called and asked me to come home for Thanksgiving. I had already made plans to do so and assured him I would be there.

When I arrived home everything seemed normal. My grandmother and mother were cooking. Other family members were visiting. Grandpa and I swapped our usual jokes and stories. Everything seemed quite normal. We had the Thanksgiving meal, watched the customary football, and had a normal visit. On Sunday , before I left, Grandpa asked me to come to his bedroom so we could talk privately. He began by telling me this would be the last time I'd ever see him. Over my objections he continued to explain that he was tired and had decided to die. Grandpa told me stories about my father and mother. He talked a lot about my early childhood. We discussed a few things that had probably been avoided over the years. When he was done we cried together, hugged our last good-by, and I left.

Three days after that discussion a secretary came and got me out of a class I was teaching. I walked out in the hallway, looked at her and said, "You don't have to tell me. My grandfather's dead, right?" She nodded her head. Grandpa finished business, legally and emotionally, and then died. He was a wonderful human being who was an incredible parent. He led a rich, full, and generous life. And he then died a rich, full, and generous death. Grandpa was constantly teaching life's lessons. And his death was one of the most important. Finish business. You'll have no regrets.

While grief is fresh, every attempt to divert only irritates. You must wait till it be digested, and then amusement will dissipate the remains of it.

—Samuel Johnson

Finish Business—Part 2

IF you don't finish business it will finish you. This is always true. Events in your life that lack closure will ultimately destroy you both literally and figuratively. The longer you hang onto the past, the more powerful it becomes. A friend of mine illustrated this dramatically. There were many things he had not gotten closure on and was having difficulty completing the healing process.

One night he dreamed he dug up a casket and carried the remains of the dead body on his back like a rucksack. He was like a dog who had unearthed a prize bone as he paced around with it at night. But as morning approached he realized he had made an incredible mistake and was frantic to return the body. It was one of those dreams where no matter how hard he tried he couldn't get the casket reburied before daylight. At that point he woke up in a cold sweat. In many ways that's exactly what you're doing by carrying around unfinished business. You're carrying extra dead weight on your shoulders. It's not only embarrassing, but it will weigh you down as well. The intelligent choice is to leave dead bodies buried. Those you have been carrying around, need to be returned as soon as possible. And the truth is, virtually any problem you are having today likely has some roots in the unfinished past. And this unfinished business probably surrounds some significant emotional memory.

If you haven't made the list of unfinished business in your life do so now. Go back to part one and complete the assignment listed there. Ask yourself some very difficult but important questions. The first question is, "How did I feel about the event at the time it occurred?" Question number two is, "How do I feel about it today?" Then ask yourself, "What did I fear about the situation then?" The last question is, "What do I fear about that event or situation now?" By answering these questions honestly you will begin to do the necessary preparation to bury the unfinished past. By unloading some "dead weight" your baby step journey will be easier.

So let me assert my firm belief that the only thing we have to fear is fear itself—nameless, unreasoning, unjustified terror which paralyzes needed efforts to convert retreat into advance.
—**Franklin D. Roosevelt**

Finish Business—Part 3

ONE of the fascinating things I've discovered while doing talk radio is that often you can accomplish the things we've been discussing without formally entering psychotherapy. I worked with a number of people who actually worked out their problems while on the air. After discussing their situations I'd give them homework assignments. After they followed the assignments they would call back. At times it would turn out to be "group therapy on the air."

The first thing I usually ask you to do is to visualize yourself being at peace. It is important to imagine yourself as "over it"—whatever "it" is. After you accomplish this, move on. If not, you need to work on simply visualizing feeling good or being happy until you actually imagine it occurring. The next mini-step is to write a chronology of the troubling events. This list focuses on *what happened,* not how you *felt* about it. Afterwards, write down the emotions associated with each event. After this is set aside and reviewed, write the other person, if there was one, a lengthy letter saying everything needed. Write as if he or she were present. Exhaust all your emotions. The letter will not be seen by anyone else. It's for you.

The final step is always the ritual. As discussed earlier, this can take various forms. The purpose of the ritual is simply to mark the passage of the event. We have birthday parties, Thanksgiving dinners, anniversary celebrations, wedding ceremonies, and other rituals that mark every passage of our emotional life. There is a ceremony or party for just about everything. Yet there are few rituals to help a person get over a broken heart, a loss, or a serious depression. This is one of the reasons it's so difficult to let go of painful emotions. There is no ritual unless you design it. This is something you can do, and need to do, if you want to continue baby-stepping your way toward happiness.

We have no more right to consume happiness without producing it than to consume wealth without producing it.
—George Bernard Shaw

Finish Business–Part 3

ONE lady I worked with had difficulty letting go of a painful incident that occurred in her marriage. Although her husband had been unfaithful, they decided to remain married. She had no trouble getting over it intellectually. However, on the emotional level she was still mired in the betrayal. She was unable to think of a ritual which adequately expressed her emotions. As a result, she kept coming back to the actual affair. She relived it regularly, and continued to punish herself and husband long after she had intellectually forgiven him. She understood the importance of letting go. It was her emotions that were stalled.

Finally in complete exasperation we both threw up our hands. I had exhausted my list of suggested interventions. She was beginning to think it was impossible. The crucial moment came in a particular counseling session. I suggested that perhaps she didn't want to let go. She described herself as unable to cry, scream, hit, or write letters. Finally I asked her, "What can you do?" She immediately responded, "I can paint." I told her to paint her feelings, and gave her some suggestions. She followed them and over a week later brought in the results.

Her artwork was masterful. It hangs in my office today. It's approximately two-by-three feet and is in a beautiful gold frame with black matting around it. It's done in bright colors and contains various artifacts from the affairs. The humorous part was several other things the portrait contained. There were dozens of tiny holes, six larger holes, and three slash marks. She explained that after finishing the painting she began to feel a great deal of emotion. It was a combination of anger, sadness, and fear. First she got a .45 caliber pistol and emptied it into the painting. Then the got a .410 shotgun and fired three rounds. Finally she got a butcher knife and stabbed the painting until she fell exhausted on top of it. Then she cried convulsively until her tears were gone. The ritual had worked. She looked great, sounded healthy, and reported she was feeling wonderful. I finally asked her what she called the painting. She said it was called "Closure." She gave it to me. "Closure" hangs in my office today.

If we have no peace, it is because we have forgotten that we belong to each other.

—**Mother Teresa**

Finish Business–Part 3

BOB was having tremendous difficulty continuing his life in a healthy way. He sabotaged himself at every turn. As we got to know each other I realized he had problems with unfinished business. Bob's father had been an Air Force fighter pilot during the Vietnam War. He was shot down and considered missing in action. There had been conflicting reports of his being alive after the crash. Returning POWs reported they'd possibly seen him in various north Vietnamese prison camps. Bob had never gotten over his anger about his father. As a result there was no closure.

The problem was that Bob appeared to be acting out his father's destiny. On several occasions he had come close to death, and was constantly shooting himself in the foot, if not out of the air. I discovered in conversations that Bob never had any kind of memorial service for his father. Over time I convinced him of the importance of doing this. Naturally, his concern was this would be disloyal to his father. He felt it would be like giving up. I convinced Bob that the purpose of the ritual was not to give up on his father. It was a way for Bob to take himself off hold. After a number of discussions about the importance of finishing business he agreed.

We did a great deal of preparation for the ritual. I wanted it to be a success, so we all did our homework. Bob gathered up pictures, medals, and letters from his father. He had located an Air Force summary of the investigation into his father's death. Since he was Episcopalian, I selected appropriate readings from the Book of Common Prayer and the Bible to help set the mood for the ceremony. We also had various renditions of his father's favorite hymn, *Amazing Grace*. I let him set the surroundings for the ritual. He chose a midnight ceremony, at my office, with several of his friends in attendance. I have conducted many rituals in my day as a therapist. But I was totally unprepared for what actually occurred. Besides being very moving, it became apparent that Bob was finally "letting go." The closure was complete. This often happens during rituals. If you let the process play itself out, the results will be far better.

If you want to be happy, be.

—Leo Tolstoy

Finish Business—Part 3

I began *Bob's ceremony* by reading a summary of the Air Force investigation. As I continued, I suddenly laid the typed report down and felt a rush of emotion come over me. Bob's father had been an F-4 fighter pilot and was shot down during operation Bloody Stiletto on July 16, 1969.

I was there at the time his father was shot down. I had taken part in that operation and was on the ground directing an air strike. I could have been the last American to speak to his father. I remembered an F-4 getting shot down, and saw a parachute open. We couldn't tell whether the pilot was alive or not, but we did attempt to locate him on the ground. We were unable to find him, due to enemy gunfire. Later I was wounded, along with several others, and extracted from the area. I explained the coincidence to the group gathered in the office and told them the details of the operation. It was eerie to think of it. And it was even more eerie when Bob's fiancee spoke up.

"He was shot down on July 16, 1969," she uttered. "What's today's date?" It was after midnight. I looked at my watch and whispered "July 16, 1985 . . ." Without knowing, we had chosen the sixteenth anniversary of his father's probable death. There was another coincidence. Bob was sixteen when his father was shot down. He turned to me and asked how old I had been. I was nineteen. Needless to say, this ritual turned out to be one of the most memorable of my professional life. The coincidences continued even further as we concluded the session. In actuality, it was a closure for many of us. At the time of the event I had felt tremendous guilt for not being able to find the pilot. Yet I knew the actual truth was he could have been more than ten-to-twelve miles away with a drifting parachute. One of the other participants suggested his football number in college had been 69. Bob's fiancee talked about the guilt she'd suffered from breaking up with a boyfriend who ended up getting killed in Vietnam. She never got the opportunity to say good-bye. This was a cleansing and healing process for each of us. It was a time of true closure. We finished business. So can you. Design your own ritual. Get closure. And in all of life, *finish business.*

When I was a child, I spoke as a child, I understood as a child: but when I became a man, I put away childish things.
—I Corinthians 13:11 NIV

Enjoy Life–It Is Not A Dress Rehearsal

ENJOY life. It is not a dress rehearsal! There are far too many people who do just the opposite. They fake their way through life, acting as if it were preparation for some melodramatic soap opera. Happy people live as though they are still children, and life is the best Christmas present they've ever gotten. If we all lived that way, we would be far better off in the long run.

HAPs enjoy life. They even enjoy the pain, challenges, and struggles. They learn to appreciate the victories, losses, and ties as well. HAPs are acutely aware of what goes on around them. They are sensitive to people, animals, and nature. They take time to admire the beauty of a rainy day and the splendor of the sun. By taking this approach, they don't expend more energy. In fact, it requires a lot less. HAPs experience life as it exists, rather than trying to change it.

When HAPs sleep, they sleep hard. They relax. They snore. They drool. They go to sleep quickly and fall into a deep trance-like state of refreshing sleep. When they eat, they pig out. They have good appetites and enjoy a wide variety of food. They usually eat a lot of healthy foods. Food is fuel for their full lives and they approach it that way. HAPs are able to set aside time to have fun, and they play intensely. They're not destructive or dangerous in their pursuit of pleasure. HAPs are able to find glee in simple things. They have vigorous sex lives within the confines of a healthy relationship. They like art, music, and literature. HAPs are perpetual learners and find educational opportunities in all of life. When they worship, they do it intensely and with meaning. To a HAP life is not a dress rehearsal. It's an opportunity to live and enjoy each moment on an intensely pleasurable level. Don't make the mistake of acting as though your life is a rehearsal for something better. It's not. Don't fall into that trap. Realize this is the one opportunity you have to reach your earthly potential. Don't let it pass you by. When problems are encountered, enjoy them as well. They are stepping stones on the path to happiness. *Enjoy life. It is not a dress rehearsal.*

Man, unlike the animals, has never learned that the sole purpose of life is to enjoy it.

—Samuel Butler

Enjoy Life–It Is Not A Dress Rehearsal

I have seen only a few cases of serious spouse abuse when the male was the victim. One of the most severe, illustrates this baby step. The husband came home intoxicated one evening and passed out on the living room floor. His golf clubs were scattered next to him, and his smoking cigarette had burned a hole in the carpet. After discovering this, his wife went into a rage. She grabbed his 9-iron and began striking him repeatedly. Before it was over she had broken several bones in his jaw, forearm and wrist. After he was discharged from the hospital they both sought psychotherapy.

Over time I grew well-acquainted with them. The man had a severe addiction to alcohol. The "Mrs.," on the other hand, was severely addicted to him. She was exceedingly angry, and was locked in a love/hate hostile-dependent cycle with her husband. On one occasion I confronted her after she physically attacked him in front of me. She vigorously dismissed my comments, explaining if she was ever out of line—which was doubtful—she would apologize. Before long, she appeared to be developing a love/hate relationship with me. I had already reached my quota of sick relationships for that year, and suggested they find another therapist. At this point she burst out, crying melodramatically, and alternated between apologizing and blaming me for "making her cry." It was quite a performance.

The next morning I got up and checked my voice mail. "Dr. Baucom, this is Jane. I just want you to know this is not over yet and you have not won . . ." At first I thought it was a joke. Then I realized she was serious. She thought this had all been a game. This was her starring role in a "Little Theater" drama. She thought this was a dress rehearsal for the final production. Jane was extremely involved in the community theater, and that was exactly how she saw this relationship. I remember thinking, "They're going to end up divorcing . . . ." He'll quit drinking and end up alone—but happy. She'll find someone else to play with. But she'll still be miserable. They did. He is. She still is too!

Happiness is like coke—something you get as a by-product in the process of making something else.
                                                        —Aldous Huxley

Enjoy Life–It Is Not A Dress Rehearsal

ONE of the biggest obstacles to enjoying life is anger. Anger has been described as a natural human reaction. It has been legitimized to the degree that it is now institutionalized as "temporary insanity." If that were true, anger would be present in all cultures. But that is not the case. Anger is not human nature. In my opinion, these explanations are used to justify the results of testosterone poisoning. In several cultures anger does not even exist.

The Arapesh of New Guinea don't behave aggressively. The Pygmies of the Ituru forest in central Africa don't compete. The Lepchas of Sikkim in the Himalayas don't fight. And the Tasaday Indians don't even have a word in their vocabulary to express anger. Yet we define it in modern society as human nature. Then it is legitimized through the justice system. Anger is simply a choice. Most people don't consider it as optional. "You make me angry!" we claim. But it is a choice, and one we have become comfortable with. We define it as normal, and even rationalize our mistakes with it. Then we justify anger by saying it is just human nature and temporary insanity. But it is not insanity at all. Anger is an impulsive choice one makes. It prevents them from enjoying life and can result in pure misery. One can choose misery by keeping an angry habit. Or he can enjoy life.

Anger is unnecessary most of the time. If you need anger to mobilize you for some reason, then make that choice. If someone is physically attacking you or a family member, get angry and defend yourself. Then forget it and enjoy life. This is not a dress rehearsal. Don't make the mistake of growing comfortable with the biggest obstacle to happiness. Anger is not now, and never will be your friend. Be different. Let go of anger and enjoy life. It is not a dress rehearsal.

Boast not thyself of tomorrow; for thou knowest not what a day may bring forth.

—Proverbs 27:1

Enjoy Life–It Is Not A Dress Rehearsal

THE second biggest obstacle to enjoying life is fear. I learned a great deal about fear from two Dobermans I had in the late seventies. I kept and trained the dogs for almost fourteen years. Or maybe I should say they trained me! The first one I bought was an extremely strong and well-bred male. I took him through standard obedience training when he was a pup, and continued over the years through guard and eventually Schutzhund training. He was a brilliant and courageous dog who had an instinctive sense of judgment that simply could not be taught. In fact, one of the trainers offered me several thousand dollars to purchase him.

The second dobie was a small red female who never actually matured. I assume she experienced pituitary gland problems, or difficulty with growth hormones. Physically and behaviorally she remained a pup her entire fourteen-year life. She was hyper-active, insecure, and fearful from the day I got her. In this case opposites really did attract. He was strong, courageous, and intelligent. She barked at the wind, ran from cats, and saw ghosts in the dark. They seemed to get along, so I kept them until they died, which incidentally occurred within days of each other.

The dogs were approximately the same age, socialized together and bred through generations for protection work. The male never caused any problems. His courage and strength allowed him to relax and enjoy life. The female, on the other hand, bit neighborhood children on three separate occasions. Her fear made her tense, dangerous, and unpredictable. Leo Raulston said, *It's the weak who are cruel. Gentleness can only come from the strong.* It doesn't take courage to be angry. Fearful people do that. Don't embrace fear. Relax. Enjoy life. This is not a dress rehearsal.

You gain strength, courage, and confidence by every experience in which you really stop to look fear in the face . . . The danger lies in refusing to face the fear, in not daring to come to grips with it . . . You must make yourself succeed every time. You must do the thing you think you cannot do.

—Eleanor Roosevelt

Epilogue

If you have gotten to this chapter in sequence, I congratulate you. If you've read each chapter leading up to this epilogue, you are well on your way to happiness. Whether or not this is your first reading of the epilogue, I encourage you to begin reading the material again. In the foreword I suggested reading the book superficially the first time. On the second reading, it is suggested you cover the material in depth. Learn each baby step as if you were going to teach it to someone else. And then do so.

Over the years as I have taught baby steps I've been asked several questions regarding the material. One of these is, "Should we be teaching these concepts to children?" I answer unequivocally, "Yes!" I can think of no better gifts to give a child than self-esteem and happiness. Children who are happy don't make the mistakes many of their peers do. They don't attempt suicide. They don't experience alcohol and drug problems. And they don't get pregnant at the age of thirteen. Not only do I encourage you to give this book to your children, but to teach the concepts to them as well.

Another question I've been asked is, "Are there study groups available to discuss *Baby Steps to Happiness?*" Even before the publication of this book, study groups were forming. For the location of a group nearest you, write to address given in the foreword of this book. Any assistance you may need in finding or establishing a study group will be provided. The most important thing is to internalize this material yourself. The best way to accomplish that is to read *Baby Steps* again, utilize the postcards and tapes, and begin living the steps on a personal basis. That will create the change you need to experience lasting happiness. Once again, congratulations on your progress.

We are built to conquer environment, solve problems, achieve goals, and we find no real satisfaction or happiness in life without obstacles to conquer and goals to achieve.
—**Maxwell Maltz**

Epilogue

Many people ask, "How will my life change after mastering this material?" The response is, it will probably change dramatically. The drama may not occur suddenly. However, there are three changes you will notice. They are not the 3 R's! They're the three L's. You may notice them only gradually. But they will be incredibly evident.

The first of these changes will be a greater interest in *laughter*. You will begin laughing and finding humor in your life far more frequently. On some occasions it will be loud belly laughs. At other times you will simply be aware of a wry smile on your face and not really understand why. It's not coincidence. The laughter and the smiles are coming genuinely from the inside out. They are barometers of your own happiness. The fascinating reality is, it's infectious. It's also contagious to others. They'll notice the change and begin to comment. You may not be able to explain exactly what's going on. You may not even understand it. But as you've already learned in *Baby Steps*, sometimes you have to *forget about understanding and just be stupid together!* Accept the change and enjoy it. Don't attempt to understand or explain. Just live it.

Another change you'll notice is a new *lust for life*. You'll begin to experience life much more fully. You'll enjoy the small things more intensely. The taste of certain foods will begin to change. Work will seem more like pleasure. Your relationships will take on a totally different depth. Your time will be spent intensely enjoying the variety of things you're involved in. Your involvements may change, but your lust for those will be noticeable. The final change you'll notice has to do with *love*. You'll begin to love people far more genuinely. You'll have a new sensitivity to others. You'll be more honest about your emotions, both to yourself and your friends. I encourage you not to be scared of these changes. They're all healthy. Review the baby steps regularly. Make them a part of your life. You are well on your way along the journey of happiness. Again, I congratulate you. Now, teach Baby Steps to someone else.

It is neither wealth nor splendor but tranquillity and occupation which give happiness.

—Thomas Jefferson

Bibliography

Adair, Lara, "The One Secret to Happiness," *Redbook*, June 1995, pp.57-60.

Berne, Eric, *Games People Play*, New York: Grove House Press, 1978.

Betmann, O. L., *The Good Old Days—They Were Terrible, New York: Random House, 1974.*

Blankenship, Virginia, "A Computer-Based Measure of Resultant Achievement Motivation," Journal of Personality and Social Psychology, August 1987, pp.361-372.

Cassidy, Anne, "Who is Happy?" *Working Mother*, November 1995, pp.26-27.

Cobb, N., A. Kahn, and S. H. Cath, "How Your Self-Image Controls Your Tennis Game," *Psychology Today*, November 1977, pp.40-53.

Cole, K. C., "Couples That Play," *Psychology Today*, 1982, pp.33-37.

Coopersmith, S., *The Antecedents of Self-Esteem*, San Francisco, California: Freeman, 1967.

Copeland, Lewis, and Faye Copeland, ed., *Ten Thousand Jokes, Toasts, and Stories.* Garden City, New York, Doubleday & Company, Inc., 1965.

Doskoch, Peter, "Mirth on Earth" (National Happiness Poll), *Psychology Today*, July/August 1995, pp.48-49.

Epstein, Norman, James L. Pretzer, and Barbara Fleming, "The Role of Cognitive Appraisal in Self-Reports of Marital Communication," *Behavior Therapy*, 1987, pp.51-69.

Epstein, Mark, "Opening Up To Happiness," *Psychology Today*, July/August 1995, pp.42-47.

Fischer, Seymour, and Roger P. Greenberg, "Prescriptions for Happiness?" *Psychology Today*, Septmeber/October 1995, pp.32-37.

Freud, Sigmund, *The Ego and the ID*, London: Hogarth Press, 1947.

Friedman, M., and R. H. Rosenman, *Type A Behavior and Your Heart*, New York: Knopf, 1974.

Goldman, Caren, "The Power of Prayer in Medicine," *Diabetes Self-Management*, September/October, 1995.

Goleman, Daniel, "The brain manages happiness and sadness in different centers (PET scan research of Mark George)," *New York Times*, March 28, 1995, p.C1.

Golfman, Noreen, "Double Happiness," *The Canadian Forum*, October 1991, p.26.

Gray, J. A., *The Nueropsychology of Anxiety*, New York: Oxford University Press, 1982.

Greenburg, D., *How to Make Yourself Miserable*, New York: Random House, 1966.

Harrison House, ed, *The Spirit-Filled Man*, Tulsa, Oklahoma: Harrison House, Inc., 1996.

Hendrick, C., "Attitude Change and Behavior Change." Unpublished manuscript, Kent State University, 1972.

Henry, Lewis C., ed., *Five Thousand Quotations For All Occasions*, New York: Doubleday & Company, Inc., 1975.

Hoyt, Carolyn, "Seven Secrets of Happy Families," *McCall's*, December 1994, p.98.

Jones, E. E., and V. A. Harris, "The Attribution of Attitudes," *Journal of Experimental Social Psychology*, March 1967, pp.1-24.

Krausner, L., and L. P. Alpman, *Behavior Influence and Personality: The Social Matrix of Human Action*, New York: Holt, Rinehart, and Winston, 1973.

Kuhn, M. H., and T. S. McPartland, "An Empirical Investigation of Self-Attitudes," *American Sociological Review*, 1954, pp.68-76.

Larned, D., "Do You Take Valium?" *Ms.*, November, 1985 pp.26-30.

Maguire, Karen, ed., *Spiritual Truths 1996 Calendar*, Kansas City Missouri: Andrews and McMeel, 1995.

Maracek, J., and D. Mettee, "Self-Esteem, Level of Certainty and Responsibility for Success," *Journal of Personality and Social Psychology*, 1972, pp.98-107.

Maslow, A. H., *Toward a Psychology of Being*, 2nd. ed. New York: Van Nostrand, 1968.

Maslow, A. H., *Motivation and Personality*, 2nd. ed. New York: Harper & Row, 1970.

May, R., ed., *Existential Psychology*, 2nd. ed. New York: Random House, 1969.

Meichenbaum, D. H., J. B. Gilmore, and A. Fedoravicius. "Group Insight Versus Group Destination in Treating Speech Anxiety," *Psychotherapy: Theory, Research, and Practice*, 1974, pp.103-117.

Merriam-Webster, ed., *The Merriam Webster Dictionary of Quotations*, Springfield, Massachusetts: Merriam Webster, Inc., 1992.

Morris, William ed., *The American Heritage Dictionary*, New York: American Heritage Publishing Co., Inc., 1969.

Moustakas, C. E., *Finding Yourself, Finding Others*, Englewood Cliffs, California: Prentice Hall, 1974.

Newfelott, Victoria, and David B. Guralnick, *Webster's New World Dictionary*, New York: Simon and Schuster, Inc., 1988.

Pasley, Kay, Marilyn Tallman, and Cathy Coleman, "Consensus Styles Among Happy and Unhappy Remarried Couples," *Family Relations*, July 1984, pp.451-457.

Peck, M. Scott, *The Road Less Traveled*, New York: Simon & Schuster, 1978.

Princeton Language Institute, ed., *Twenty-First Century Dictionary of Quotations*, New York: Philip Lief Group, Inc., 1993.

Ranson, Hugh and Margaret Minor, ed., *The New International Dictionary of Quotations*, New York: E. P. Dutton, 1986.

Rogers, C. R., *Client-Centered Therapy: Its Current Practice, Implications, and Theory*, Boston, Massachusetts: Houghton Mifflin, 1951.

Rosenberg, M. and R. Simmons, *Black and White Self-Esteem: The Urban School Child*, Washington, D. C.: American Sociological Assn., 1971.

Rosenberger, Lisa M., and Micheal J. Strube, "The Influence of Type A and B Behavior Patterns on the Perceived quality of Dating Relationships," *Journal of Applied Social Psychology*, 1986, pp.227-286.

Safire, William, and Leonard Safir, ed., *Good Advice*, New York: Wing Books, 1992.

Scarf, Maggie, "Secrets of Happy Families," *Ladies' Home Journal*, September 1995, pp.104.

Scarf, Maggie, "The Happiness Syndrome," *The New Republic*, December 5, 1994, p .25.

Selye, H., *The Stress of Life*, New York: McGraw-Hill, 1956.

Simcox, Carrol E., ed., *Four Thousand and Five Hundred Quotations for Christian Communicators*, Grand Rapids, MI: Baker Book House, 1992.

Strachey, N. J., ed., "Beyond the Pleasure Principle (1920)," *The Standard Edition of the Complete Psychological Works of Sigmund Freud*, Vol. XDIII. London: The Hogarth Press, 1953.

Swain, Austin, and Graham Jones, "Relationships Between Sport Achievement Orientation and Competitive State Anxiety," *Sport Psychologist*, March 1992, pp.42-54.

Sweeting, Guthrie, ed., *Who Said That?*, Chicago, Illinois: Moody Press, 1995.

Toffler, A., *Future Shock*, New York: Random House, 1970.

Wagner, D. N., et al., "Paradoxical Effects of Thought Suppression," *Journal of Personality and Social Psychology*, 1987, p.13.

Wartik, Nancy, "Is Everybody Happy?" *American Health*, May 1995, p.38.

Watson, J., "Psychology as the Behaviorist Views It," *Psychology Review*, 1913, pp.158-177.

Watson, Lillian Eichler, ed., *Light From Many Lamps*, New York: Simon & Schuster, 1951.

Watzlawack, P., J. H. Beavin, and R. D. Jackson, *Pragmatics of Human Communication*, New York: Norton, 1967.

Young, David M., et al, "Aggression," *Journal of Communication*, 1977, pp.100-103.

Zondervan Publishing House, *Women's Devotional Bible: New International Version*, Grand Rapids, Michigan: Zondervan Corporation, 1990.

Index

Situational Index

The Situational Index is intended to help you in various life situations. For each situation that may be affecting your happiness, read the baby step indicated. For more help with general areas read the entire section indicated.

Books by Starburst Publishers

(Partial listing—full list available on request)

Baby Steps to Happiness —John Q. Baucom
(trade paper) ISBN 0914984861 **$12.95**

Little Baby Steps to Happiness —John Q. Baucom

Inspiring, witty and insightful, this portable collection of quotes and affirmations from *Baby Steps to Happiness* will encourage Happiness one little footstep at a time. This book is the perfect personal "cheerleader."
(trade paper) ISBN 091498487X **$6.95**

God's Vitamin "C" for the Spirit —Kathy Collard Miller & D. Larry Miller

Subtitled: *"Tug-at-the-Heart" Stories to Fortify and Enrich Your Life.* Includes inspiring stories and anecdotes that emphasize Christian ideals and values by Barbara Johnson, Billy Graham, Nancy L. Dorner, Dave Dravecky, Patsy Clairmont, Charles Swindoll and many other well-known Christian speakers and writers. Topics include: Love, Family Life, Faith and Trust, Prayer and God's Guidance.
(trade paper) ISBN 0914984837 **$12.95**

God's Chewable Vitamin "C" for the Spirit

Subtitled: *A Dose of God's Wisdom One Bite at a Time.* A collection of inspirational quotes and Scriptures by many of your favorite Christian speakers and writers. It will motivate your life and inspire your spirit. You will *chew* on every *bite* of *God's Chewable Vitamin "C" for the Spirit.*
(trade paper) ISBN 0914984845 **$6.95**

God's Vitamin "C" for the Spirit of MEN —D. Larry Miller

Subtitled: *"Tug-at-the-Heart" Stories to Encourage and Strengthen Your Spirit.* This book is filled with unique and inspiring stories that men of all ages will immediately relate to.
(trade paper) ISBN 0914984810 **$12.95**

God's Chewable Vitamin "C" for the Spirit of DADs

Subtitled: *A Dose of Godly Character, One Bite at a Time.* Scriptures coupled with insightful quotes to inspire men through the changes of life.
(trade paper) ISBN 0914984829 **$6.95**

God's Vitamin "C" for the Christmas Spirit —Kathy Collard Miller & D. Larry Miller

Subtitled: *"Tug-at-the-Heart" Traditions and Inspirations to Warm the Heart.* This keepsake includes a variety of heart-tugging thoughts, stories, poetry, recipes, songs and crafts.
(hardcover) ISBN 0914984853 **$14.95**

Purchasing Information:

Listed books are available from your favorite Bookstore, either from current stock or special order. To assist bookstores in locating your selection be sure to give title, author, and ISBN #. If unable to purchase from the bookstore you may order direct from STARBURST PUBLISHERS. When ordering, enclose full payment plus $3.00 for shipping and handling ($4.00 if Canada or Overseas). Payment in US Funds only. Please allow two to three weeks minimum (longer overseas) for delivery. Make checks payable to and mail to STARBURST PUBLISHERS, P.O. Box 4123, LANCASTER, PA 17604. **Prices subject to change without notice**. Catalog available for a 9 x 12 self-addressed envelope with 4 first-class stamps. 8-96